DATE DUE

FEB 2 1 1995	
MAR 2 0 1995	
APR 1 1 1995	
FEB - 6 1996	
FEB 2 2 1996	
Mar. 7/96	
MAR 2 7 1996	
OCT 2 4 1996	
NOV 2 6 1996	
APR - 3 1997	
MAR - 2 1998	
APR 1 3 1998	
JUL 2 7 1998	
FEB - 6 1999	
FEB 1 8 1999	
NOV - 9 1999	
APR 2 5 2000	
OCT 1 1 2000	
BRODART MAR 1 6 2001	Cat. No. 23-221

Male
Sexual
Abuse

Male
Sexual
Abuse

A Trilogy of Intervention Strategies

John C. GONSIOREK

Walter H. BERA   Donald LeTOURNEAU

SAGE Publications

International Educational and Professional Publisher
Thousand Oaks   London   New Delhi

For information address:

 SAGE Publications, Inc.
2455 Teller Road
Thousand Oaks, California 91320

SAGE Publications Ltd.
6 Bonhill Street
London EC2A 4PU
United Kingdom

SAGE Publications India Pvt. Ltd.
M-32 Market
Greater Kailash I
New Delhi 110 048 India

Printed in the United States of America

Library of Congress Cataloging-in-Publication Data

Gonsiorek, John C.
    Male sexual abuse : a trilogy of intervention starategies / John C.
Gonsiorek, Walter H. Bera, Donald LeTourneau.
        p. cm.
    Includes bibliographical references and index.
    ISBN 0-8039-3716-4. — ISBN 0-8039-3717-2 (pb)
    1. Male sexual abuse victims—Rehabilitation. 2. Teenage sex
offenders—Rehabilitation. 3. Male prostitutes—Rehabilitation.
I. Bera, Walter H. II. LeTourneau, Donald. III. Title.
RC560.S44G66   1994
616.85'83—dc20   94-11731
                                                                      CIP

94 95 96 97 98 10 9 8 7 6 5 4 3 2 1

Sage Production Editor: Yvonne Könneker

Contents

Part II: Family Systems Therapy for Adolescent
Male Sex Offenders
WALTER H. BERA

Acknowledgments

Special thanks goes to William J. Doherty and Mac A. Baird for permission to adapt their model of levels of family involvement in family-centered health care to adolescent sex offender families. Their article, "Developmental Levels in Family-Centered Medical Care," appears in *Family Medicine, 18*(3), pp. 153-156, 1986, and is used with the permission of the Society of Teachers of Family Medicine.

The Victim-Sensitive Offender Therapy Model was originally presented as a chapter by Walter H. Bera, titled "The Systemic/Attributional Model: Victim-Sensitive Offender Therapy" in J. M. Yokley (Ed.), *The Use of Victim-Offender Communication in the Treatment of Sexual Abuse: Three Intervention Models,* Orwell, VT: Safer Society Press, 1990, and is used with the permission of the publisher.

The opening extract of the epilogue is from *A First Zen Reader* by Trevor Leggett. Copyright © 1960 by Charles E. Tuttle Co., Inc. Used by permission of Charles E. Tuttle Co., Inc. All rights reserved.

Valuable comments on previous drafts of this manuscript were made by Craig Allen, Debra Boyer, Bill Friedrich, Stephen Grubman-Black, Mary Koss, Brenda Vander May, Larry Morris, and Stephen Mussack.

*　　*　　*

I wish to thank my life partner, Jim, for his patience, love, under-standing, and support; Nicholas Kozel, for typing, editing, and com-puter assistance; Brenda Vander Mey for encouragement and wise counsel during a difficult period; Charles Silverstein, for his example of courage and tenacity; Walter Bera and Don LeTourneau, for their friendship, collegiality, and patience; and M., for teaching me more about the effects of abuse and recovery than any book or ex-pert could.

                                                                   –J. C. G.

                                *   *   *

I wish to thank my family, Jane and Sophia, for their deep love, patience, and support in the creation of this book. Thanks to those who read early drafts and provided valuable comments and support: mentor and friend William Doherty and Gail Ryan and William Friedrich, whose clear feedback came at a critical time. Thanks to Fay Honey Knopp, who provided critical early support in the devel-opment of the victim-sensitive offender therapy model. Special thanks goes to old colleagues and friends Mike O'Brien and Ruth Matthews, who read the early drafts and, as part of PHASE, stimulated and sup-ported the development of many of the concepts presented. Finally, thanks to John Gonsiorek and Don LeTourneau for their friendship and intellectual honesty; and to the many victims, offenders, and their families who taught me what is needed in healing.

                                                                   —W. H. B.

                                *   *   *

I wish to thank Mike, without whose badgering and support I never would have found my way in the world of hustlers; Michael (Seattle) and Gabe (Los Angeles), for acting as insightful sounding boards over the years as I have thought out boy prostitution; Debra Boyer, for reviewing an early draft and offering support and insight; the staff of the Center for Youth Development and Research, for helping to teach me the praxis of youth work; Michael Baizerman, for being a mentor, friend, and colleague who would not let me get away with intellectual laziness; Jackie Thompson, with whom I have shared much and whose work and research have informed and shaped much of what I have written; Walter Bera and John Gonsiorek for believing in me and teaching me much of what it means to be male in this culture; and to all the young people I have worked with on the streets who taught me so much, thanks for sharing your stories with me—to those who did not make it, your stories are not forgotten.

                                                              —*D. L.*

Introduction

This book describes three clinical intervention approaches to working with adolescent and young adult males who are victims or perpetrators of sexual abuse. These perspectives differ both in the populations for whom the applications are intended and in the style and theoretical orientation of the intervention techniques.

Part I: Assessment of and Treatment Planning and Individual Psychotherapy for Sexually Abused Adolescent Males describes assessment, treatment planning, and individual psychotherapy with primarily young adult or later adolescent males who have been sexually abused. The theoretical perspective draws upon adaptations of Heinz Kohut's self-psychology. In terms of technique, this perspective often employs interventions from a cognitive-behavioral perspective.

Part II: Family Systems Therapy for Adolescent Male Sex Offenders proposes a model of family systems therapy for working with adolescent males who are perpetrators of sexual abuse. A variety of family systems perspectives and techniques are synthesized into a victim-sensitive therapy for offenders.

Part III: A Model for Working With Adolescent Male Prostitutes relates a model of working with male street youth who are engaged in prostitution. The detached youth work perspective is derived from an older social work tradition best articulated by Gisela Konopka, and recently adapted by Jackie Thompson. The intervention described falls more under the rubric of youth work, not therapy. Indeed, the population described is generally viewed as untreatable in therapy.

Male Sexual Abuse is not a primer on sexual abuse of children. Finkelhor's *Sourcebook on Child Sexual Abuse* (1986) attempts to do that. The two-volume series by O'Donohue and Geer, *The Sexual Abuse of Children: Theory and Research* (1992a) and *The Sexual Abuse of Children: Clinical Issues* (1992b), offers a thorough and well-documented grounding in the complexities of this field.

Nor is *Male Sexual Abuse* a comprehensive view of males as victims of sexual abuse. *Males at Risk* by Bolton, Morris, and MacEachron (1989) fits best in that category. *Male Sexual Abuse* is not written for a lay audience, as is Lew's *Victims No Longer: Men Recovering From Incest and Other Childhood Sexual Abuse* (1988); nor it is a self-help book for sexual abuse victims such as Nestingen and Lewis's *Growing Beyond Abuse: A Workbook for Survivors of Sexual Exploitation or Childhood Sexual Abuse* (1990). These and similar volumes published in recent years effectively address such topics.

Our intent is to provide a diversity of clinically sophisticated points of view in working with adolescent and young adult males involved as victims or perpetrators of sexual abuse. The intended audience is mental health and human service professionals. The sexual abuse field needs greater sophistication in clinical approaches than the first wave of writings produced. We also believe a greater emphasis and respect for diversity of ideas is needed; the field has moved prematurely and somewhat dogmatically to a level of purported consensus about childhood sexual abuse, unwarranted by the nascent databases and clinical explication currently available.

We do not attempt, except in the most rudimentary manner in the Epilogue, to coalesce our three different perspectives. Indeed, they have been developed in a divergent, not convergent, fashion. Some readers may find this unsatisfying. The intent of this book is more to raise questions than to give answers, and to stimulate, not to conclude, discussion.

We come from a variety of backgrounds. John C. Gonsiorek is a traditionally trained clinical psychologist who works primarily in the areas of sexual orientation and sexual identity, and sexual exploitation by health-care professionals and clergy. In the area of sexual abuse, his primary focus has been on young adult and late adolescent males who are victims of sexual abuse and perpetrators, both male and female, whose abuse occurs in a professional context. Walter H. Bera is a psychologist and family therapist whose involvement in the field has been primarily with adolescent sexual abuse perpetrators and male victims. Other influences have been family systems approaches and behaviorism. Don LeTourneau is a traditionally trained social worker with a background in juvenile delinquency, community mental health for adolescents and families, and public policy. He has spent most of his career doing youth work and, in recent years, his focus has been street work with adolescents, primarily males who are often involved in prostitution.

The reader should not attempt to utilize our suggestions as the single correct approach to individual psychotherapy, family therapy, or street work. We have taken subsections of the areas of male sexual abuse and integrated them with our preferred theoretical perspectives. We encourage the reader to do the same with his or her preferred clinical populations, theory base, and set of skills, rather than to adopt our models in their entirety. As we have challenged each other in assembling this volume, we have mercifully disabused each other (not without some protest and discomfort) of the idea that each of us is "correct." Our greatest hope is that our struggle to maintain respect for diversity of perspectives is catching.

Throughout this book, we often use the word "victim" to refer to those who have been on the receiving end of sexual abuse. We recognize there is considerable debate about the most descriptive and respectful term. Some argue that the word victim suggests a passivity and resignation and is hence undesirable, preferring the word "survivor." This is a valid point, but the word survivor has an even more complex set of connotations. We are uncomfortable with the term survivor, as it tends to imply only the most severe outcomes and suggests that an ongoing struggle is the only appropriate way to respond, thus disenfranchising individuals whose experience may not have been an ongoing struggle.

Around the turn of the century, knowledge of sexual abuse began to emerge, only to become submerged again and repressed on a massive scale. We therefore prefer the word victim, as it captures, in a raw but riveting manner, the violation that is inherent in sexual abuse. We believe the emphasis should be on the wrong that was done, not on any particular way of coping with that wrong. We also realize, however, that the many points of view on this issue of terminology all reflect different facets of sexual abuse experiences.

Male Sexual Abuse is organized into three parts. Part I: Assessment of and Treatment Planning and Individual Psychotherapy for Sexually Abused Adolescent Males is written by John C. Gonsiorek. Chapter 1 reflects on historical perspectives regarding adolescence and male sexual abuse. Chapter 2 critiques current models for understanding sexual abuse. Chapter 3 reviews some of the more salient findings from the male abuse literature and related areas; chapter 4 describes a model for psychological assessment and individual psychotherapy with young adult and late adolescent male victims of sexual abuse.

Part II: Family Systems Therapy for Adolescent Male Sex Offenders is written by Walter H. Bera. Chapter 5 reviews the clinical literature on adolescent sex offenders; chapter 6 describes family systems treatment approaches. Chapter 7 relates in detail victim-sensitive offender therapy.

Part III: A Model for Working With Adolescent Male Prostitutes is written by Don LeTourneau. Chapter 8 reviews what is known about male prostitution. Chapter 9 describes various treatment approaches and a detached youth work model.

An epilogue, by John C. Gonsiorek, finishes the volume. In keeping with the open-ended and inconclusive way we view this field, each author draws the conclusions he sees fit in each chapter, and the book is not "tied together" with a grand summary. We believe that at this juncture, divergent, not convergent, thinking will most benefit the study and understanding of sexual abuse.

PART I

Assessment of and Treatment Planning and Individual Psychotherapy for Sexually Abused Adolescent Males

JOHN C. GONSIOREK

1

Historical and Background Perspectives on Adolescent and Male Sexual Abuse

THIS CHAPTER ADDRESSES issues that are typically neglected, avoided, or misunderstood. For a comprehensive historical perspective, readers are referred to the work of Vander Mey (1988, 1992a, 1992b) and the references cited in this chapter. This chapter critiques some internal contradictions in the sexual abuse field; places the concept of adolescence in a historical context; raises the often neglected issues of diversity, erotophobia, and homophobia; and introduces recent understandings about sexual orientation.

The study of sexual abuse is a relatively new field, at least in its current incarnation. Masson (1984) describes an effort to explore this area almost 100 years ago, as well as its eventual suppression. Yet, much writing on sexual abuse lacks historical perspective. It appears that this area emerged suddenly as victims came forward in the 1970s. Writers with more historical grounding point to Freud's "discovery" of sexual abuse in his early work and his later refutation of it. This is important not only for its historical significance, but for its theoretical import. The refutation of the reality of client reports of sexual abuse is a central component in Freud's theory of the unconscious. Arguably the most powerful theoretical structure in mental health, the psychoanalytic perspective is predicated on the belief that reports of childhood sexual abuse generally are not real. Psychological perspectives appear to have a history of extremism in the ways they view sexual abuse.

Methodologically sound research on sexual abuse is expensive and more challenging to undertake than most endeavors in the behavioral sciences. An adequate empirical base is only beginning to emerge in a few areas. One might anticipate that, under these circumstances, theoretical and clinical perspectives would be cautious and tentative. Instead, they display a distinct tendency to be overreaching, conclusive, and dogmatic. This is a common failing in the behavioral and social sciences; however, the study of sexual abuse displays it to an unusual degree.

For example, there is no parallel in the behavioral sciences to the assertion made in some quarters early during sexual abuse theory development that "victims never lie." The assertion itself is not surprising; one might expect this from the popular press. What is surprising is its pronouncement by some mental health professionals and behavioral science researchers as a rationale for incomplete assessment or sweeping conclusions when the available database was insufficient. Even after malpractice actions against mental health professionals have skyrocketed in the area of sexual abuse/child custody situations, some mental health professionals continue to assert that they "can tell" who is telling the truth even in the most adversarial and contentious sexual abuse/child custody situations. Whether victims do or do not lie (or, more correctly, which victims respond with what degree of veracity under which circumstances) is an empirical question not conclusively answered and inadequately researched (see chapter 3 for further discussion of this subject).

Theory and treatment in the area of sexual abuse tend to stand apart, unintegrated with the main body of theory and clinical practice in the behavioral sciences. For a problem perceived to be so damaging, its conceptualization and remediation have often been asserted in minimalist and simplistic terms. If the initial observations and findings about sexual abuse are accurate (and we believe they generally are), how abuse experiences affect victims, what paths result in certain individuals perpetrating, and how all involved can experience meaningful remediation of their problems and pain are as complex as anything in the behavioral sciences or clinical practice.

We do not purport to offer a sophisticated historical analysis of how this pandemic of simplistic thinking came to be. Part of the problem may be that the forces that are most effective at bringing attention to a neglected issue are often not the most effective at explicating and integrating it. While the field of sexual abuse would not exist without feminism, as chapter 2 argues, feminist perspectives alone seem unable to conceptualize the diversity inherent in sexual abuse, and to create clinical models that can respond to that diversity.

Initially, it is important to take a broad perspective of sexual abuse. A number of historical and theoretical concepts important for understanding adolescent males as victims and perpetrators of sexual abuse are discussed below.

Males as victims and perpetrators of sexual abuse cannot be understood without a grounding in the pervasive erotophobia, denial of diversity, and homophobia of our culture, and in the development of sexual identity. Most sexual victimization of males is very likely done by males. While this creates no simple prediction about the sexual orientation or sexual identity of either victim or perpetrator, American culture's homophobia and stereotyping become mobilized by these situations. Understanding this homophobia is an important component to understanding the causes of adolescent male sexual abuse.

THE HISTORY OF ADOLESCENCE AS A CONCEPT

In late-20th-century North America, most individuals, including most mental health professionals, are likely to view the life phase known as "adolescence" as self-evident and, without question, "real." Adolescents are seen as a class of humans, as distinctive as infants, children, and adults, that faces unique developmental challenges and shares common psychological processes. Training programs in the health and behavioral sciences increasingly treat adolescence as a distinct area of specialization. Indeed, much current knowledge about adolescence has developed because areas such as developmental psychology and adolescent medicine made the assumption that adolescence is a distinct entity worthy of study.

It is important to realize, however, that this was not always so. Some historians argue that the concepts of adolescence and even childhood are relatively new: "It seems more probable that there was no place for childhood in the medieval world" (Aries, 1962, p. 33).

Aries (1962) suggests that the concept of childhood as a distinct phase of human development emerged in the Middle Ages as a complex distillation of social, religious, economic, and political forces. In particular, the development of the concept of childhood was linked with "the growing influence of Christianity on life and manners" (p. 43). As time passed, the importance of a nuclear family to the social order (as opposed to the more amorphous extended families of earlier times), coupled with the use of the concept of childhood to further religious ideas, crystallized into a concept of childhood as a fragile stage in human existence. In the 18th and 19th centuries, these two trends merged with others (such as concerns about cleanliness, hygiene, and physical health and the need for predictable training and education of the workforce) to strengthen the concept of childhood.

As the 19th century progressed, the nuclear family as the central social unit began to have increasing political, social, and economic importance. A rationale for the nuclear family was to provide protection and development for children. With the emergence of organized medicine and the increasing medicalization of social issues in the late 19th century, the concept of childhood as a distinct real entity became more urgent, warranting not only the attention of the family but also the attention of the helping professions to ease and monitor children through the transitions, conceptualized as increasingly difficult and fragile, to adulthood. In this process, adolescence as a distinct period of life and development began to emerge.

This particular structuring of both the family and childhood as distinct entities is neither universal nor inevitable. As some historians (Veyne, 1987) note, during other historical epochs, such as the Roman period, the basic role and structure of the family as well as the existence and conceptualization of a childhood period, while accepted, were construed so differently as to be qualitatively distinct. A historical perspective suggests that not only the family but the conceptualization of developmental stages is rooted in a social, political, economic, and religious context inextricably bound to time and place. (See Calvert, 1991, for a history of childhood in the United States;

deMause, 1982, especially chapter 1, for a general history of childhood; Hart, 1991, for a history of children's rights; and Radbill, 1974, for a history of child abuse.)

This is not to suggest that conceptualization of childhood as a distinct entity is a mere cultural figment of the imagination. Indeed, some argue that conceptualization of childhood as a distinct period is a hallmark of civilized societies. Rather, the strength of the conceptualization of childhood, and even more so its particulars and structure, varies across time and cultures. This is even more true for adolescence, a relative newcomer as a distinct entity and less stable as a fixed concept.

Throughout the majority of history, persons were considered fully adult at a time in life that is now labeled adolescence. Even in cultures and historical periods that have a transitional phase between childhood and adulthood, this phase appears to be briefer than our own conceptualization and the transition to adulthood was made at an age younger than ours. This was true in our own society until the industrial revolution and remains true in many third-world countries today. As Veyne (1987) describes, the Romans (who had a conceptualization of childhood, although not like our own) rapidly transited children into full adulthood during a period that we consider mid-adolescence, ages 14 through 16. Today's research on differences in family structures across ethnic, class, and racial groups begins to capture some of this idea of variance, but often does not recognize the magnitude of possible variability once cultural and historical variation are added. In other words, current concepts of diversity are blind to the effects of time and historical development.

Moreover, in the 20th century there appears to be a trend to prolong the duration of adolescence, particularly among upper-socioeconomic strata. Adolescence no longer ends at age 18, the traditional legal beginning of adulthood, but increasingly extends through the college years. Our society is not only ambivalent about when an individual is accorded the rank of adult, but also capricious, as shifts in the legal age for the consumption in alcohol over recent decades suggest. (Ironically, one of the few relatively stable hallmarks of adulthood has been the age at which one can join the military.) The development and expansion of adolescence runs contrary to a trend toward earlier physical sexual maturation that began in the late 19th century in industrialized societies. Consequently, the biological hallmarks of adulthood have steadily diverged from the cultural concept of adulthood.

Adolescence Today

In its current North American conceptualization, adolescence is generally viewed as an intermediate period between childhood and adulthood that is catalytic, in that both psychological and biological development reach a kind of crescendo, more or less setting into place the physical and emotional framework of the human being who will now be deemed adult. Most developmental psychological theories posit explicitly or implicitly that adolescence is the last great burst of development, after which the variations of adult development are relatively minor. Despite recent increasing interest in the complexity and strength of postadolescent adult development, there is little evidence that these adult development theories alter the primacy afforded childhood and adolescence in theory.

It would be simplistic to conclude that because there are historical, political, economic, and social bases of the current conceptualization of adolescence, and because adolescence as we understand it in late-20th-century North America may not be universal, adolescence is therefore less "real." Most viewpoints that adopt this perspective, often known as social constructionist or deconstructionist, at times imply that dissecting such influences somehow renders a concept transparent, null, or less real.

Not only are adolescents depicted as immature and incapable of adult decision making, adolescents themselves generally accept this view. Current cultural institutions expect and tolerate immature behavior from adolescents. Large social structures such as educational institutions, the legal system, health care, and the family accept and promulgate this reality, as do adolescents. The fact that adolescence may be culturally constructed as a psychosocial reality does not mean that it is easily discarded, that it can or should be discarded, or that, for individuals operating within this cultural context, its reality and power are diminished.

Sexual Expression

There is probably no area conceptualized more distinctly as a purely adult prerogative than sexual expression. In our culture, sexual expression is reserved for adults, specifically heterosexual, married adults. Sexual expression is not seen as a proper adolescent prerogative; rather adolescent sexual expression is construed as an institutional and psychopathological problem requiring a response from parents, schools, clergy, physicians, mental health professionals, and the court system. The intent of this concern is to understand, categorize, legislate, pathologize, cure, and ultimately suppress adolescent sexuality.

This view is widely held, despite the fact that throughout human history individuals were fully sexual, reproducing at ages that are now viewed as too immature to permit sexual expression. One does not have to look far to see the tensions and incongruities of this view. Skyrocketing rates of adolescent pregnancy and sexually transmitted diseases suggest that whatever position one takes on adolescent sexuality, the effectiveness of its repression is without doubt a failure.

The Social Constructionist View

The current view of adolescence is relatively new. For example, a comparison of age-of-consent laws in the United States in the last 100 years suggests that not too long ago in a more agrarian, less industrialized, society, sexual expression and marriage were deemed appropriate activities at an age at which individuals today are deemed incapable of such activities on the basis of their "psychological immaturity."

While some more politicized commentators have referred to this incongruous state of affairs as a "colonization" of childhood (Mendel, 1971), such radical deconstructionist or social constructionist perspectives miss the point. All cultures have powerful internal rationales for what they do that are pervasively encoded into the social structures and individual psyches of members in that culture. One is hard-pressed to find cultures that do not utilize such ultimately arbitrary structures. As Berman (1982) notes, such radical social constructionist perspectives offer only "a world historical alibi for the sentence of passivity and helplessness" (p. 35).

However, there is an appropriate use for social constructionist perspectives. At a point of rapid social, cultural, and political change (which is a fair description of our time), the most basic assumptions not only can shift but probably are shifting; in Berman's (1982) phrase, "all that is solid melts into air." The mental health disciplines have been especially myopic in this regard, glibly describing observations that may be astute about white, North American, English-speaking, middle-class, mid- to late-20th-century culture as universal truths about human nature. While ambivalently and incompletely embracing the "minor" variations of ethnic, race, and (to a lesser extent) class diversity within one culture at one point in time, mental health perspectives quickly dismiss as ridiculous the possibility that "major" variations of change over time and cultures unlike Western ones might be so extensive as to demand a revision of basic conceptual categories.

THE PRESENT SOCIAL CONTEXT

The discussion so far has focused on historical challenges to current conceptualizations about adolescence. One could argue that current realities about the lives of some adolescents are alone sufficiently incongruous to challenge our notions of adolescence. Current realities regarding adolescence are considerably more grim than musings on the historical context:

- Every 8 seconds an adolescent drops out of school (552,000 in the 1987-1988 school year)
- Every 14 seconds a child/adolescent reports being abused or neglected (2.2 million in 1986, up 66% since 1979)
- Every 26 seconds an adolescent runs away from home (1.2 million per year)
- Every 7 minutes a youth is arrested for a drug offense (79,986 per year)
- Every 2 hours a young man between 15 and 25 is murdered (4,233 in 1987)
- Youth of color and/or poor youth represent a disproportionate number of these youth

The catalog of similarly somber statistics is extensive (Children's Defense Fund, 1990).

Because of demographic changes, the United States faces a future in which children and youth will be a shrinking share of the population. There will be 14% fewer young people in the 18-24 range in the year 2000. Nearly one third of the nation's 18- to 24-year-olds will be from minority groups, compared to less than one quarter in 1985. Today, more than 12 million children and youth have no health insurance. The earning power of young males has dropped sharply since 1973. Foundations, business, education, health, and welfare groups have issued reports that warn of the impending problems from society's inability to create environments for young people that foster growth and development.

Kurth-Schai (1988) presents a conceptual continuum to describe contemporary paradigms of children in society. On one end of the continuum is the image of children as victims of adult society. The assumption in this image is that children are vulnerable and in need of adult protection. The most obvious examples include the numbers of children who are physically, sexually, or emotionally abused and, more recently, who have joined the ranks of persons with AIDS. In this image of children, those who are not overtly victimized may be sentimentalized as "economically/socially worthless but emotionally priceless."

At the other end of the continuum is the image of children as threats to adult society. The assumption in this image is that youth are dangerous and in need of adult control. Images of youth as threats to established political, educational, and moral conventions have been perpetrated by youth participation in civil rights and antiwar protests during the 1960s, classroom violence during the 1970s, and gang warfare during the 1980s and 1990s.

In an intermediary position on the continuum is the image of children as learners of adult society. The assumption in this image is that children are incomplete, incompetent, and in need of adult guidance. Because guidance can include elements of both control and protection, this paradigm can be used to support philosophical/political positions associated with either of the other two positions. This image has gained academic endorsement in modern child development theories: for sociologists, through theories of socialization; for anthropologists, through theories of enculturation; and for psychologists, through universal stage theories. All assume that human development is orderly, predictable, and universal. All are blind and/or antagonistic to the historical perspectives and assume the "reality" of the categories they utilize.

Kurth-Schai (1988) points out:

> By conceptualizing children as objects of sentimentalization we trivialize their thoughts and actions. By seeing children as objects of socialization we obscure their social insight and environmental-shaping competence. By regarding children as victims we obscure their potential for adaptations and survival. By perceiving children as threats to society we ignore their potential as catalysts for positive social change. (p. 117)

Toffler (1974) notes:

> The secret message communicated to most young people today by the society around them is that they are not needed, that the society will run itself quite nicely until they—at some distant point in the future—will take over the reins. Yet the fact is that the society is not running itself nicely . . . because the rest of us need all the energy, brains, imagination, and talent that young people can bring to bear on our difficulties. For a society to attempt to solve its desperate problems without the full participation of even very young people is imbecile. (p. 15)

Adolescent Sexual Abuse

Given current conceptualizations of young people and gender stereotyping, young males are more likely to be considered threats to society and young females are more likely to be considered victims of society. Sexual abuse of males complicates and muddles these stereotypes (i.e., Are they victims or offenders? Are most offenders victims? Are they potential offenders?). As a result, sexual abuse of males elicits much resistance; it is more threatening to current conceptualizations of adolescence, gender, and social structure than most people can easily articulate.

Many theories of sexual abuse treatment for children and youth (both males and females) fail in three key aspects:

1. By viewing youth as victims, threats, or incompetents, these theories fail to be client driven, not allowing the client to create meaning or to have a proactive role in treatment.
2. By failing to recognize the economic, social, and developmental realities of young peoples' lives, these theories ignore environmental factors that mitigate or counteract many treatment strategies; these environmental factors may be a cause of presenting problems, instead of, or in addition to, intrapsychic issues.
3. By focusing on the dysfunctional, these theories often overlook creative adaptation and factors that foster resilience.

The reason why many survivors of abuse do not begin to heal until adulthood may be more related to our culture's incapacity or unwillingness to empower, listen to, and respond to young people than it is to the inability of these survivors to address those issues until adulthood.

DIVERSITY, EROTOPHOBIA, AND HOMOPHOBIA

Even as a relatively accurate description of the conjunction of a particular culture and time, current perspectives on sexual abuse still have problems. North American society, the context in which current knowledge of sexual abuse has developed, is not only pluralistic but becoming more so. Most information about mental health practice in the behavioral sciences, including sexual abuse, describes a subset that is primarily white, English speaking, and middle class or above.

There is not only political injustice in this state of affairs, there is also scientific inaccuracy. It is simply poor science to develop theory and practice on samples wherein certain classes of individuals are overrepresented more than their numbers warrant. In particular, it is in the areas of class, cultural, ethnic, and racial diversity that concepts relating to the nature of adolescence, the role of the family, and the nature of childhood reflect greater diversity than current scientific knowledge encompasses (see Homma-True, Greene, Lopez, & Trimble, 1993, for elaboration).

Another factor that complicates any discussion of adolescent sexual abuse is our culture's pronounced erotophobia. Our culture is obsessed with sex, yet phobic and deeply distrustful of sexuality. Considerable attention is focused on sexual behavior rather than on the integration of intimacy and sexuality. North American, particularly U.S., society is deeply ambivalent about sexuality, so much so, that the United States lacks the basic sex education school curricula considered minimal in most Western industrialized societies.

Sexual faults deserve a penalty in the public eye far greater than the most egregious financial or political corruption. Concern about the influence of the media on children and adolescents focuses on sexual material, although most empirical studies suggest that such material is most problematic in the area of interpersonal violence. The deeply embedded erotophobia in our culture makes discussions of sexuality, particularly adolescent sexuality and even more particularly adolescent sexual abuse, problematic and complicated.

Homosexuality in American Culture

Most men who are sexually victimized as children or adolescents are so abused by males (see chapter 3). This belief mobilizes our culture's extensive hostility to homosexuality even though this situation is no more representative of homosexuality than situations of sexual abuse by adult males of female children are representative of heterosexuality. Yet the cultural myths persist to such an extent that they must be factored into any understanding of adolescent male sexual abuse.

In our culture, most individuals are socialized, to varying degrees, to be negatively predisposed toward homosexuality. The range of these negative biases extends from denial that homosexual individuals exist to indictments of homosexuals as diseased, sinful, or criminal. Allport (1954) discusses the general nature of prejudice and its effects, while Herek (1991) addresses the complex social psychological processes that perpetrate such stereotyped perceptions. As Herek notes, an extraordinary amount of organized bigotry, random violence, and discrimination is directed against individuals who are homosexual or perceived to be homosexual.

"Homophobia" refers to an irrational and distorted view of homosexuality or homosexual persons. Among heterosexual individuals, homophobia is commonly manifest as a prejudice or general discomfort with homosexuality, developed and maintained through the psychological processes described by Herek. The intensity of these feelings is modulated by a number of factors, including personal history, contact with homosexual individuals, and individual psychological makeup. For example, there appears to be an inverse relationship between levels of homophobia and interaction with gay and lesbian individuals (Staats, 1978; see Herek, 1991, for discussion of the complexities of this finding); that is, certain kinds of contact with homosexual individuals reduces homophobic bias. As a result of the pervasive homophobia, in situations of sexual abuse where both the victim and the perpetrator are male, there is a distinct tendency for the same-sex aspect of the interaction rather than the exploitative aspect to predominate in the minds of most observers.

SEXUAL IDENTITY DEVELOPMENT

Another area that warrants explication in understanding the male adolescent experience in sexual abuse is the development of sexual identity in males. This area is generally one of considerable confusion for both lay people and professionals. The field is itself in a somewhat disorganized state. (For a comprehensive look at sexual identities across the life span, D'Augelli & Patterson, 1994, is recommended.) The first problem in understanding male adolescent sexual abuse is the general confusion that exists about sexual identity.

Shively and DeCecco (1977) divide sexual identity into four components: biological sex—the genetic material encoded in chromosomes; gender identity—the psychological sense of being male or female; social sex role—adherence to culturally created behaviors and attitudes that are deemed appropriate for males or females; and sexual orientation—the erotic and/or affectional disposition to the same and/or opposite sex. It is important to note that the first three components bear no necessary relationship to sexual orientation in any given individual; however, each has been confused with sexual orientation.

Confusion frequently arises between sexual orientation and sexual behavior. Engaging in either same- or opposite-sex behavior is not always a good predictor of ongoing disposition to same- or opposite-sex behavior; nor is it a good predictor of a psychological sense of identity as bisexual, homosexual, or heterosexual.

A number of different psychological processes impinge on this. Many individuals who have significant same-sex interests deny these on account of societal or intrapsychic pressures. There is therefore a class of individuals who engage in same-sex behavior but deny or distort to themselves recognition that this indicates an ongoing same-sex desire. A different situation occurs in individuals who are oriented toward the same sex, but who deny this to themselves and become heterosexually involved as a part of this denial. In this situation, sexual behavior may be directed toward the opposite sex while fantasy life and affectional disposition may be directed toward the same sex. Finally, there is a class of individuals who may engage regularly in same-sex behavior for reasons other than erotic attraction to the same sex, who retain full awareness of this, and who assume incorrectly that this represents a same-sex erotic preference. It should be noted that the division of sexual orientation into categories such as homosexuality, heterosexuality, and bisexuality is currently viewed in some quarters as inaccurate and in need of revision. (Gonsiorek & Weinrich, 1991, provide discussion on the definition and scope of sexual orientation.)

For the purposes of this discussion, the original research on males by Kinsey and his associates (Kinsey, Pomeroy, & Martin, 1948) makes the relevant points. They found the following:

- 50% of the population is exclusively heterosexual in both activity and fantasy.
- 37% of the population has had at least one overt homosexual experience between adolescence and old age and an additional 13% have had at least incidental homosexual fantasy without behavior.
- For at least a 3-year period between the ages of 16 and 55, 10% of the male population has been predominantly homosexual.
- About 4% of the male population is solely homosexual beginning with adolescence and continuing through adulthood.

The Kinsey data clearly indicate a discordance between homosexual behavior and a stable ongoing pattern of homosexual practice. Taken at their most extreme, these data could suggest that of all males who have had at least one homosexual sexual experience, only one in nine will be exclusively homosexual throughout their adult lives (the 37% figure versus the 4% figure). Similarly, the number of individuals who are predominantly homosexual for at least a 3-year period is 2½ times the number of individuals who are exclusively homosexual throughout their adult lives (the 10% figure versus the 4% figure).

Descriptions of homosexuality in prison note individuals who engage in homosexual behavior for prolonged periods of time, but, when given a choice of sexual opportunities outside prison, engage only in heterosexual behavior. The point is clear: Sexual behavior at any one point in time, or even for an extended period of time, is a weak predictor of ongoing sexual interest and behavior throughout the life span, and bears no necessary relationship to self-identification as homosexual, heterosexual, or bisexual.

Coming Out

A related issue is the coming-out process, or the development of an identity as gay. This area is important both to recognize those individuals who are undergoing such a process and to recognize those who are not, as the predominant same-sex nature of much sexual abuse of male adolescents can often obscure this difference. Following is a cursory introduction to this area. (Readers are referred to Gonsiorek, 1988; Gonsiorek & Rudolph, 1991; Malyon, 1981; and Martin, 1982, for further information.)

Boys who eventually have predominant same-sex orientation are raised in the homophobic culture described above. In individuals who eventually become gay, these antihomosexual prejudices mobilize a series of psychological processes that occur in addition to the other developmental events of childhood and adolescence. Boys who will eventually become bisexual or homosexual often develop an awareness of being different at an early point in their lives, often in childhood. They may not understand the nature or precise meaning of this difference, but they quickly learn that it is negatively regarded. As these boys mature, they reach a fuller understanding of the nature of this difference and also of the negative societal reaction to it. These negative feelings are often incorporated into self-image, resulting in varying degrees of internalized homophobia. These negative feelings about a part of one's self—that is, sexual orientation—are often overgeneralized to encompass the entire self. Later effects may range from a tendency toward self-doubt in the face of prejudice to unmistakable overt self-hatred. This process occurs later and in addition to earlier developmental processes; that is, it is overlaid on a full range of preexisting personality development.

This internalized homophobia can have various expressions. Some individuals can overtly experience it and may consciously view themselves as evil, second class, or inferior on account of their homosexuality. They may abuse substances or engage in other self-destructive or abusive behaviors. Because overt internalized homophobia is so psychologically painful and destabilizing, it is probably less prevalent than covert forms. Few persons easily tolerate conscious self-deprecation. The covert forms of internalized homophobia therefore are likely to be the most common. Such individuals appear to accept themselves, yet sabotage their own efforts in a variety of subtle ways.

In adolescence, however, these psychological processes are likely to be underground. Denial of same-sex interests often predominates and has a number of effects. Teenagers who eventually become gay or bisexual often withdraw from typical adolescent social experiences. Socializing with either gender can be emotionally difficult: Interaction with persons of the same gender may arouse strong sexual or emotional feelings, while interaction with the opposite gender may be a painful reminder of the absence of heterosexual interest. As a result, teenagers who eventually become gay or bisexual may avoid the interpersonal experimentation that is an important developmental task of adolescence. This suppression and repression of same-sex desires and interests is often accomplished at the expense of normal adolescent interpersonal skill development.

Denial tends to be problematic, as adolescent sexuality is somewhat diffuse. That which is being denied is a moving target. As a result, denial often is generalized beyond sexual areas. As sexual drive increases during adolescence, greater intrapsychic energy is required to maintain denial. The effect of this escalating emotional blockade is that some adolescents who eventually become gay or bisexual reach adulthood as strangers to their own inner emotional life and have developed habits of constricting any strong feelings. So, while homosexuality per se is clearly understood as a nonpathological variation in human sexuality (see Gonsiorek, 1991, for a review of this literature), some adaptations to it are psychologically constricting and in that sense pathological. The same can be said for heterosexual and bisexual variations.

When emergence of same-sex interest does occur, it is almost never as a result of a conscious decision. Typically, a strong emotional or sexual interest toward someone of the same sex emerges in a way that breaks through the denial. For teenagers who eventually become gay or bisexual, the coming-out process is initiated by a defensive collapse that often represents the beginning of a shift in that individual's core sexual identity. As a result there are likely to be dramatic levels of emotional distress. There appear to be gender differences (Gonsiorek, 1988; Gonsiorek & Rudolph, 1991) in the direction of males being more dramatically and floridly symptomatic due to differences in sex-role socialization. Males also tend to sexualize these conflicts to a greater extent than females.

The coming-out process as an overt event is triggered by defensive collapse in an individual who, in order to maintain repression of same-sex interests, has been avoiding interpersonal skill development typical in adolescence and has become increasingly alienated from his or her own emotions. Not surprisingly, individuals in the coming-out process, particularly men, often go through a period of considerable emotional turmoil. It is important to note, however, that homosexuality and psychopathology are not intrinsically related (Gonsiorek, 1991), and that most individuals after a period of temporary distress appear to weather this crisis and proceed with their lives.

Sex-Role Stereotyping

Sex-role stereotyping is also an important consideration in understanding adolescent male sexuality. Most studies on social sex roles suggest that these roles are most rigidly defined and behaviorally prescriptive during adolescence. While social sex roles are complex in their effects and individuals vary in the degree to which social sex roles are adhered, there is a general tendency for males in this culture and adolescent males in particular to view sexual expression apart from intimacy and, perhaps more importantly, to view sexual expression as a male prerogative. Put another way, most male adolescents view sexual contact as something that they have willed or chosen except in situations of obvious force. This creates a situation where adolescent males are often unaware of the interplay between sexual and other emotional needs and of the subtleties with which sexuality can be manipulated. This represents a particular way in which adolescent males can be vulnerable to sexual abuse.

SUMMARY

Sexual abuse of males presents a significant challenge to our perception of adolescence, gender, and social structure. Understanding how other times and places view human development, the role of diversity, how homophobia functions, and the development of sexual identity can facilitate more open, inclusive, and useful perspectives in this area.

2

A Critique of Current
Models in Sexual Abuse

THIS CHAPTER BRIEFLY OUTLINES and critiques some current models for understanding sexual abuse. The term *model* is used loosely not to refer to a distinct school of thought but to ideas that appear to be consistent with and represent a relatively cohesive view of sexual abuse or certain aspects of sexual abuse. These models are presented with broad strokes, to outline core beliefs that impinge on the area of male abuse. Some, especially feminist and psychoanalytic perspectives, contain variations and elaborations far from the ideas described here. Our interest is in describing the assumptions, limitations, and points of tension and paradox of current models.

Most of the discussion focuses on feminist models, the dominant perspective today. Psychoanalytic models, which generally preceded feminist perspectives, are discussed briefly as a point of comparison. Profamily models usually represent a lay perspective, although they may be more present in clinical practice than their scarce representation in professional literature suggests. Propedophile models are discussed at some length, partially because their explication can help disentangle sources of some of the homophobic bias described in chapter 1, and partially because they are usually ignored in the professional literature, and so operate as underground models.

FEMINIST MODELS

The field of sexual abuse would not exist if it were not for feminism. At a time when North American culture viewed sexual abuse as a rare and arcane phenomenon not worthy of serious discussion, feminist advocates, theoreticians, and researchers courageously and tenaciously insisted on the reality, relatively high frequency, and deleterious effects of sexual abuse. Developing from the late 1960s to the present, feminist models, through increasingly diverging perspectives, represent the current dominant models in the area of sexual abuse.

In feminist perspectives, sexual abuse is usually seen as a variant of the ways in which men control and oppress women. Feminist perspectives, then, view sexual abuse as overwhelmingly perpetrated by males upon females. These models implicitly or explicitly minimize male victims and female perpetrators or recast them as mirrors of the male perpetrator/female victim model without recognizing that they may have unique characteristics. Although some feminist models can accommodate a differential understanding of types of sexual abusers, these are generally posited within a sociopolitical context of sexual abuse as an example of the oppression of men upon women. Vander Mey (1988, 1992a, 1992b) offers comprehensive analyses of feminist perspectives on rape, incest, and sexual abuse.

Feminist models usually have as their ultimate goal the righting of sociopolitical wrongs, of which sexual abuse is merely an example. As this is essentially a political and moral perspective, those who disagree with aspects of feminist perspectives tend to become suspected of sociopolitical corruption. Feminist perspectives implicitly or explicitly carry with them a "siege mentality" in which individuals are either for or against the "right" cause. If an individual is deemed against the right cause, then, feminists believe, his or her opinions are lacking in credibility because they are suspect. Feminist perspectives have a difficult time accommodating divergence of opinion or empirical information that do not fit their framework.

Feminist perspectives are, at their core, a political and social change paradigm. Indeed, that is one of their strengths. At a time when sexual abuse had no scientific data or theoretical respectability to support it, only sheer political will could have been effective against the intransigence of the professional communities surrounding this issue.

Once feminist models forcibly opened the issue of sexual abuse to scientific inquiry and the development of clinical practice models, the preeminence of the political rights of women increasingly developed into a hindrance. Restricting scientific discourse to theory, research, and practice that is congruent with a limited sociopolitical perspective is poor science.

Clinical practice, in particular, has at its core the ethical requirement and legal structure for practitioners to operate in the best interests of the individual patient, in a specific sense. The tendency to view the realities and rights of some patients as more legitimate than those of others due to their disenfranchisement, and to construe the best interests of the patient in an overarching manner focused on general political goals for certain classes of clients, leads to an ethically compromised and legally vulnerable clinical practice.

The paradox is that science and clinical practice do not seem to be (or at least have not been) able to work themselves out of the ruts they periodically create without a nonscientific, nonpractice driven challenge—that is, political will. The beneficial effect of the challenge by political will leads to the establishment of a more holistic and less biased science and clinical practice; which, paradoxically, ultimately rejects the excessively narrow claims of the political will that corrected it. The field of sexual abuse is at such a juncture as more paradoxes and contradictions emerge within feminist perspectives on sexual abuse.

A central tenet of feminist perspectives is that women are not seen as flawed, deficient versions of men but as whole, complete, and different entities in their own right. Yet, feminist perspectives often resist viewing the perceptions of male victims of sexual abuse as the touchstone to understanding male experiences. Instead, models of sexual abuse are derived from the experiences of female victims and are often held dogmatically.

Similarly, research suggests that those individuals who are victimized are not entirely random but include a disproportionate number of individuals noteworthy for their vulnerability prior to the actual sexual abuse. In keeping with their broad sociopolitical perspective, feminist models view the effects of abuse on victims as relatively monolithic, because the meaning of abuse is ultimately monolithic in this sociopolitical sense. The possibilities that some individuals may suffer minimally from abuse, that the effects of abuse may be diverse, and, especially, that abuse may intermingle with preabuse life experiences and problem areas are difficult for many feminist perspectives to accommodate.

The myth that male victims usually become perpetrators is a misconception not applied to female victims. Simple political slogans that sexual abuse is something men do to women become complicated by a full array of psychosocial problems, issues of equity and justice, and other concerns of which the rights of women are only one part.

An irony of some radical feminist perspectives is their insistence that victims of sexual abuse are purely and entirely victims. This seriously underestimates the real damage that childhood sexual abuse can cause. The propensity of some individuals to develop chronically self-destructive patterns as a result of their victimization is perhaps one of the most horrifying effects of victimization, as it increases the likelihood that victimization will continue in the future. Once such patterns are established, individuals with such patterns are ill-served by focusing solely on the wrongs done to them, rather than on how the wrongs done to them have led to self-destructive patterns that they now continue and bear personal responsibility to alter.

The role of the therapist within feminist perspectives is often to assist the client in undoing the specific damages caused by the abuse and to educate the client about broader sociopolitical issues and empower the client to act on those. Clients who may disagree with or have mixed feelings about the larger sociopolitical feminist viewpoint can sometimes be perceived as holding their opinions as a result of abuse or larger political oppression. In other words, differences of opinion are prone to be pathologized.

Feminist perspectives on therapy with abused clients are paradoxical in this regard. Although these perspectives endorse advocacy for the rights of clients, clients can be infantilized and treated as diseased or incompetent if they have substantially different viewpoints on larger sociopolitical issues. Similarly, although treatment is empowering for the specific effects of abuse, it can become intrusive and infantilizing if it assumes the therapist knows best what the sociopolitical larger picture is, and if a goal of therapy is to persuade the client of this. Feminist therapies run the risk of becoming what they aspire to remedy, that is, oppressive and controlling therapy.

Feminist therapies often implicitly assume that the rights of some people, such as women or victims, are more important than the rights of others, such as men or perpetrators. This creates another paradox in which the sexism and male privilege of "traditional" male therapists can be replaced by reverse sexism and moral privilege of radical feminist therapists. As a result, a range of actions from legislative remedies to suggestions made in therapy are undertaken in which the possible harm to others is considered as significantly less important than the potential benefit to women. In so doing, feminist perspectives erode their own moral basis. By substituting moral righteousness for raw power as the basis for privilege, they open the possibility that others with different value systems can assert higher moral privilege and thereby also decide, as some feminists do, that some human beings are more important than others.

These criticisms are primarily directed at the more radical feminist theorists in this area (Dominelli, 1986; Mackinnon, 1987; Rush, 1974). However, to the extent that moderate feminist theorists are silent on these problems, it is fair to characterize the problems outlined here as generally true of feminism.

We do not perceive these problems as failings of feminism; rather, as successes, albeit ironic ones. This development of a need for more heterodox and integrated theory and clinical practice and less politically restricted discourse on sexual abuse could never have come about without the single-minded insistence on the reality and seriousness of sexual abuse provided by feminism. Feminism is now challenged to take its rightful place as a necessary, but by itself insufficient, building block of a more eclectic, diverse, clinically sophisticated, and theoretically complex field of sexual abuse and to relinquish its role as the arbiter of the field.

Challenges to feminist perspectives have been most acute in the field of male sexual abuse. Victims who are not female and who do not necessarily respond as female victims do, and perpetrators who are not always male and not always powerful adults and whose motivations can include ignorance, stupidity, misinformation, and confusion as well as malice, arrogance, and insensitivity require even-handed explication. We have little doubt that sexual abuse is done by men to women more often than any other dyad. But other dyads exist, are not rare, are of equal human worth and scientific interest, and should be understood on their own terms and in a multiplicity of ways, not merely from feminist perspectives. If the field of sexual abuse is to obtain scientific respectability and its practice models are to obtain clinical integrity, sexual abuse in all its diversity must be understood and integrated.

Feminist views are not only articulated by women. Some recent writings on male victims (Hunter, 1990; Lew, 1988) are within a feminist framework in that they assume global, pervasive, and monolithic effects of sexual abuse; have a high advocacy component; treat therapy as a generally extensive process with elements of "therapist knows best" about phenomena outside therapy; and have a difficult time accommodating interactions with pre-sexual abuse damaging experiences. Such writers have adapted the core of feminist perspectives while changing aspects of the context. Not surprisingly, this male-feminist perspective is relatively inarticulate about a broader sociopolitical agenda, as the internal contradictions of adopting some but not all of the feminist perspective leave it without a clear sense of direction.

PSYCHOANALYTIC MODELS

Psychoanalytic models include a variety of perspectives that in some ways provide a mirror image of feminist perspectives. These models tend to minimize the specific effects of abuse experiences and maximize, in line with standard psychoanalytic thinking, the earliest developmental events as central. For example, a sexual abuse situation that began in the latency period (the modal time for abuse experiences to start) or later would a priori be deemed less important than earlier history because most of the individual's psychological structure had been laid down prior to the abuse. When effects of abuse are discussed, they tend to be subsumed as examples of other, more historically based, issues.

Analytic perspectives are hostile to political or client advocacy and generally view such perspectives as countertherapeutic. Analytic therapy is nonintrusive and nondirective, with little explicit attempt to shape or guide the therapy experience, although such passivity may mold in its own ways. Analytic perspectives often assume a point of cure, a feature they share with feminist perspectives. These two perspectives differ, however, in that analytic perspectives explicitly view the point of cure as a resolution of the broader intrapsychic issues of which the abuse may be merely an example, whereas feminist notions of cure involve, usually implicitly, not only a resolution of the specific abuse but also far-reaching changes in consciousness in which a broader feminist sociopolitical perspective is adopted.

The rejection of the reality of sexual abuse by Freud in his development of the theory of the unconscious, although unevenly accepted by modern proponents, gives psychoanalytic perspectives a tendency to minimize or ignore the reality of child abuse. Analytic perspectives are capable of handling issues prior to the abuse in a sophisticated and complex manner, but they tend to so minimize the abuse that they often waste this advantage.

Proponents of psychoanalytic models view intrapsychic change as the only truly profound change. For victims or perpetrators of sexual abuse with significant behavior problems, as many males present, this perspective offers little to ameliorate symptoms until a client is "ready" for intrapsychic change. Psychoanalytic perspectives often translate their failure with such situations into pessimism about the treatability of individuals who do not respond well to its techniques.

Analytic perspectives tend to be limited by perspectives of culture, social class, and worldview; all the more so for their tendency to assert their universality and dismiss such concerns. The applicability of these perspectives beyond the Eurocentric upper-middle-class confines on which they were developed has long been suspect.

PROFAMILY MODELS

Profamily perspectives are often, but not always, associated with right-wing political movements. A core feature of these perspectives is the assumption that the family and larger social structures are primary and the individual is subordinate. To disagree with this view is to invite social chaos and societal collapse. Therefore, sexual abuse situations that are congruent with this political perspective are not only emphasized but demonologized; sexual abuse situations that run contrary to this political perspective are minimized or denied. Specifically, intrafamilial sexual abuse is minimized. When admitted at all, the welfare of the family as a unit, not the individual who has been abused, is asserted as paramount.

At the same time, nonfamilial sexual abuse, particularly sexual abuse perpetrated by males perceived to be homosexual, is considered a threat of the first order and its destructiveness is maximally emphasized. Because sexual abuse of males, more often than that of females, occurs in a nonintrafamilial context, profamily models are paradoxically sensitive to sexual abuse of males. The one paradigm these perspectives can easily admit, that of a nonfamily member male abusing a male victim, appears to be more represented in male abuse situations. The relative lack of concern for female victims is consistent with these perspectives' pervasive sexism.

Profamily perspectives are riddled with contradictions. Advocacy in the intrafamilial context is considered an intrusion of the state on the most sacred institution—the family—whereas no degree of advocacy is unwarranted in responding to sexual abuse outside family confines. This is not as contradictory as it appears, however, because the guiding principle is that the rights of the family and social institutions are paramount. This guiding principle unites these perspectives.

Therapy within profamily frameworks often runs a significant risk of unethical practice. The ethics codes of all major mental health professions share a requirement that the services rendered be in the best interests of the client. This is the basis for the entire ethical and practice structure of the mental health professions. Profamily models implicitly, and at times explicitly, deny this basic assumption, stating that the welfare of the family and of traditional social institutions are paramount and the individual's welfare must be subsumed to these institutions. Children and adolescents are ultimately viewed as property, to be handled in a way best suited to the family and other social structures. Legally, this perspective often runs into conflict with child protection statutes, which generally mandate reporting of child abuse and neglect regardless of circumstances or effects on families or other institutions.

PROPEDOPHILE MODELS

Propedophile models assert that the repression of childhood and adolescent sexuality is damaging to minors and therefore to society. As part of the broader liberation of children and adolescents, free sexual expression is encouraged. This sexual expression includes the "right" of children and adolescents to be sexual with adults.

These models suggest that treating minors as incapable of consent in relationships with adults is another aspect of disempowering minors and depriving them of their rights. Within these models, the negative effects of child abuse are viewed as illusory or fabricated, either to discredit pedophiles or to squelch childhood sexuality; or as a misunderstanding, in that society's negative reactions to childhood sexuality, not sexual contact between adults and children, cause negative effects.

Propedophile models claim to be uniquely sensitive to the needs and rights of minors, and at times claim to provide the emotional support and nurturing denied children and adolescents by a heartless society (O'Carroll, 1982). Minors are conceptualized within these models as primarily sexual in their needs. The possibility that minors may have areas of vulnerability and fragility, may be vulnerable to manipulation, and may confuse sexual and nonsexual needs are viewed as distortions. Paradoxically, then, propedophile models, which begin their arguments based on a wish to support childhood sexuality, end up supporting sexual access of pedophiles to children.

The propedophile movement devotes little energy to encouraging the right of children and adolescents to be sexual with each other or to be seen as individuals motivated by needs other than sexual. Ironically, propedophile models share with profamily models a view of children as property; however, profamily models view the appropriate use of children/property as in the best interests of the family and the state; whereas propedophile models view the best use of children/ property as in the sexual interests of pedophiles.

COMPARISON OF THE MODELS

The different models operate in different contexts and with different profiles. Prior to feminist models, child abuse models did not exist; there was primarily denial about child sexual abuse. (Although some researchers tried to direct attention to incest in the 1940s and 1950s; see Vander Mey's 1992b discussion of the work of Riemer and Weinberg.) Isolated pockets remain where service delivery systems deny the existence and seriousness of child abuse, sometimes but not necessarily out of any organized perspective such as the profamily or propedophile models; more often, simply from denial. These are fading rapidly, at least in professional circles. By and large, feminist models predominate.

Analytic models tend to keep a low profile, except in areas where analytic perspectives predominate, in which case anything other than analytic perspectives are viewed as simplistic, second-rate, and "not really therapy." When confronted with strong opposition, however, analytic perspectives tend to avoid conflict with feminist perspectives. Rather, they withdraw into the background, generally acting acquiescent or passively scornful toward feminist perspectives. Through their passivity, assiduous avoidance of advocacy, focus on the importance of factors prior to the abuse, and lack of directiveness with clients, analytic models tend to undermine feminist perspectives.

Profamily perspectives are generally the province of so-called Christian psychotherapists and other religiously oriented providers. Profamily perspectives are weakly represented in the mental health professions but assert occasional power in the legislative arena and in the courts. They can marshall their few professional experts and mobilize them effectively to serve as experts in key cases. Profamily perspectives can operate as a powerful lobby and directly challenge feminist perspectives in lobbying for legislation and social change. Although they are underrepresented in mental health, profamily perspectives can, through court cases and legislation, affect mental health services. The ability of right-wing profamily lobbyists to control the political agenda regarding adolescent pregnancy, birth control, and health care throughout the 1980s and early 1990s, despite opposition from health-care providers, is a good example. The role of these perspectives in the mental health professions is more as a devil's advocate; these models were the first to challenge the assumption that victims never lie. Although scholars of intelligence and integrity exist on both sides of the repressed memories versus false memory controversy, much of the subtext and public discourse on this debate is increasingly assuming a feminist versus profamily cast.

The propedophile movement is the most curious one in terms of its position and profile. Although it claims to have a database (Sandfort, 1982, 1983, 1984; Sandfort, Brongersma, & van Naerssen, 1990), the movement is generally regarded as fringe and without empirical foundation (Finkelhor, 1990a). The propedophile movement has virtually no clout politically, and is not well represented among mental health professionals or among feminists. It derives its weak power base from its peculiar relationship to some segments of gay male communities and by occasionally playing on the sympathies and support of "liberal" academics. It suggests few therapeutic strategies; its focus is on sociopolitical change for the benefit of pedophiles, although ostensibly for the rights of children.

The propedophile movement claims that the repression of pedophilia is similar to the repression of gay men and lesbians, women, and racial and ethnic minorities; if one repression is allowed, all will follow. This movement argues that, by analogy, the empirical foundations for overthrowing the illness model of homosexuality and racial and sexist stereotypes apply also to pedophilia, although besides analogic reasoning no data are behind this, as there are for the obsolescence of these other stereotypes. Under the guise of academic inquiry and criticism, this perspective is portrayed as having scientific credibility (see Sandfort et al., 1990; and Tsang, 1981).

Segments of gay male communities have frequently served as the launching pad of the propedophile movement. In a sense, the propedophile movement can exist only because of homophobia and the repression of homosexuality. The analogy that if pedophilia is repressed then homosexuality will also be strikes a chord in some gay males who are aware that homosexuals are the only remaining minority group where bigotry remains acceptable and officially sanctioned.

The propedophile movement may also capitalize on the existential experiences of some gay males. Many gay men can clearly recall a period in their own adolescence in which they were isolated, cut off from any support, their sexuality vilified and repressed, and their level of psychological functioning impaired. Peer support for emerging same-sex feelings was simply not available for most gay adolescents. Some gay adolescents resolve this dilemma by seeking out the adult gay community, some of whom provide support and a remedy to external oppression, and others of whom merely provide sexual contact or, at times, frank sexual exploitation.

Even in these latter situations, for the gay male adolescent who has experienced disparagement as a result of his sexuality, this valuing of sexuality alone may be powerful and positive enough to override, at least temporarily, exploitative aspects of the interaction between the adult and the adolescent. Whether or not a particular gay male has directly experienced this, he often knows this to be real from vicariously understanding the experience of his peers. Many gay male adolescents are keenly aware of their isolation and wish for contact, sexual and otherwise, with other gay males.

The propedophile movement exploits the oppression of homosexuality by playing up the fear that lack of acceptance of pedophilia foreshadows increasing intolerance toward homosexuality. On a deeper level, the propedophile movement resonates in the life experience of some gay men, who recall a time of intense isolation and longing for contact, sexual and otherwise, with other men. In this sense, there is a grain of truth, albeit distorted, in that the repression of adolescent sexuality can be damaging and its expression can be healing. The solution the propedophile model offers, however, is an exploitative one. But compared to the further repression of homosexuality, it may seem like the lesser of two evils for some gay males.

A genuine solution to the repression of adolescent sexuality involves full civil rights for homosexuals and the creation of support services for gay and lesbian youth in which they are afforded the same interpersonal opportunities and exploration that heterosexual youth are. The propedophile movement, however, deflects gay male communities from these goals by its focus on the sexual access of pedo- philes to youth.

The relationship between the propedophile community and the gay male community is paradoxical and complex. Some gay men find it virtually impossible to reject the propedophile movement until there is greater support for homosexuality; yet, in not rejecting the propedophile community, the gay male community elicits political rejection because of its perceived support for child abuse. The gay male community rarely conceptualizes these issues clearly. The propedophile community, whether consciously or not, exploits this dilemma artfully. In this way, the relationship of the propedophile movement to gay male communities is parasitic, not symbiotic.

Strengths and Weaknesses of the Models

The strength and value of feminist models are their unyielding insistence on the reality of sexual abuse and its damaging impact. The weaknesses of feminist models are their tendencies to bring sociopolitical concerns not necessarily directly related to a particular client into the therapy of that client and to be insufficiently sensitive to the history and personality factors of the individual prior to the abuse experience; and to restrict scientific discourse to that which is politically correct and congruent with feminist perspectives. This insistence on the reality of abuse is not obsolete; as discussed in chapter 3, greater questioning of this basic reality appears to be in the offing, as the false memory syndrome advocates sort out whether they will offer a scientific corrective to politically correct ideology and assumption, or right-wing "disinformation."

The main strength of psychoanalytic models is their ability to conceptualize the individual in a rich psychological context where a variety of historical and personal factors can be used to understand and treat the individual. The primary vulnerability of psychoanalytic models is their suspicion or outright rejection of the reality of sexual abuse effects or, in some more modern formulations, minimization of the trauma of the abuse while earlier historical factors are maximized. In addition, dynamic perspectives can run the risk of financial exploitation of clients as the nondirective, leisurely therapy style is inefficient. These models can be a disservice to individuals, many of whom are men, whose sequelae of sexual abuse include disinhibition and acting out problems because of the models' inability to provide sufficient structure and direction for such clients.

The profamily and propedophile perspectives do not have a great deal to offer in a direct sense, although both offer a nugget of truth amid their self-serving rhetoric. Profamily perspectives are exquisitely sensitive to understanding that sexual abuse occurs in a series of contexts—family, community, and societal—all of which have a stake in sexual abuse. Profamily perspectives react instinctively to the tendency of some mental health professionals to be unnecessarily overbearing and discounting of the importance of such contexts.

Propedophile perspectives are the most clear in espousing the rights of minors, including the rights of minors to be sexual, and are perhaps the clearest voice for the reality of adolescent sexuality. However, propedophile perspectives use this as a rhetorical device, a distraction from their systematic misconstruction of the rights of children, by equating the rights of children with the alleged right of pedophiles to have sexual access to children.

Neither the profamily nor the propedophile perspectives offer much of substance to mental health practice. Each does, however, remind mental health practitioners in a convoluted way of some blind spots and limitations in their assumptions.

THEORY-DRIVEN VERSUS CLIENT-DRIVEN MODELS OF TREATMENT

The economics of services for abuse victims and their political implications are also worthy of consideration. The analytic model offers individuals who have been sexually abused the same slow-moving, expensive, inefficient therapy of unknown but generally long duration that it offers everyone. The economics of analytic therapy has been one of the strongest reasons for its distrust by policy makers and its perennial attraction to entrepreneurial mental health providers.

However, feminist therapies increasingly run the same risk. When broad-ranging change in consciousness is a therapeutic goal and other therapeutic goals range far from the client's presenting problems, the client who came because of victimization may end up paying the therapist to inculcate him or her into the therapist's political agenda. We suggest that therapy that is unnecessarily prolonged, particularly for reasons external to the immediate needs of the client, is itself exploitation, a form of economic oppression, regardless of the sophistication, alleged righteousness, or urgency of its theoretical rationale.

The three clinical intervention models discussed in this volume differ in this regard. The goal-oriented, focused quality of these models tends to make the interventions briefer and more focused on therapeutic goals. These approaches are difficult where intervention goals are expansive, either in an intrapsychic or sociopolitical sense.

The models critiqued in this chapter are theory driven. As a result, goals extraneous or tangential to the individual have an increased probability of being included in interventions derived from them. The likelihood of unnecessary economic burden to the client increases as a function of the degree to which a model is theory driven.

The three models described later are client driven. The role of theory is subsumed to a source of suggestions; heuristic devices to inform, but not dominate, an intervention plan that is individually tailored. This factor plus the willingness to recombine therapy models into hybrids to maximize change decrease the likelihood of unnecessary economic burden for clients. Attentiveness to the economic implications of interventions is an important concern for all clients, particularly for individuals who have been victimized.

It is our observation that many therapists are relatively insensitive or inattentive to this concern. We reject arguments that therapists as a group are naive about economics. Rather, it is our observation that entrepreneurially driven therapists attempt to act generally in the best interests of their clients except when their economic self-interest is involved, in which case they generally act in their economic self-interest. This is a weakness of the mental health and human services industries that is merely exaggerated and more sharply drawn in clinical work with sexual abuse victims. It is unlikely these concerns will be resolved soon or easily as the number of therapists increases and competition increases for the already besieged health-care dollar.

One of the effects of therapists who operate primarily in their economic self-interest with sexually abused clients is a tendency to overdiagnose in order to obtain authorization of continued treatment. To the problems and stresses already experienced by the abused individual can sometimes be added unnecessary or overpathologizing diagnoses that have a significant impact on the individual's future insurability in health, life, and other insurance situations.

Managed health care, with its very different but still very entrepreneurially based system, can impose a different kind of dilemma for victims seeking treatment. Entrepreneurially based therapists in the private sector receive maximum economic rewards by prolonging treatment as long as possible. Entrepreneurially based managed health-care systems derive profit from keeping treatment as short as possible. Managed health-care systems that are not quality conscious can provide inadequate levels of service for sexual abuse victims. Ironically, even though private health-care providers and managed health-care systems often see themselves as opposite, if they are insufficiently attentive to clients' needs and quality of care, both share a tendency to short-change the client, albeit in different ways, due to their particular economic motivations.

SUMMARY

This chapter critiques ideas and models, both manifest and latent, in the sexual abuse field. If we have added complexity and ambiguity to readers' understanding of this area, then this critique has been effective.

3

Male Victims of Sexual Abuse

THIS CHAPTER REVIEWS some of the basic theoretical and empirical understandings of male victims, and will serve as a database for further discussions. This review is not comprehensive, but focused to be most useful for ideas developed later. Readers seeking comprehensive reviews should consult Bolton, Morris, and MacEachron (1989), Finkelhor (1986), and the two-volume series by O'Donohue and Geer (1992a, 1992b). Konker (1992) summarizes the lack of theoretical consensus in the field of child abuse and offers an anthropological perspective.

DEFINITIONS OF ABUSE

As Finkelhor (1986) notes, definitions of abuse vary widely in the research literature. Compared to the definitions used in clinical practice, however, they are relatively consistent. There is almost no standardization of definition in clinical practice.

Particularly with adolescent sex offenders, it is important to factor in the overlap between true situations of sexually abusive adolescents versus childhood and adolescent sexual exploration when defining sexual abuse. The typology of male adolescent sex offenders discussed in chapter 5 suggests a continuum starting from a gray area to clear situations of sexual abuse. It is important to note that on the other side of the gray area is normative nonpathological sexual exploration between adolescent peers that is often accompanied by considerable confusion, much clumsiness, a full range of both positive and negative affects, and a full range of sequelae.

As noted in chapter 1, ours is a deeply erotophobic culture. One effect of this is an increase in the likelihood that adolescents, during normative sexual exploration, will not be able to handle their sexuality well. As a result of cultural erotophobia, adolescent sexual expression is often labeled as psychopathological, especially if it is same sex.

The field of childhood sexual abuse must struggle with the important distinction between normative sexual exploration in adolescence and childhood and abuse. This distinction is not easy, but it is imperative. If this challenge is not met, the field of child sexual abuse runs the risk of becoming an "enforcer" of cultural erotophobia. Overly broad definitions can label all adolescent sexuality as abuse or abusive, or recapitulate cultural bigotry, as in homophobia or stereotyping adolescents of color as hypersexual.

A disturbing trend we have noted is the tendency of some therapists to use purely subjective definitions of sexual abuse. Although there is no consensus on an absolute definition of sexual abuse for research purposes, the various research definitions that exist are relatively objective (see Finkelhor, 1986, pp. 22-27 for definitions). Theoretical positions that label a situation as abusive if others react badly to it, if it creates any negative affect, or if it does not fit how "normal" sexual or interpersonal relationships are theorized can be dangerous. Such therapists place themselves in the role of enforcing cultural erotophobia. In an erotophobic culture, most sexual exploration by adolescents receives negative reactions from someone and has some accompanying negative affect and sequelae, and the form and nature of the interactions are displeasing to some people. Comparable to the risks of some feminist therapists seeing as therapeutic the inculcation of clients into a particular construction of reality, therapists working with adolescents are challenged to make certain they operate in the best interests of the specific adolescent client, and not in the service of any particular worldview.

We believe the tensions over adolescent sexuality are primarily a cultural problem. To label them as problems of individual psychopathology is a political act, and a deeply regressive one. After a period of sexual excess in the 1960s and 1970s, the 1980s ushered in a period of sexual repression. Both stances are extreme. Practice styles and theoretical models that are overly aligned with either extremity are flawed. Competent theory and practice in the area of sexual abuse are vigilant of the potential for therapists to become agents of social control and cultural fads, rather than agents of scientific inquiry and therapeutic healing.

PREVALENCE

Although research on male victims of sexual abuse has not been as extensive as research on female victims, its amount is respectable and dates back to some of the earliest studies. As discussed by Peters, Wyatt, and Finkelhor (1986), studies of prevalence are problematic due to varying definitions of sexual abuse, different modes of questioning, differing sample characteristics, and varying response rates.

The prevalence rates of sexual abuse, based on studies from the United States and Canada, vary between 3% and 31% of males and between 6% and 62% of females (Peters et al., 1986). In most broad community studies, female victims are from 2½ to 4 times more likely to have been sexually abused than males; however, in studies of college populations, females are about 1½ times more likely to have been abused than males.

The studies that show the highest percentages of males as victims of sexual abuse are four of the earliest reports. Freud (1896), in the period when he believed client reports of sexual abuse, describes one third of sexual abuse victims as males. Hamilton (1929) found prevalence rates of 20% for females and 22% for males, whereas Landis (1956) found prevalence rates of 35% for females and 30% for males. A study by Bender and Blau (1937) also suggests an equal male/female risk. The predominance of female victims is concentrated in the more recent studies, with the exception of the Tobias and Gordon study (1977), which suggests equal risk. Some (Kempe & Kempe, 1984; Plummer, 1981) have theorized that boys are more likely to underreport sexual abuse, and therefore the "real" prevalence is roughly equivalent.

A number of studies suggest increased reporting of male sexual abuse. The American Humane Association (1981) found that sexual abuse reports have risen over the years and that the proportion of male victims reported has increased. Finkelhor (1979) surveyed 796 college students and obtained a sexual abuse victimization rate of 9% for males and 19% for females. In 1980, 15.7% of sexual abuse reports were from males; in 1984 that number increased to 21.7%. Of 2,627 people contacted in a *Los Angeles Times* random phone survey (Timnick, 1985), 16% of the men reported being molested as children. In a large ($N = 2,019$) British sample, Baker and Duncan (1985) report that 12% of females and 8% of males recount sexual abuse before the age of 16.

Self-report studies from perpetrators suggest a higher rate of male victimization than studies based on victim reports. Freeman-Longo (1986) reports a prevalence rate for female abuse of male children of 40%, and Petrovich and Templer (1984) a rate of 59%, based on retrospective reports in a sample of male rapists.

The current literature suggests that in most populations studied, female victims outnumber male victims, but the specific ratio is not easy to determine, and may vary significantly between different samples. Some have argued that the admission of victimization is at odds with sex-role stereotyped masculinity so powerful in adolescence. Because most sexual abuse of male adolescents is likely perpetrated by males, avoiding the appearance of homosexuality imposes a significant constraint on boys reporting their abuse (Freeman-Longo, 1986). Others have commented that society is more sensitized to girls being victims because of the perception of boys as strong and girls as weak and that victim status and role are "reserved" for females (Vander Mey, 1992a), whereas males are not permitted to express vulnerability and helplessness (Nasjleti, 1980). Clearly, there are many unanswered questions in the empirical literature. Although there are insufficient data to determine if the arguments for severe underestimation in males are true, the arguments are consistent with other known features of male adolescent behavior, and so warrant serious consideration.

Setting aside the issue of male/female differences in prevalence, the range of sexual abuse cited in the studies is roughly of a factor of 10, that is, a range of variation that is unacceptable for informed decision making. The public policy implications of knowing whether the prevalence of sexual abuse for women is 6% or 62% are enormous.

The reaction of some researchers to methodological problems in prevalence studies is peculiar. In the volume by Finkelhor (1986), otherwise characterized by a cool objective tone, personal attacks on particular researchers appear to be limited to researchers who advocate equal prevalence for boys and girls (see pp. 61-64). Finkelhor and Russell (1984) appear intent on making certain there is little deviation from childhood sexual abuse being predominantly conceptualized as something that males do to females. Although Finkelhor and his associates seem sympathetic to the notion that rates of sexual abuse may be underestimated across the board, they seem overly protective of the idea that many more girls than boys are sexually abused. In a field where much research is weak, studies that conflict with the prevailing notion of female predominance in victimization are singled out for weaknesses that many studies share.

Allen (1990) comments on the increasing recognition of female perpetrators of sexual abuse. His discussion raises an interesting possibility. If one assumes that sexual abuse perpetrators of either sex act consistent with sex role stereotypes (this is a reasonable assumption, as research suggests many sexual abuse perpetrators are quite conventional in their sex role stereotypes), it may be the case that female perpetrators perform sexual abuse in a more "female" manner, that is, in a less goal-directed, violent, or overtly genital manner. Examples of this might include exhibitionism, both overt and subtle; seductiveness; caressing; and fondling, as opposed to acts of penetration and violence and clearly orgasmic activities.

If female sexual perpetration is underestimated because definitions of sexual perpetration are geared toward describing male perpetrators, the data on prevalence of male and female child victims might be skewed. For example, if female perpetrators consistently select more male victims and the observation that males underreport as compared to females is empirically validated, then prevalence estimates may require substantial revision.

It is our belief that male victimization and female perpetration are likely to be a minority of the sexual abuse situations, although not a small minority. What this means, as Allen (1990) points out, is that there are millions of cases of this "minority" situation. Clearly, any viable conceptual framework of sexual abuse must be able to accommodate the full range of sexual abuse experiences, both the majority and the minority. It is for this reason that we believe that feminist perspectives, which were crucial in the early development of this field, are insufficient in the current phase of theoretical development.

The Truthfulness of Child Abuse Reports

In the early years of current interest in childhood sexual abuse, it rapidly became an article of faith that the truthfulness of self-reported victims could not be questioned. To do so often elicited pejorative labeling, such as "minimization theorists," from child abuse advocates. Such advocates imply that raising questions about the truthfulness of abuse reports is tantamount to saying that abuse does not exist. We believe this is an extremist position.

Historically, questions about the truthfulness of child abuse reports have occupied a central role. The "discovery" by Freud, and earlier by French mental health practitioners (Masson, 1984), were revolutionary. Equally revolutionary was Freud's complete repudiation of his previous theory. This repudiation occupies a central place in psychoanalytic theory, as it is a core feature in Freud's theories of the unconscious and the Oedipal struggle. It is unwise to take a position that all reports of sexual abuse are true. Historically, extremist positions about such matters seem to fall in and out of fashion.

The late 1980s and early 1990s have seen the latest twist in changing fashions, with the emergence of "false memory syndrome" (False Memory Syndrome Foundation, undated; Freyd, 1992; Wakefield & Underwager, undated), which allege that many cases of childhood sexual abuse are lies or distortions, often created by overzealous therapists. This perspective legitimately points to the error of assuming that sexual abuse must have occurred when there is no memory of it because of the existence of certain symptoms common in sexual abuse victims. However, it appears to go beyond this in its suggestion that remembered or even clearly substantiated cases are generally suspect.

In fact, there are sound methodological and empirical reasons to believe that the recollection of repressed memories of sexual abuse is considerably more complex than a simple slogan of "victims never lie" (Briere, 1990, 1992; Doris, 1991; Faller, 1990, especially chapters 5 and 9; Goodman & Bottoms, 1993; Jones & McGraw, 1987; Loftus,

1993; Loftus & Foley, 1984; Meyers et al., 1989, especially pp. 32-127; Perry & Wrightsman, 1991; van der Kolk & Kadish, 1987). The field of sexual abuse may be reaching a stage comparable to Freud's doubts before he "recanted" and denied the reality of abuse memories. Our view is that both extremist positions are unworthy of scientists and health-care professionals.

There is a middle position that can be exemplified by a classic film, *Rashomon*. In this film, based on a medieval Japanese tale, two individuals come upon the scene of a rape-murder. The crime is reported to the authorities, who interview the two witnesses, the alleged murderer, and the murder victim, who is represented through a medium. Each individual tells an internally consistent and entirely believable story. Each individual's story differs in significant details. The movie ends with the narrator bemoaning the human condition, complaining that truth and reality are impossible to ascertain and that all is chaos. Although we do not share this last conclusion, the movie makes an important point.

The truthfulness of a report of sexual abuse is very difficult to ascertain in a number of situations. In most situations of sexual abuse reporting, this is not the case; rather, the truth is relatively easy to come by because of multiple victim reports, incriminating circumstances, material evidence, and the like. It is important, however, to admit that gray areas exist for a balanced understanding of sexual abuse phenomena. Examples of these gray areas include situations between early and older adolescents or between late adolescents and young adults where the older party is developmentally immature. In these, immaturity, clumsiness, and insensitivity can be recast as coercion and abuse.

Many areas may appear gray, but on careful examination are not. Chapter 7 presents a methodology with a purpose of uncovering the truthfulness of what occurred in a sexual abuse situation. Similarly, Schoener and Milgrom (1989) describe a technique in situations of client-therapist exploitation that can sometimes uncover greater degrees of accuracy in situations that appear gray. Neither of these methodologies is foolproof, and cases remain where it is impossible to ascertain what occurred. These situations occur predominantly where there is a single alleged victim or when victim reports become contaminated. A noteworthy example is the famous Jordan,

Minnesota cases (see Hechler, 1988), in which contamination by prosecuting attorneys and therapists working for the prosecution rendered much of the evidence from alleged multiple victims unusable.

Similarly, in situations of client-therapist exploitation, we have seen situations where alleged victims of the same perpetrator are placed in the same support group. In the process of obtaining support and advocacy, stories that were initially dissimilar become strikingly similar, making truthfulness harder to ascertain. Given the preponderance of simplistic theory in the area of sexual abuse (i.e., the belief that victim effects are monolithic and that if a person does not show a predictable pattern of effects then he or she is "in denial"), there is a danger that attempts to provide support and clarification for victims can instead provide a kind of secondary victimization in which alleged victims are told what to believe, think, and feel, or are labeled as psychopathological.

It is our observation that truthfulness cannot be separated from a sociopolitical context. In a period when victim reports, whether of childhood sexual abuse or client-therapist exploitation, are not believed but rather discredited, individuals who make reports have a very high probability of being truthful. This is a context in which there is no benefit from making a report of abuse, truthful or not, and making the report is an uphill struggle. Not surprisingly, the few instances of false reporting in this context are likely to be situations in which the false reporters have significant problems with reality. This is an environment in which any reporting, true or false, is likely to bring neither justice nor benefit to the reporter.

It is important for child abuse and client advocates to realize that when their advocacy efforts are successful, as they generally have been, the sociopolitical context changes. When justice and accountability for victims become possible or even standard, when criminal sanctions are strengthened and civil statutes are amended to allow for easier recovery of damages, the context changes.

In the past, the context was one in which it was more or less true (with the exception of those people with poor reality testing) that victims almost never lied. When there is greater justice and accountability in the system, at least two possible effects occur. There are greater sanctions against perpetrators and it is possible (although it is certainly not clear empirically) that some potential perpetrators might be constrained from perpetrating. More importantly, some individuals might have greater motivation to claim victimization when it did not occur or to exaggerate victimization, as there is the possibility of obtaining significant damages monetarily and of harming alleged perpetrators in other ways, such as via licensing board complaints.

To put it another way, in an environment where victim reports are not believed and there is little justice for victims, only a crazy person would make a false report, and there is little constraint on potential perpetrators. In a situation that approaches justice and equitability, constraints on potential perpetrators might be effective in some cases; more importantly, there are sound reality-based reasons for some people to file false or exaggerated victim complaints.

Therapists who treat victims of abuse in a simplistic monolithic manner contribute to this situation. Sloganeering, such as anyone who engages in inappropriate behavior has a progressive out-of-control illness and will necessarily reoffend, any vaguely remembered emotional discomfort in early childhood is indicative of sexual abuse, particularly if it is not well remembered, and the like tend to create distortion, especially when popularized as "scientific." These belief systems, particularly when reinforced in a support group, can shape and even manipulate a client's beliefs and create retrospective falsification of vaguely remembered events.

We continue to believe that most victim reports are true; that a class of perpetrators exists who reoffends until forcibly prevented from doing so; and that there is some truth to simplistic myths about child abuse. These viewpoints describe a subset of abuse situations, not the entirety of them. A pressing need in the area of child sexual abuse is to develop the conceptual and theoretical capacity to deal with gray area cases without resorting to extremist positions of denying the possibility of abuse or embracing it when there is insufficient clarity to make such determinations.

BARRIERS TO IDENTIFICATION OF MALE VICTIMS

Once boys realize that something sexual has happened to them that was confusing or inappropriate, there are no clear avenues for clarifying their confusion. Rape crisis centers and other victim services are generally staffed and identified as resources for women. The advertisements, literature, and atmosphere of an organization can prevent male victims from coming forward.

Some organizations have significant cultural barriers to recognizing male victims. Organizations identifying themselves as feminist or as having a feminist ideology are readily able to identify and support females oppressed in a world controlled by males but may have difficulty recognizing the adolescent or young adult male victim of sexual abuse—especially if that abuse is perpetrated by a female, or if the male victim is sex role stereotyped and not "feminist." Male victims of sexual abuse can be silenced by the gender stereotyping of both patriarchy and feminism.

When the need for services for male victims of sexual abuse is acknowledged, a fear of competition can develop. Providers who serve predominantly female clientele are at times resistant to address the issues of male victims because their services are already overburdened with female victims. This competition for funding has been recognized as between those who serve people identified as "offenders" and those identified as "victims."

Mental health services providers suffer from a lack of awareness of the extent and nature of male victimization. As a result, they fail to ask questions in a way that is sensitive to male experiences and perceptions. (See the section in this chapter, The Effects of Sexual Abuse on Males, which suggests that interview formats, as opposed to checklist formats, may be more sensitive to male experience, as men have greater resistance to describing abuse effects.)

The media and arts in general fail to identify male victimization. This lack of realistic images in the media prevents males from having models with which they can identify, and thereby feel less alone. *Deliverance* and *Ode to Billy Joe* exemplify this insensitivity to male victims; in *Prince of Tides,* sexual involvement of an adult male with his female psychotherapist is depicted as beneficial. A significant lack of research and theory addresses the issues of male victims.

Primarily as a result of cultural gender stereotyping and homophobia, a number of myths concerning sexual abuse have led to its lack of recognition and therefore underreporting by both victims and health professionals (Dimmock, 1990).

Myths About Male Sexual Abuse Victims

You Cannot Make Males Have Sex Against Their Will. For children and adolescent males, as with young females, the majority of sexual abuse is perpetrated by family members, known persons in authority, relatives, or friends. The victim is tricked or manipulated by someone whom they trusted. The experience most often results in a feeling of confusion. With older teens and young adults, sexual abuse often occurs with force. This is especially true when the victim is in a residential, correctional, or armed services setting and is threatened by someone who has power and authority in that context.

If a Male Has an Erection and Ejaculates, He Consented. Male children and adolescents can experience erections in a variety of situations. In cases of abuse, the male adolescent may ejaculate; this is confusing for the victim. It may also be difficult for others to believe his report about this experience. Manipulation or trickery, whereby the victim "goes along" with a situation, in no way implies consent. Rapid ejaculation is often described by victims as the way to get through the abuse quickly.

All Males Who Sexually Abuse Boys Are Homosexuals. A number of research studies show that the vast majority of sexual abuse against boys is perpetrated by heterosexual identified males or females (Groth & Birnbaum, 1978). This myth equates sexual abuse with sexual orientation, and sexual abuse with sexuality; such myths are no longer tolerated in regard to female sexual abuse victims but continue regarding males.

If Abused by a Male, the Abuse Occurred Because the Boy Is Gay or Acted Gay. This particular myth causes considerable anguish and confusion for boys. The victim sometimes ascertains the pedophile's focus on the typically androgynous qualities of young adolescents. The offender may say "how smooth your skin is" or "how pretty you look," leading to misattribution of blame and responsibility onto the victim. For adolescents who are experiencing some sexual identity conflict or are at the beginning of a coming-out process, this myth adds a considerable burden.

If Abused by a Male, the Male Victim Will Become Gay. Some correlational research suggests that male victims of sexual abuse are twice as likely to engage in same-sex behavior (Finkelhor, 1984; Johnson & Shrier, 1985). It must be emphasized that this research is "correlational," and no direct causal factor has been determined at this time. One rationale may be that a young male who is in a coming-out process may have been read as such by a pedophile, who takes advantage of this special vulnerability of a child or adolescent in a homophobic society (see chapter 4).

If Forced or Tricked by a Female Into Being Sexual, the Boy Should Consider Himself Lucky. This myth is perpetuated by a number of teen "sexploitation" films that depict older or adult females as sexual with adolescent boys. Although many adolescents (and society in general) initially have a difficult time perceiving this situation as abusive, there is no evidence that the gender of the perpetrator eliminates or diminishes effects of the abuse.

If a Boy Is Sexually Abused, He Will Become an Offender. This is sometimes called the "vampire syndrome," which holds that once abused, a boy will become an abuser. This myth is often offered as an explanation of how men become sex offenders. As suggested by the PHASE research (O'Brien, 1989) and other studies (Becker et al., 1986; Fehrenbach et al., 1986), only a minority of adolescent sex offenders in outpatient treatment programs report being victims of sexual abuse. (Chapter 5 provides a typology of adolescent offenders that demonstrates differential motives and behaviors.) This myth is readily applied to male but never to female victims, who are viewed in a comparatively benign manner. Neither clinicians nor the general public assume that female victims have an enhanced probability of becoming a perpetrator. This myth reflects gender stereotyping that males play aggressor and offender roles, and females play passive or victim roles.

Boys Are Less Hurt by Sexual Abuse Than Girls. This myth reflects gender stereotyping that boys are stronger, tougher, and not as emotionally vulnerable as girls. Ironically, this sexist stereotyping has been promulgated by some feminists (Rush, 1980). It implies that if boys are abused, the abuse will not affect them as much. In fact, both boys and girls display symptoms that reflect psychological and physical trauma when they experience sexual abuse (Friedrich, Beilke, & Urquiza, 1988; Woods & Dean, 1984). Although some research suggests the nature of effects may be different, it does not suggest the severity is less. For boys, such sexist stereotyping often encourages repression and denial.

Boys Can Protect Themselves From Sexual Abuse. This myth seems to view sexual abuse as a correlate to physical assault, whereby "tough boys" should be able to defend themselves physically. This reflects the stereotyping that if a boy is threatened, he is expected to defend himself and his manhood (Block, 1983).

Males Are Initiators of Sex; if Abused, They Got What They Were Looking For. Gender stereotyping implies that males are initiators or aggressors of sexual encounters. In reality, males are as vulnerable as females to seduction by manipulation or force.

FEMALE PERPETRATORS OF SEXUAL ABUSE

Virtually all the literature on sex offenders describes male offenders, and there is little doubt that males are the majority of sexual perpetrators. The prevailing view has been that female perpetration is rare; Finkelhor and Russell (1984) conclude that females account for about 20% of perpetration on males. However, there are good reasons to consider that females may not be such a small minority of perpetrators.

A number of researchers have raised the possibility of greater amounts of female perpetration on males. Justice and Justice (1979) suggest that the appearance of lower rates of female perpetration is due to female perpetration assuming a different form and mimicking child care through activities such as exposure, fondling, and sexualized physical interactions. Groth (1979) expresses a similar view and suggests that bathing and dressing children can mask more varieties of female perpetration than can typical goal-oriented male orgasmic behavior. Children are reluctant to report, especially if the perpetrator is a parent, and males may be even more reluctant to report as a group.

Knopp and Lackey (1987) found that female perpetrators account for 51% of male victims in their research. Johnson and Shrier found that 60% of their adolescent male victims were sexually abused by females. Allen (1991), comparing female and male perpetrators, found the women to be less aggressive, had more troubled histories, more often selected male victims, and were less willing to admit sexual abuse perpetration.

Finkelhor and Russell (1984) reviewed the clinical literature and report that approximately 24% of all male victims and 13% of all female victims are sexually abused by females acting alone or with a male partner. Clinicians have reported that female sex offenders are usually nonviolent, the abuse is not explained in terms of power and authority, and no psychosis is found in mother-child incest cases (Marvasti, 1986; McCarty, 1986).

Fehrenbach and Monastersky (1988) summarize findings on 28 female adolescents referred to an outpatient juvenile sexual offender treatment program over a 7-year period. None of the subjects were self-referred. Less than one half (39.3%) had been adjudicated for the referral offense or another sexual offense. Referral offenses were either rape (53.6%) or indecent liberties (46.4%). Rape involved oral, anal, or vaginal intercourse, or penetration of the victim with an object or finger. Indecent liberties involved sexual touching between offender and victim, short of penetration. Modal age of the victims, with the exception of one adult victim, was age 5. The victims were all known to the offender, with the majority occurring while the subject was baby-sitting. Ten of the offenders assaulted males, sixteen assaulted females, and two assaulted both sexes. About one half of the female offenders had reported histories of being sexually abused themselves. The authors report that, unlike female sexual offenders of previous studies (McCarty, 1986; Wolfe, 1985), these adolescents committed offenses without coercion from male co-offenders and starting at an early age.

Typology of Female Offenders

Mathews and her colleagues developed a preliminary typology of female sex offenders based on a study of 14 adolescent and 16 adult female offenders (Mathews, 1987; Mathews, Matthews, & Speltz, 1989). This typology is presented in abbreviated form below. The first three types are termed "self-initiated" by the female offender, and the last two are termed "male-involved," and include a male in the commission of the offense.

The Exploration/Molestation Type

The exploration/molestation type is usually a younger adolescent with a young male child (6 years or younger) in a baby-sitting situation. Abuse occurs one or a few times and involves fondling the victim.

The Predisposed/Severe Abuse History Type

The predisposed/severe abuse history type can be an adolescent or adult female with a severe sexual and physical abuse history, who commonly has substance abuse, depression, and personality disorder diagnoses. She is apt to have clear deviant sexual fantasies, minimizes and rationalizes the sexual perpetration, and commits abuse in a forceful, repetitive, and ritualized manner. Fondling, exposure, finger penetration, and oral sex are common abuse behaviors.

The Teacher/Lover Type

The teacher/lover type is an adult female, and victims are usually teenaged males (age 11-16), who may be the perpetrator's own child, stepson, child's friend, neighbor, student, or "friend." Deviant fantasies and projection of blame are apparent, with the abuse described as a "love affair." This type appears most similar to Groth's fixated or regressed pedophile type.

The Psychologically Disturbed Type

The psychologically disturbed type is usually an adult female who may abuse a peer-age adult or child of either sex, with participation but no coercion by a male cohort. This type tends to have a significant history of psychological problems, conduct disorder, or antisocial personality that is a contributory factor to the sexual abuse. The abuse may be initiated by either the male or the female, occurs alone or with the partner, and tends to be more violent than the above types.

The Male Coerced Type

The male coerced type is usually an adolescent or adult female intimidated or threatened into the abuse behavior by a boyfriend or husband, who generally initiates the abuse prior to the female's involvement. The victims are familiar children, adolescents, or adults chosen by the male initiator.

We focus on female perpetrators in this discussion because their existence is minimized or denied in most discussions. Sexual abuse by females is as complex as abuse by males, and may well approach it in frequency.

THE EFFECTS OF SEXUAL ABUSE ON MALES

There appear to be striking gender differences in phenomenology and effects of sexual abuse. Considerably more males than females are sexually abused outside the home; female sexual abuse is more characterized by intrafamilial incest situations, which is less characteristic of male victims (Finkelhor, 1986). There are other suggestions that force plays a greater role in the sexual abuse of males (Pierce & Pierce, 1985, p. 195).

There also appear to be gender differences in the effects of sexual abuse. Although some studies suggest that males are less adversely affected (Fritz, Stoll, & Wagner, 1981), this does not appear to be entirely accurate. Johnson and Shrier (1985) describe approximately two thirds of the males in their sample as reporting that sexual abuse was adverse in its impact. Finkelhor (1984) reports that, although two thirds of girls rate the effects of sexual abuse as adverse, only one third of the boys do. Even in the Finkelhor study, however, male victims scored lower on a sexual self-esteem inventory than female victims. Woods and Dean (1985) suggest a more complex pattern; male victims in their research report fewer adverse initial effects but, on greater scrutiny using a more intensive interview procedure, a greater percentage report negative effects. Friedrich et al. (1988) found that of those boys who viewed their abusers positively, this effect was reduced significantly over time. From a radical feminist perspective, Rush (1980) asserts, based on feminist theory and not data, that boys are less affected by abuse than girls.

There are some suggestions that the particular effects reported differ between boys and girls. Boys appear to respond more often with acts of aggression (Gomes-Schwartz, Horowitz, & Carderelli, 1990; Tufts New England Medical Center, 1984), whereas girls tend to respond more with depression (Conte, Berliner, & Schuerman, 1986). Urquiza and Crowley (1986) report few differences between men and women, with some exceptions. Women are more often depressed, whereas men more often have aggressive fantasies toward others and report a greater sexual interest in children. Because there are suggestions that the frequency of behavior problems secondary to sexual abuse increases with time (Friedrich et al., 1986), and males display more behavioral problems, male effects may again be masked. Rogers and Terry (1984) note sexual identity confusion, insecurity about masculinity, and recapitulation of victimization as unique effects on male victims.

Citing studies by Conte, Berliner, and Schuerman (1986), Tufts New England Medical Center (1984), and Kelley (1988), Finkelhor (1990b) emphasizes that most studies show little differences between males and females; however, most of these studies utilized a symptom checklist format that does not appear to be especially sensitive to revealing sex differences. It is noteworthy that most of the studies that show specific male effects tend to use interview rather than symptom checklist formats (e.g., Woods & Dean, 1984). If it is true that males have a more difficult time admitting to sexual abuse or perceiving the effects of sexual abuse, then greater effort is required to elicit histories and effects of sexual abuse from them. Part of the difficulty in obtaining clear sex differences may be due to a presumption in the research that victims speak directly and freely about their sexual abuse experiences and effects, an assumption that may be more true for females than males.

In studies on client-therapist sexual abuse, there are suggestions of similar patterns. Gonsiorek (1989) comments on the extreme reluctance of male victims, particularly adolescent male victims, to perceive sexual interaction with a therapist as abusive, especially when the therapist is female. He describes situations where male victims of female therapists maintain denial that the interaction was exploitative even when presented with information that they were one of multiple victims. This information is often effective at breaking down the denial about victimization of female victims, but less so with male victims.

O'Brien (1989) found that 37% of 170 juvenile sex offenders surveyed were victims of sexual abuse. This figure is comparable to other surveys of outpatient adolescent sex offender treatment programs (Fehrenbach et al., 1986). In O'Brien's study, nearly one third of the respondents reported that the sexual abuse was perpetrated by a female. In order of frequency, the perpetrator was a baby-sitter, a relative (such as an aunt), a sister, and the mother.

In a study by O'Brien (1989) examining the sexual abuse victimization rate of adolescent sex offenders, the results are as follows: 42% of incest offenders, 40% of child molesters, and 29% of non-child molesters (e.g., exposure offenders, obscene phone callers, or acquaintance rapists) were themselves victimized. These outpatient figures reveal only a minority of adolescent offenders as victims. They are different from residential or prison population statistics (Groth & Burgess, 1979), which report significantly higher rates of victimization (see Bolton, Morris, & MacEachron, 1989, pp. 81-85 for a review of this area).

As with the truthfulness of sexual abuse, it is important that a gray area be developed in understanding the effects of sexual abuse victimization. In the area of male victims, volumes such as the ones by Lew (1988) and Hunter (1990) have played an important role in opening the field and providing the crucial step of giving permission for male victims to speak about the reality of their abuse. However, these volumes, like similar ones on sexual abuse of women, are simplistic because they suggest a relatively monolithic, invariably severe, and global characterization of victim effects.

A good theory about the effects of sexual abuse victimization must be able to take into account a full range of effects, a continuum from virtually no adverse effects to psychologically devastating ones. Such a theory is presented in chapter 4. Preliminary findings in the empirical literature indicate that the longer the abuse, the greater the trust violation; the more sadistic or brutal the abuse, the worse the effects. Finkelhor (1990b) notes that one quarter to one third of child victims report no adverse effects.

SUMMARY

When viewed through the lens of sexual abuse of female children, sexual abuse of males is seen as a rare phenomenon, similar to the abuse of females but less frequent. As sensitivity to the particular characteristics of male victims and female perpetrators increases, such sexist assumptions are likely to change. It would be surprising if males were a large majority of child sexual abuse victims and females a majority of perpetrators. However, greater recognition of female perpetration, near gender parity of victim prevalence, and greater appreciation for unique male victimization effects and clinical needs are likely.

4

Diagnosis and Treatment of Young
Adult and Adolescent Male Victims:
An Individual Psychotherapy Model

THIS CHAPTER DESCRIBES a method of assessment, treatment planning, and treatment for male victims of sexual abuse in an individual psychotherapy model, using techniques derived from cognitive-behavioral perspectives and theory derived from the self-psychology perspective of Heinz Kohut. The target populations are late-adolescent or young adult males who are independent of their families or whose families are not accessible or amenable to treatment. Typically, the sexual abuse experiences are not current but removed in time, and the client presents with symptoms related to his sexual abuse. Clients vary in the degree to which they attribute their current symptomatology to the aftermath of sexual abuse.

Most sexual abuse of males occurs in latency or adolescent years; however, most victims do not then seek services. Rather, the typical course is that most boys and young men bury the abuse experience, and attempt to avoid its aftermath. They often seek assistance some years later, often in young adulthood, when they encounter problems, usually relational or interpersonal in nature, and/or perceive adverse effects of the abuse. This population is the focus of the therapeutic strategies described here. For those boys and early adolescents who receive therapeutic services shortly after the abuse, the material here is less applicable, as it is meant for an older population and family and systemic intervention strategies are generally preferable with younger populations.

The material presented here is not the "correct" way to assess and plan treatment, nor is it the correct way to undertake psychotherapy with young adult male victims. Rather, it is an example of how to apply assessment, treatment planning, and psychotherapeutic techniques, extant and established, thoughtfully and in an effective manner to the particular challenges presented by male victims of sexual abuse.

The chapter concludes with an attempt to understand the experience of male victims of sexual abuse through a self-psychology framework. Again, this is not offered as the correct perspective on male victims of sexual abuse but as an example of understanding sexual abuse in a more theoretically rich manner and integrating it with a "depth" theory in psychology.

A word about terminology is in order. "Psychotherapy" is used throughout this chapter to designate the intervention strategies described. That word is chosen to reflect the emphasis in the model described here on linking current problems with past history. It is not intended "territorially," that is, to imply that only persons with particular degrees, training experiences, or the like can make use of these ideas. The focus is on the behavior and conceptualizations of the therapist. Although this does assume a theory base and skill level in the therapist, it is not specific or exclusionary in this regard. In fact, the model presented is itself a hybrid of different theoretical and technical styles.

ASSESSMENT

As Bolton, Morris, and MacEachron (1989) note, careful assessment is the prerequisite for appropriate treatment planning in the area of sexual abuse. They argue that assessment should be multidimensional and yield direct implications for treatment. Further, they suggest a number of areas that should be assessed, including the nature of the abuse, the type and severity of problems that ensue from the abuse, and the strengths and skills of the person being assessed. We recommend their approach as a sound introduction to assessment of male victims, but with some modifications.

Psychological Testing

Psychological testing is not always necessary or desirable; but when it is done, it should be done cautiously and well. Psychological testing is a complex skill, rendered more commonly than well, with as much potential to hurt as to help. For those adept at this skill, this discussion can raise and clarify some difficult issues; for those who do not provide psychological testing services themselves, it can assist them in making more informed and discriminating choices about the best uses and limitations of such services for their clients. Matarazzo (1986) points out that testing alone is inadequate; psychological testing is useful only to the extent that it is integrated with other sources of information, and its implications filtered through clinical judgment.

Generally, psychological testing can be useful early in treatment when the presenting problems are complex and/or confusing, when the client's ability to describe his history and/or psychological state is poor, or when there is a known history of clinical risk or volatility, such as suicide attempts or decompensation, such that a quick and thorough database is desired. Later in treatment, psychological testing may be useful if the therapy becomes inexplicably "stuck," if unexpected new information arises that confounds an earlier treatment plan, or if unexpected symptoms or behaviors occur in therapy.

Psychological testing is probably not worth the expense when clients present with a relatively full information base, either from their self-report or from other sources; or when the symptom picture is relatively uncomplicated and congruent with known history. Routine testing in all cases may pose an unnecessary financial burden on some clients, and will often be redundant with what is already known.

Because the field of sexual abuse treatment is so young, it is important for a therapist to use the best validated and most established psychological measures, on the principle that when a field is new and quasi-experimental, this should be counteracted whenever possible by utilizing established techniques. Novel and specific psychological measures are often recommended or utilized with sexual abuse victims; problems with this approach are twofold.

First, they are too specific. The treatment of sexual abuse victims and theories about the effects of such abuse are at an early stage of development. Assessment should therefore cast as broad a net as possible. Specific tests implicitly focus the assessment process on the relatively narrow range of measures that such tests are capable of detecting. The assessment process then becomes prematurely narrowed toward the assessment of a relatively small number of variables. The tests that capture the broadest possible range of information are the most desirable.

Second, the tests used should be among the most highly validated and well understood. Specific tests tend to be marginally validated or narrowly validated on limited samples. This tends to be true of specific and limited psychological tests, as they tend to attract less research interest precisely because of their specificity.

There is a noteworthy psychometric dilemma in such decisions about testing. In general, the more narrow a construct that a test measures, the more likely the instrument will capitalize on particular features of the population on which the test is standardized. What such a narrow instrument measures, then, becomes contaminated by error variance particular to the population on which validation occurred. This is a problem with all psychological testing and measurement. More broad-ranging instruments however, because of the multiple variables they measure, tend to be standardized on multiple populations. Initial results on target populations often appear promising with single variable measures, and the measure is then often utilized before adequate cross-validation occurs. If and when the necessary cross-validation does occur, validity often shrinks to a level where enthusiasm for the instrument is considerably diminished (see Greene, 1981, for a good introduction to these concepts).

An example can illustrate this point. Suppose one has a theory that male victims are unusually prone to sexual inhibitions and one develops a 20-item test of sexual inhibitions secondary to male sexual victimization. Suppose that this test is initially standardized on a number of samples of male sexual abuse victims in therapy, and the results appear promising; that is, male sexual abuse victims score higher than a sample of nonvictim males.

It would be too early to conclude that the test has any necessary validity. For example, loss of libido is a common sign of depression, and the instrument may really be measuring the higher degree of depression, including loss of libido, that is common in psychotherapy samples. If the sexual inhibition measure were part of a larger battery of established tests, correlations with measures of depression and other variables could document this possible area of contamination. With single measure instruments, it is too tempting to conclude erroneously that one has effectively measured a variable.

The ideal assessment battery consists primarily of broad-ranging, well-validated standard psychological test instruments. These can be supplemented by more specific single variable measures if these are of interest to the assessor. Our recommendation, however, is that specific measures never be utilized alone, as they are often not adequately validated for diverse samples. Further, there is no way to place these narrow measures in a fuller psychological context without a broad-ranging psychological assessment.

The battery we recommend includes a Minnesota Multiphasic Personality Inventory (MMPI) variant: the MMPI-II (Butcher, Dahlstrom, Graham, Tellegen, & Kaemmer, 1989) for adults and the MMPI-A (Butcher, Williams, Graham, Archer, Tellegen, Ben-Porath, & Kaemmer, 1992) for adolescents, and a well-validated projective instrument such as the Exner System Rorschach (Exner, 1986). The MMPI is recommended because of its unparalleled ability to screen quickly for major elements of psychopathology. It is our view that there is still no instrument that can screen as effectively with such little time required of the assessor. The Rorschach provides the most in-depth psychological description of the defensive style, functioning level, and conflicts of an individual, provided the administration and interpretation are competently rendered. This means that the assessor must utilize correctly the Exner scoring system and interpret the Rorschach within the confines of that system.

In some cases, this battery will be incomplete. The MMPI, although unparalleled at describing psychopathology, tends to provide minimal, flat descriptions of individuals who have little overt symptomatology; the MMPI is not intended to measure different kinds of normal personality variables. The Rorschach, although adept at describing areas of psychological conflict and defensive styles, gives less, but still some, information about normalcy. Therefore, in many situations, another test is in order specifically to measure more normal personality variables.

It is our view that the California Personality Inventory (CPI) (Gough, 1987) is unparalleled in this regard. It is well validated and adequately standardized, and provides a broad-ranging description of normal personality variables.

In some situations, other measures may be in order. For example, with certain populations, rapid and detailed assessment of Axis II problems, that is, character disorder pathologies, is desirable. This is a weakness of the MMPI variants, which do not differentiate among character disorders well; similarly, the Rorschach, although it addresses the kind of problems inherent in Axis II diagnoses, rarely yields a clear diagnostic formulation of characterological problems. For the purpose of differentiating among kinds of Axis II problems, the Millon Clinical Multi-Axial Inventory (MCMI-II) (Millon, 1987) is probably the most effective choice.

It should be noted that the MCMI-II, however, is not an appropriate instrument to assess broadly the presence or absence of psychopathology. The intent of the MCMI-II is to differentiate varieties of personality disorders. The MCMI-II generally assumes an Axis II disorder exists and proceeds to describe it. It is limited in describing mental health problems apart from character disorders and where no psychopathology is present. The MCMI-II can serve as a useful adjunct to the MMPI when working with populations with a high rate of Axis II disorders, such as those in court or corrections systems.

All of these tests are extensively validated on a diversity of populations and provide very broad descriptions of personality functioning, and their strengths and limitations are relatively well understood. More specific limited measures may be appropriate, depending on interview and testing findings. When single variable measures are used embedded within a comprehensive battery as described above, the established measures can anchor the less validated ones.

These recommendations may come as a surprise to individuals who work in the area of sexual abuse. Most of the instruments recommended here are considered "old-fashioned" and are somewhat suspect as a result. We feel this is not a relevant objection. The assessment of sexual abuse victimization presents difficult clinical and ethical challenges. These more established old-fashioned assessment instruments do present a problem of relevancy in the area of sexual abuse, in that few variables they measure directly address sexual abuse concerns. The instruments that do appear to address such concerns more directly, however (i.e., meet the criteria of relevancy), tend to be more specific and less validated.

We believe the best response to this dilemma is to use the strongest available instruments and supplement their weaknesses regarding relevancy by careful interviewing. Relying solely on assessment instruments of questionable validity does not truly address the question of relevancy; it merely obfuscates it by giving a false sense of security that something has been adequately measured, when in fact it is usually unclear what has been measured and how it fits with other attributes of the individual.

Specific instruments in isolation are likely to confirm only what the clinician already believes he or she knows, which violates the most commonsense principle of psychological assessment: that it should suggest things one does not already know. Otherwise, the considerable expense and bother are not worthwhile. In addition, theoretical development is inhibited by narrow instruments; broad-ranging instruments can suggest relationships one would have never expected. We feel this quality is especially desirable in a fledgling area of practice.

No assessment should be attempted without a careful articulation of the central question in every assessment situation: What is one trying to assess? We suggest two central assessment concerns. The first is an assessment of serious psychopathology. Current theories about sexual abuse effects posit the possibility of relatively severe mental health sequelae. An assessment can rapidly ascertain if these are present to optimize treatment planning and manage risk to the client.

The second assessment concern is to describe generally the personality style, defensive patterns, assets, and liabilities of the individual. Individuals who have been sexually abused have a psychological history prior to the abuse, and this history interacts in often unpredictable ways with the abuse experience. A general description of personality functioning can begin the process of mapping this basic information.

The first concern can most efficiently be assessed by an MMPI variant, supplemented in some populations by the MCMI-II. The second concern can be addressed over a complete range of strong-to-poor psychological functioning by a combination of the CPI and the Exner-scored Rorschach. Those who enjoy the challenges and risks posed by single variable measures may want to experiment with ones that seem relevant to the experience of male victims, provided they are embedded in a battery of standardized instruments like the ones described above. Alternatively, one can obtain such information from interviews.

A word of caution. The American Psychological Association's *Ethical Principles of Psychologists and Code of Conduct* (1992), *Standards for Educational and Psychological Testing* (1985), and *Guidelines for Computer-Based Tests and Interpretations* (1986) make a number of related points (see also Pope, Butcher, & Seelen, 1993, for details on these and related issues for the MMPI variants). Appropriately trained psychologists must always be in charge of psychological testing. Even when psychologists delegate such activities to others, psychologists retain responsibility—this responsibility cannot be delegated. Psychologists are also entirely responsible for the decisions made about the appropriateness of instruments used. Not only are clients poorly served by poorly chosen and rendered psychological testing, but the professionals involved can make considerable trouble for themselves.

An important and informative tension exists about the use of psychological testing. Standard psychological practice and assessment were, for many years, insensitive to the area of sexual abuse. Many individuals working in the area of sexual abuse are suspicious of traditional practice, and appropriately so; indeed, the area demands all the skepticism and creativity its practitioners can muster. However, if psychological assessment is performed at all, it ought to be performed well. Careful psychological assessment is typically a tedious and rather stodgy process that often does not attract the interest of many practitioners. Yet practitioners who work with sexual abuse victims often need to know the kinds of information that cannot be easily or quickly ascertained in interviews alone; hence the need for psychological testing.

Those skilled in psychological testing are challenged to utilize these measures in the most effective way, and to do so in a manner that corrects for the insensitivities of the measures toward sexual abuse victims. Those not skilled in psychological testing are challenged to find those who have such skills and who can use them in ways that benefit their clients.

Interviews

Psychological Testing and Interviews: Relative Merits

Psychological testing and interviewing both work best in relation to the other. Psychological testing is a rapid way of learning things from initial interviews that one does not already know or one cannot easily or quickly assess because it is not entirely in the awareness of the individual. Interviews are best at obtaining individual details of history that do not easily collapse into the discreet variables measured by sound psychological testing instruments and obtaining information on how the measured general tendencies of an individual are uniquely manifest.

Two examples illustrate these points. Psychological testing, although it can comment on ongoing propensities of individuals, usually functions best as a description of the individual at one point in time. Certain clinical problems that are by their nature variable over time are therefore difficult for psychological testing to measure. Bipolar affective illness, manic-depressive disorder, is a good example. Most psychological tests more or less accurately describe the current mood state but almost never capture the range of affective swing that is central to this disorder. Similarly, psychological testing can describe some of the propensities for certain kinds of interpersonal disturbances commonly found in Axis II character disorders but rarely gives the level of detail required to make an accurate and specific Axis II diagnosis. In both cases, interviews, careful history taking, and perhaps corroborative interviews are needed to develop an accurate understanding of the person's functioning over time. Some diagnoses rely heavily on history, others rely more on the symptom picture at one point in time. Most psychological testing, especially paper-and-pencil, objective instruments, work better with the latter.

Another area where psychological testing has difficulty is in circumscribed disorders, such as the paraphilias or sexual perversions. Generally, the more circumscribed and specific a problem area, the harder it is to measure without considerable cross-validation research on different populations to eliminate the population-specific error variance that often contaminates promising measures. Many of these diagnoses are best determined by careful interviewing, clear understanding of symptoms, and verification from external sources of corroborative information, such as police reports and victim accounts.

Well-interpreted psychological testing, on the other hand, can have an objectivity that is less easily swayed by the reactions one may have to a client in a prolonged series of interviews. A valuable feature of psychological testing is its ability to suggest what clients are unable to describe because they are not aware of it. Both psychological testing and interviews have strengths and weaknesses and are best used in conjunction with each other, with a clear understanding of the powers and limitations of each. As Matarazzo (1986) notes, an assessment process is considerably more complex than mere test interpretation, involving skilled integration of multiple sources of information by an accountable assessor. Dahlstrom (1993) offers a concise overview on the proper uses of testing.

An Approach to Interviewing

Later in this chapter, a theory about sexual abuse effects is presented. To preview one part of that theory, we hypothesize that a class of individuals (not all sexual abuse victims) exists whose history of emotional deprivation and psychological injury prior to their sexual abuse make it more likely that they will be sexually victimized, due to their enhanced vulnerability combined with the ability of some abuse perpetrators to "read" such vulnerability. In line with this theory, we recommend extensive interviewing to differentiate levels of problems that may have arisen from different kinds of abuse, deprivation, or psychological trauma. This includes a detailed history from childhood, focusing on patterns of emotional support or deprivation in the family of origin, and a detailed history of all significant interpersonal relationships.

Detailed questions about what occurred during the abuse, what it was like for the victim, and effects the victim has noted are important. It is our observation that many individuals who have been victimized are not fully aware of its impact on them; however, we also suggest it is inappropriate for therapists to fill in these gaps with hypotheses derived from the relatively young theories in this area.

Rather, the incompleteness is valuable in its own right. It serves as a clue to understanding what may be submerged and the varieties of distortions and defensive operations the client uses. It can suggest what might be significant about what is verbalized versus what is unspoken, and what these mean. The client's description of the abuse, with its bumps and warts, is not flawed. It is the distillation at one point in time of how the client understands what happened to him and the coping resources he brings to bear on those experiences. The difficulty and therefore the challenge for the interviewer is that this distillation cannot always be easily teased apart from actual and complete "truth." The task is easier if the therapist keeps in mind that the goal is to understand the client, not to verify a favorite theory, and that truth may be as elusive clinically as in *Rashomon,* but consistency is often a realistic goal.

Corroborative Interviews

A partial solution is corroborative interviews. Interviewing the spouse of the victim, other family members, close friends and associates, romantic partners, and others who have a detailed observational base of the client can provide useful information about effects about which the victim may not be aware. Again, the outcome is a more consistent hypothesis, not necessarily the truth.

Case Example

Greg, 22, requested psychotherapy to help sort through the effects of being sexually abused by his mother's father. He had had a dim recollection of the events for some years. What precipitated his coming into therapy at this point was his attendance at his younger sister's substance abuse program's family week, where she told him that she had also been abused by the same grandfather. Initial interviews gave the impression that Greg had a fairly detailed and accurate knowledge of the abuse, much of which was admittedly spurred by discussions with his sister and her memories, but a good deal of which Greg appeared to recall on his own. However, he also reported episodic deep depressions that came and went for no apparent reason. He talked about these only with reluctance, which was unlike him, as he was generally nondefensive in therapy.

After the third abrupt unexplained depression, the therapist suggested a joint interview with Greg's wife as a way to understand these episodes further. At one point in this interview, the wife stated as if it were obvious and self-evident, "You know you always get these after you have any interaction with your mother. It has something to do with her." This was new information for Greg, although he agreed that the pattern his wife observed was true. He became increasingly depressed talking about it in the joint session. Psychological testing was sought at this point; it suggested long-standing depression, with likely linkages to early emotional deprivation.

The next few individual sessions produced new material that proved to be the key to understanding these mysterious depressions. Greg began to recall that his mother, on at least two occasions, walked in on the sexual abuse by her father of Greg; not only did his mother not interfere with her father's abuse of her son, but she subtly accommodated her father in this abuse. Greg also began to verbalize very early memories of being ignored for long periods in his crib while his mother sat immobile nearby, perhaps seriously depressed herself. For Greg, the impact of these memories rivalled the impact of the abuse per se.

Interviews can obtain a detailed understanding of the coping strategies employed by the victim. This is an area where both strengths and deficits are explored. A typical pattern is that victims utilize coping strategies that are suited to the victimizing environment but are often not adaptive outside that environment. Some victimized individuals develop areas of real strength and high functioning in areas of life that have been untouched by the victimization, sometimes as a compensatory device.

A careful history of relationships, with corroborative interviews if possible, can be very useful. Many clinicians working with victims of sexual abuse report that intimate relationships can be the most sensitive in mirroring the effects of sexual abuse. Whom one chooses, whether there are elements of exploitation versus mutuality, how and whether conflicts are resolved and the nature of conflicts, the longevity of relationships, how relationships begin and end, repetitive areas of stress within relationships, the subjective experience of connectedness, the parts of relationships wherein the client holds back, and sexual functioning within relationships are all rich avenues for exploring the impact of sexual abuse. Particularly with males, who often do not perceive effects as clearly as women, a detailed relationship history can set the stage for understanding effects of which they have not been aware.

Diagnostic Formulations

Case Example

Paul, 21, was a gay male who had a pattern of choosing unavailable men. In adolescence, he almost exclusively fell in love with heterosexual men; however, as he developed a gay support system, he received feedback that this was self-destructive. Paul partially incorporated this feedback but began to choose as the objects of his interest gay men who were in relationships or not interested in relationships. The only relationship in which he had not been abandoned was one in which a man he was dating left a relationship he was already in for Paul, at which point Paul terminated the relationship.

Paul could articulate his depression, anger at his family, and sexual dysfunction (he could not tolerate being touched while asleep or even sleepy and he connected this to the fact that the stepfather who had sexually abused him usually initiated the abuse when Paul was asleep). Paul had no recognition, however, of his active avoidance of intimacy, focusing on his perceived inadequacies and the "impossibility" of finding someone in the gay world as explanations for his relationships.

Although Paul's relationship history had been obtained in bits and pieces over the course of six sessions, the therapist suggested at the end of the sixth session that he would like to spend the next session getting more detail about Paul's relationship history. In this interview, the therapist focused Paul's discussion on the unavailability of his choices and how hard Paul worked to pursue such impossible situations. Paul was able, for the first time, to conclude, "Sometimes I think I just pick men who just can't give me what I want."

Mental status exams can be helpful in determining significant current symptomatology. Ideally, assessment should be sufficiently thorough not only to map out the particular effects of sexual abuse and current functioning but also to diagnose accurately on both Axis I and Axis II, should these exist (American Psychiatric Association, 1994).

Many clinicians who work in the area of sexual abuse often display a distinct dislike for making diagnostic formulations, particularly on Axis II. The reason often articulated is that such labels tend to blame the individual for the effects of the abuse, and the Axis II labels in particular tend to shift the blame to the victim. Although we endorse such vigilance in making certain the victim is not blamed for his own abuse, we believe that, in this situation, reluctance to make diagnostic formulations is misplaced.

An unwillingness to diagnose problems for which there is clear evidence tends to underestimate the effects of sexual abuse. Sexual abuse is so damaging because it can elicit or create diagnosable mental illness, among its other possible effects such as constriction of educational and vocational opportunity. The appropriate response to the unique complexities of diagnosis in victims of sexual abuse is not to resent the diagnostic process and render it poorly but rather to render it with skill and sensitivity to the particular issues of the victims.

In addition, some perpetrators do not randomly select those whom they victimize but rather choose individuals who are vulnerable. In other words, mental health problems existing prior to the abuse are likely to be overrepresented in individuals who later become sexually abused. At least some of the perpetrators select victims for vulnerability. It is precisely this vulnerability that will eventuate in later diagnosable disorders and/or interact with the abuse history to create certain diagnostic disorders.

Thorough Assessment

Sexual identity and sexual orientation can best be assessed in terms of perception of identity and in terms of behavioral and emotional experiences with the same and opposite sex. Male victims are apt to differ from female victims in that their victimization is more likely expressed through male socialization. Males in our culture are socialized to respond in ways that include more acting out, problems with behavior control, and sexualization of problem areas. Because male sexual abuse victims often express sequelae in ways consonant with male sex role socialization, areas of acting out, impulsiveness, and self-destructiveness within sexual expression and across different areas of life functioning should also be assessed.

Case Example

Bob, 23, came from a chaotic family where he was sexually victimized as a child by a young aunt, an older male neighbor, and two male cousins. Bob had chronic difficulties with properly asserting himself, particularly on the job. He was meticulous and a perfectionist, who would be assigned more than his share of work. He did not protest this but instead became increasingly angry and resentful, which he directed toward his wife. Bob was particularly ashamed about his temper outbursts and alluded vaguely to "flying off the handle," but gave the impression that this consisted solely of episodic verbal abuse.

About 3 months into therapy, Bob came to a session despondent, and announced that his wife had left to stay with her sister and was discussing separation. After obtaining permission from Bob, the therapist conducted a phone interview with the wife, in which the therapist learned that Bob's abusiveness was not merely verbal; when he became enraged, he destroyed property in the house on a regular basis. The incident that led to the wife's moving out was an evening when Bob came home from work especially frustrated, picked an argument with his wife, and then systematically destroyed a collection of orchids she carefully tended. Bob was deeply ashamed of his inappropriate outbursts, because he associated them with the behavior of one of his abusive cousins. At the same time, however, he minimized the impact these had on his wife. The therapist had neglected to do a careful assessment of acting-out problems and corroborative interviews in the beginning of the treatment, and so was surprised by these events.

Thorough assessment interviews can be therapeutic in that the client tells his story in detail for the first time and frequently has a variety of reactions to it. The simple act of the therapist taking a profound and detailed interest in the client's life and obtaining information without prejudgment can elicit a variety of complex emotional reactions from the client. It is usually wise, however, for the therapist to refrain from active intervention at this point except in a broadly supportive way that facilitates the assessment process or to intervene in crisis or near-crisis situations that require immediate attention. It is preferable to wait until the assessment process is complete and the therapist can offer a formal treatment plan before embarking on active intervention strategies.

It is important to conceptualize assessment as not merely data gathering but as a vehicle for conveying to the client the first impressions of what the interactions with the therapist will be like. The optimal stance for the therapist during this process is to be direct, thorough, and interested in all aspects of the client's life. The therapist may ask challenging questions and at times be pointed in his or her probing but should not jump to quick conclusions and should elicit and value the client's understanding and explanation of what his life means to him. This is the first set of experiences in which the client can see that the therapist is genuinely interested and proceeds with caution and respect. The effects of sexual abuse can be conceptualized as an injury to the sense of self. Many individuals who have been sexually abused had previous injuries caused by emotional deprivation and other situations.

The importance of conveying to the client early on that he is of great interest to the therapist and will be treated with care and respect cannot be underestimated. It not only provides a framework for later interaction, it serves as an anchoring point against which the internal negativity and hostility toward the sense of self, which is present in many sexual abuse victims, can begin to be focused and directed. Paradoxically, the interest and respect shown by the therapist both makes it safe for the client by creating a healing environment and begins to mobilize the negativity within the client to undermine this environment in which the self, which is partially unacceptable, is treated consistently well.

FORMULATION OF A TREATMENT PLAN

Once a treatment plan is formulated, it is important that the client fully comprehend and agree to it. Although this is a truism in practice with all clients, it is especially pertinent in working with victims. An individual whose trust has been violated is often especially sensitive to coercion.

It is not uncommon for a therapist to have a more comprehensive view of the areas needing treatment than does the client. In particular, therapists are often more persuaded of subtle effects of sexual abuse and expect multiple effects in the victim's life. Therapists are often distrustful of the client's description of low levels of sequelae. However, a recent review of research suggests that approximately one third of victims of childhood sexual abuse are nonsymptomatic, even at follow-up (Finkelhor, 1990b).

This is partially due to the tendency of clients who have been victimized to be unaware of some of the effects of victimization. However, there are situations when these are distortions on the therapist's part, as theory and practice in this area are overinclusive and tend to "see too much." It should not be assumed that any discrepancy is merely the client's denial, although it may be. We have observed an unfortunate tendency in many therapists to believe it is their prerogative and even obligation to press clients who have been victimized into accepting the therapist's view of how the abuse has affected the client and what should occur in treatment. We disagree with this strategy.

In situations where the client and the therapist disagree about goals and treatment plan, we recommend that the therapist, in a straightforward fashion, explain the rationale for his or her recommendations and discuss differences with the client; if differences remain, then the therapist should defer to the client's perspective whenever possible.

This does not mean that the therapist should agree with the client's perspective if that is not what the therapist truly believes. Rather, the two agree to disagree but formulate a plan in which goals that are mutually agreed on can be addressed. The therapist can take the position that if the client is correct, then, on completion of this limited treatment plan, the therapy is done. If the therapist is correct and the client ends therapy too early, goes out into the world, encounters problems stemming from unresolved abuse sequelae, and realizes that more work lies ahead, the client is welcome to return. The client and therapist can then recontract and formulate a new treatment plan.

Case Example

Aaron, 17, sought therapy at the suggestion of his brother. Both had been abused as children for a period of months by an adolescent female baby-sitter. The brother was in therapy and persuaded Aaron to come for an assessment. A careful evaluation, including corroborative interviews with Aaron's mother and current girlfriend, found few or no symptoms suggestive of sequelae of sexual abuse, although all parties seemed to assume that hidden effects must be present, primarily because the brother had significant effects.

Aaron's agenda appeared to be a simple one, namely to tell his story, to obtain some educational information about sexual abuse, but not to continue in therapy. The therapist appropriately outlined the possibility that more subtle effects might be present but also acknowledged that a significant minority of individuals appear to experience no sequelae; and invited Aaron to return should there be problems at a later date.

Approximately 4 years later, Aaron again sought services from the same therapist when he was making a difficult vocational decision that involved relocation and a complicated career shift. The therapist had an opportunity to follow up on the possibility of sexual abuse sequelae and again determined that there was no evidence of any sequelae. The therapist also learned that Aaron's brother discovered later in therapy that he had been sexually abused previous to the baby-sitter by an older male neighbor, whereas this had not been the case with Aaron. The diversity of sexual abuse effects between the two brothers began to make sense.

Case Example

Carlos, 23, appeared for an evaluation at the suggestion of a cousin when a priest who served the parish in which Carlos grew up was prosecuted for a long history of sexual abuse of altar boys. This cousin had been abused for a prolonged period by this priest, and made a formal complaint. Carlos told his cousin that he too had been abused. Although Carlos was cautious about coming in for an assessment, he agreed to do so.

The assessment suggested that Carlos had some significant areas of possible sequelae. In particular, he had a history of going to sexually oriented bookstores and public cruising places, where he allowed men to perform fellatio on him, even though he identified himself as heterosexual. These behaviors seemed related to periods of stress and conflict in his marriage. Carlos refused the therapist's recommendation for therapy, stating he understood after talking with his cousin about their mutual abuse why he did such behaviors and he was confident he would no longer do them. Furthermore, Carlos did not want his wife to become aware of these behaviors. The therapist reiterated his perception this might be a significant problem warranting treatment, suggested what Carlos might look for if the problem worsened, and left open the possibility for Carlos to return.

Eighteen months later, Carlos returned, stating he had been arrested in a sexually oriented bookstore by an undercover police agent. Although his attorney quietly settled the charge, Carlos was deeply shaken by this close call with public exposure, and detailed to the therapist an even more extensive history of anonymous sexual behavior with males, which was incongruent with Carlos' perception of his sexual identity as heterosexual. Carlos requested the therapist do "some sort of behavior modification to cure this homosexual thing" and resisted examining the issue in any depth. The therapist declined to offer Carlos the treatment he sought, stating it was inappropriate for his problems.

Carlos returned 2 years later, stating he had sought services from a Christian psychotherapist who did aversion therapy to "cure homosexuality." Although Carlos initially experienced some reduction of same-sex behavior from this treatment, his sense of shame and self-esteem problems worsened and his cycles of sexual acting out deepened. This time when he appeared for services, Carlos was willing to look at the full range of ways in which the sexual abuse may have affected him, including his sexual orientation confusion. The therapist believed that his gentle and respectful handling of the disagreements about the treatment plan with Carlos made it possible for Carlos eventually to return for substantive therapy.

We refer to this approach as a "dental model" of mental health practice: One year a person may need a cleaning, another year a filling, the next year a root canal. The fact that different goals are the focus of the treatment at different points in time does not decrease the legitimacy of any of those goals or place either party in the position of having to be right or wrong. We believe it is imperative that, if therapy with victimized individuals does nothing else, it should model a relationship of trust and respect. The exceptions to these recommendations are situations where the client's plan for treatment is contraindicated or objectively harmful. Disagreement with the therapist's favorite theory does not in and of itself constitute objective harmfulness.

Further, it is our view that the belief of some therapists that they know more than the client does about his sexual abuse is arrogant. Clearly the therapist is—or ought to be—expert; but in the area of sexual abuse the knowledge base is thin and highly impressionistic. One therapist's expertise may be another's incompetence, narrowness, or countertransference. The problem is that the field in which the therapist is expert is murky. We recommend therapists be nondefensive about this, as it is no one's fault—it reflects the development of knowledge in this area and the field's immaturity.

At the end of the assessment process, the client and the therapist agree on particular therapeutic goals. Complete agreement on all goals the therapist views as important is not necessary, but the therapist must believe that those goals that are agreed on are clinically sound and relevant. At times there may be insufficient agreement between the client and the therapist to proceed. In such cases, it is recommended that the therapist lay out his or her perceptions and recommended treatment strategies and rationales, listen to the different points of view from the client, seriously consider those, and discuss them with the client; but if no common ground is reached, then the therapist should decline to treat the client.

This happens most typically with clients who have unrealistic expectations about a rapid cure in therapy, who conceptualize their role in therapy as a passive one, or who have become philosophically aligned with certain theoretical perspectives or self-help movements. They might insist, for example, that the therapy focus solely and exclusively on issues such as "healing the child within" or "helping recover from codependency." The idea of mutually agreed-on therapeutic goals does not mean that the therapist surrenders his or her judgment but rather that the two parties find areas of genuine agreement. If these cannot be found, therapy cannot proceed.

Case Example

Ralph, 24, presented for therapy with the request that he be given "heavy-duty psychological techniques" to help contain his sexual acting out. Ralph had been sexually abused by his stepfather and had a history of sexual interaction with female prostitutes once or twice a year on business trips, which he felt was out of character for him and about which he felt considerable guilt. For the past year, he had attended a sexual addicts' group facilitated by a charismatic leader whom the therapist regarded as an ill-trained cult figure. This leader believed that any sexual expression other than monogamous heterosexual sex was "addictive" and would "eventually destroy you." Included in the prohibited activities were any masturbation and all sexual fantasies if they were not of one's monogamous spouse.

It was the therapist's assessment that this extremist and shaming perspective further eroded Ralph's behavioral controls, increased his difficulties maintaining adequate self-esteem, and exacerbated his problems. The therapist outlined to Ralph the reasons for his concerns and disagreements, made a number of alternative suggestions, and informed Ralph that what the therapist had to offer and what the group had to offer were different in philosophy and style and that Ralph would have to make a choice because the two treatments would likely clash. Ralph opted to obtain individual psychotherapy from a therapist recommended by the group leader.

It is important, both from an informed consent perspective and as an aspect of respect shown the client, that the therapist be explicit. There will be times when the therapy causes more upset and disruption than relief of symptoms and times when the therapist will ask the client to do difficult things. It is also wise to clarify that therapy will be an active process and that no change will occur unless the client actively participates.

AN INDIVIDUAL THERAPY MODEL

This individual therapy model is a hybrid, in that the conceptualization of client problems is in line with the self-psychology theory; however, the therapist's behavior and interaction with the client are more akin to a cognitive behavioral style. In other words, the therapist thinks dynamically but acts pragmatically, in a goal-oriented fashion. This model is meant for late adolescents, young adults, and older men who are functioning more or less independently of their families of origin.

The intent of this therapy is to reduce symptoms that the client presents within a framework of producing dynamic change in the sense of self. These two features taken separately are considered necessary but not sufficient conditions in working with sexual abuse victims. Symptom reduction alone does not address the unique characteristics of sexual abuse victims, such as their propensity for repetitive interpersonal difficulties. Given the possible depth and pervasiveness of the effects of sexual abuse, it is reasonable to assume that symptom reduction runs the risk of problems reemerging at a later date. Similarly, dynamic change alone provides no way to ascertain if the client's change process is merely intellectualized or emotionally integrated. The ability of the client to reduce symptoms and apply coping strategies learned in therapy to a variety of new life challenges is considered in this model to be the best test of whether dynamic changes are truly integrated.

Individual therapy is central in this model; although group, couples, and family therapy modalities may be used to amplify individual therapy, they are auxiliary. The use of these other modalities is briefly discussed later. This is not to suggest that individual therapy is necessarily the optimal choice for a given client, but that if multiple modalities are used, they be coordinated and consistent.

Early Stages

The initial stages of interaction involve taking a thorough history of the client and in particular, reflecting on how the past history of sexual and other abuse currently affects the client's life. A picture of current symptomatology should be mapped out and the reasons why the client presents for therapy now should be discussed.

Typically, individuals who have been sexually abused have been living with this history within some sort of equilibrium. When they seek individual therapy, often something has occurred to disrupt that equilibrium and increase symptoms. A thorough understanding of these reasons and events can clarify a number of important points. The coping strategies and vulnerabilities of the client can be illustrated, and initial ideas of the most efficient points of entry into the client's experience of having been sexually abused can be suggested.

Most individuals with a history of sexual abuse who have managed to lead their lives with reduced or no symptoms in at least some areas have struck some balance between their history and coping strategies. The immediate situation that has increased symptomatology provides an important opportunity for the therapist. It allows the therapist to get underneath those coping strategies in a way that is acceptable to the client, as opposed to battering down the client's defenses in areas where these defenses have been effective. In other words, the circumstances of the immediate situation can reduce the sense of violation during the therapy process. They also signal to the therapist possible related areas that are ripe for the next interventions, presuming the client continues in therapy.

Equally important is understanding what has worked well in the client's life. Areas of high functioning and good coping strategies can provide a context for understanding the overall fragility or strength of the client, as well as a context for mapping out the areas of defensive adaptation that may not be amenable, at least not quickly, to therapeutic intervention.

Implicit in this discussion is the assumption that the therapist should not dismantle the client's defenses. What is suggested here is that the therapist approach only those defenses that have already failed and respect those that are working well. The rationale for this approach is twofold: it conveys to the client a sense that he will be respected and not violated, and it reflects a therapeutic stance in which the client is seen as an individual who has been besieged by certain events and who has evolved a pattern, however flawed, of coping with those events, that warrants respect.

The therapy process, whenever possible, should improve functioning level, not erode it. The client's sense of himself in day-to-day functioning is crucial. If there are areas in his life where he feels competent and proud of his functioning, these are areas to be encouraged, not undermined, even if the functioning strategies are problematic. In this model, therapists who believe that breaking through the client's defenses for the "therapeutic good" of the client are not seen as acting with more thoroughness but with disrespect, poor planning, and lack of imagination and understanding. Such therapists are seen as not adequately strategizing how they can most effectively work with the areas of vulnerability the client presents while respecting the areas of strength the client has carved out. If the client does not perceive maladaptive aspects of what he considers a strength, the therapist might use examples from the client's experience to suggest these aspects. The therapist's "hunches," "experience," or "theory" alone are insufficient. The client's experience weighs the most.

Case Example

Fred, 26, came from a family in which there was extensive physical and sexual abuse and alcoholism. Despite the emotional and economic poverty of his background, he was very proud that he completed college and achieved a middle-level management technical position at a large corporation. He was particularly proud of what he perceived to be his "strength." As the therapist began working with him, Fred began to form the perception that a good deal of his "strength" really consisted of a variety of intellectualized defenses against a profound underlying depression. These defenses caused considerable emotional constriction, which apparently led to chronic dissatisfaction from his male spouse about Fred's aloofness and coldness.

Auxiliary couples treatment was not effective in altering this pattern. Fred perceived that the couples therapist and his male partner wanted him to be "weak." The individual therapist determined it was unwise to push Fred at this time on this issue. Some weeks later in a one-to-one session, Fred began to explore tentatively his sadness and disappointment in himself regarding an incident with his 4-year-old son from an earlier heterosexual marriage. His son came to him for support and comfort following an altercation with a peer. Fred saw that his aloofness clearly wounded his son, who then sought support from Fred's partner. For the first time in a therapy session, Fred teared up, but he rapidly began to compose himself. The therapist decided to take a risk with this opportunity and asked Fred if he really wanted to do to his son what was done to him.

Fred began crying profusely but then became panicked at his "weakness and loss of control." The therapist redefined this "loss of control" as progress and reassured Fred that his well-established patterns of reinstating control would not likely desert him; he might learn a more sophisticated and flexible way of maintaining control if he could stay with these feelings for a while. In the following sessions, Fred discussed physical abuse and emotional coldness from his biological father, whereas before Fred's emphasis had been on the physical and sexual abuse he received from a stepfather. Fred spontaneously noted he could see the legitimacy of his partner's complaints.

Behavioral Assignments

The initial assessment, because of its thoroughness, often elicits considerable historical material. In this model, it is recommended such material be pursued if it seems relevant to current life problems, but that it not become the sole or even primary focus of therapy. Rather, we recommend that early in therapy, the therapist strategize behavioral tasks for the client to do as homework assignments. The selection of these initial assignments is important. The ideal assignments are ones that involve a current problem area in the client's life which is a clear example of a long-standing dysfunctional trend and is theorized to be related to the aftereffects of sexual abuse, other damage to the sense of self, or deprivation. The ideal assignment targets initial behavior change in a pattern that represents how the client currently functions out of a historically damaged sense of self.

Equally important, these initial assignments should be chosen for a high likelihood of success. Part of the intent of this assignment is to give the client an initially successful experience with behavioral change. This is why a thorough understanding of the client's functioning level during the initial phases is so important. Without this information, it may be difficult to predict the likelihood of success in these assignments. Considerable care and planning are crucial to this therapy model. Spontaneity may have a role in the therapist's style but not much of a role in the therapist's strategies.

Case Example

Kent, 24, was repeatedly passed over for raises and promotions on his current job and treated with considerable verbal sarcasm by a male supervisor. Nevertheless, the supervisor and others in the office understood that when a difficult job needed to get done, Kent was the person to do it. This had been an ongoing pattern with Kent, and indeed had been the reason he resigned a number of jobs in frustration and anger. He had never been able to discuss his dissatisfaction with supervisors. The first behavioral assignment started by helping him clarify in therapy his dissatisfactions with the current job and how his passivity may have played a role in this dissatisfaction.

Kent eventually understood this was not simply a situation of unpleasant coworkers and supervisor but rather an interaction between their behavior and his own. The therapist assisted Kent in targeting reasonable appropriate assertive requests of the supervisor and then role playing them in therapy. After these were refined, Kent carried out the assignment. Results were mixed: Kent performed well, albeit with some passive-aggressive aspects that were not effective; the supervisor was responsive to some but not all of Kent's requests and reduced but did not eliminate sarcastic remarks.

As important as planning the assignment was its recapitulation. Over the next few sessions, time was spent reviewing Kent's performance, examining his expectations about what changes were reasonable, and targeting the next behavioral assignments. The initial tasks provided an opportunity to discuss the maladaptive aspects of Kent's passivity, withdrawal, and passive-aggressive style; challenged his idealized and grandiose expectations of his ability to change the world; and connected these themes to how his sexual abuse as an early adolescent by a minister affected him and resulted in poor coping strategies.

Ideal assignments exemplify chronic situations in which the client acts in a self-defeating way that seems linked to his history of abuse and any earlier damage to his sense of self. The specific examples initially chosen, however, should be relatively uncomplicated and "safe bets" for successful experiences. Even though the assignment is relatively simple, it should be treated cautiously. The situation is reviewed in therapy, the client develops some understanding of his and the other person's role in the problem, and the situation is role played. This increases the likelihood of the experience being successful and ensures that the client's perceptions of the events are reasonably accurate. Treating a client concern, even a minor one, as worthy of careful planning is an important message.

These "simple" initial assignments are not simple in their meaning for the client; there is often a surprising amount of resistance. The reasons for the resistance are processed and the client is reminded that little can occur in this therapy without his active participation. Once the client begins following through on assignments, gradually more complicated and challenging assignments are given until the client experiences significant affective responses. This sometimes occurs early, although a few assignments may be needed. Examples of these responses include a recognition of anger at other events in the client's life, feelings of sadness at having been cheated and deprived, or a sense of insight or connection to earlier events.

If this process continues with the affective responses processed and the client gradually being given more assignments, a point will usually come at which the client begins to experience directly his negative sense of self. This can take the form of a lack of confidence in relatively simple assignments, feelings of not being worth the positive outcomes of the assignments, feelings that progress in therapy is not "good enough," or similar distortions. What is happening dynamically is that the areas of life in which the client is functioning with a low sense of self are being slowly remedied and replaced with the client acting as if he has a positive sense of self.

Although the client may initially be elated and have a sense of empowerment, this is often followed by the negative sense of self emerging as strong resistance. In other words, a parallel history begins to develop that is based on a positive evaluation of the self. This eventually creates conflict with the prevailing negative sense of self.

Middle Phase

Simultaneous with behavioral assignments, the historical issues that emerged in the initial phases are pursued in the middle phase of therapy. Part of the therapy sessions is spent planning for and process-ing the assignments, and part is spent discussing longer-term issues. By the time significant negativity emerges from the behavioral assign-ments, the client has begun to process historical issues that can be brought to bear on understanding the negativity.

In this model, the behavioral assignments serve a number of func-tions. They begin to create a parallel history in the client's life in which he sees in his own experience that he is capable of mastering tasks he thought were not possible earlier; the behavioral assignments serve as an engine that drives a more dynamic integration. When chosen carefully, the behavioral assignments will not only address real problems in the client's life but will produce a variety of mean-ingful emotional responses, the integration of which begins to make the client more whole.

Resolution of the negative sense of self involves letting the client experience it directly. Typically, this negativity has been defended against and the client backs away from it when it emerges. The client is encouraged to "let it have its say," to experience and integrate the accompanying affect, and to analyze them in a cognitive-behavioral fashion (cognitive restructuring, see Beck, 1976, and Young & Beck, 1982; rational-emotive approaches, see Ellis, 1962, and Ellis & Greiger, 1977; structured behavior change, see Phillips & Weiner, 1966), whether this negativity is what the client wishes to support or to counteract.

Throughout this process, two events require careful management. First, although it may temporarily slow down to give more time to process and resolve affective responses, the process of changing be-havior in the present does not stop. In other words, forward momen-tum is maintained in the behavioral change, despite the affective responses. The negative self is not allowed to stop the behavioral development of a positive self.

Second, it is important to make certain that the anxiety elicited during these processes is not discharged by acting out. The earlier careful assessment of acting-out potential becomes crucial. Often, when these affective responses do not occur, the client has been discharging the accompanying anxiety in some other way. If acting-out anxiety is occurring, it is important that this be blocked.

Case Example

Mark, 19, came from a family background of sexual and physical abuse and significant alcoholism. Therapy seemed to be progressing surprisingly well given his history; he appeared to handle initial behavioral assignments well and historical issues were being explored. Mark seemed to be handling these seemingly meaningful changes and discussions in stride, with little distress and no emergence of negativity toward himself. The therapist inquired generally about acting-out behaviors; Mark reported none.

A few sessions later, the therapist received an emergency phone call from Mark; this had not occurred previously. Mark was mysterious on the phone about what had transpired but was clearly upset. The therapist saw him later that day on an emergency basis. With considerable embarrassment, Mark revealed he had begun a sexual affair with a female coworker about a month into therapy. Her boyfriend had discovered it, followed Mark after work, ran him into a ditch, and showed him his shotgun, which he promised to use on Mark if he had further contact with his girlfriend. Mark returned home, had a series of panic attacks, and called the therapist.

In the next session, processing focused on Mark's distrust and fear of rejection by the therapist in not discussing this earlier. Information also emerged that self-destructive affairs to avoid affect were a pattern for Mark. Mark and the therapist agreed to a contract in which Mark would tell his best friend and the therapist when he began to plan an affair.

Mark canceled the next session at the last minute; this was unlike him. The therapist called Mark; after initial defensiveness, Mark began crying, stating he had "fucked up his therapy like he fucked up everything in his life." With much difficulty, the therapist persuaded Mark to return. Over the next sessions, Mark expressed considerable self-hatred. Eventually, his long-standing pattern of placating male authority figures by being "perfect," followed by sexual acting out, followed by his withdrawal from the male figures because he believed they would reject him if they knew, was explicated and processed in light of other aspects of his family background.

In Mark, the lack of the expected emergence of negativity against the self raised the possibility that this negativity was being discharged instead of being experienced. Although attempts to evaluate this produced no information, when it did emerge, Mark used his deception with the therapist as a vehicle for self-attack. Making a contract to contain his acting out produced anxiety and more deception and precipitated a crisis. The crisis was eventually put to therapeutic effect, but it was a risky point in the therapy. If the therapist had been rejecting or critical of Mark for his deceptions, or had been too lax in limiting the acting out, the therapy might have ended poorly.

It is important that the therapist be forgiving of errors the client makes both during the behavioral assignments and in the processing of the affective responses. The therapist's typical response to errors should be one of acceptance coupled with an expectation that, despite these errors, the client will maintain forward momentum. If levels of depression or anxiety reach the point where the client begins to experience functional impairment, breaks can be taken and a more supportive therapy temporarily put in place; but when the client is able, the forward progress is again resumed. The therapist communicates to the client that the client will be able to cope with the situation. The negative self can be experienced but not allowed to interfere substantially with development of a positive self.

Case Example

Bill, 21, had been sexually abused during childhood and adolescence by his pediatrician, who was also a neighbor and family friend. He did not want to file a complaint or reveal the name of the pediatrician in therapy. Bill's goals were to improve his relationship functioning and eventually to confront the physician. The therapist cautioned Bill early in therapy that his plan of a one-to-one confrontation without support or knowledge of friends, family, or authorities placed an undue burden on Bill, and agreed to proceed only if Bill was open to considering other options if his original plan proved ineffective.

After making some significant improvements in his relationship with his girlfriend, Bill began discussing confronting his abuser. After two sessions discussing his ambivalence about this, he came to the next session distraught. He had become angry at the pediatrician after the last session, had seven beers, went to the physician's home, and demanded $5,000 to help defray the cost of therapy. The physician calmed Bill down, offered to send him instead to a colleague who would treat him free, offered Bill more beer, and then seduced him. This was the first time Bill had had sexual contact with the physician in 5 years.

In the session, Bill was confused, harshly self-critical, and deeply ashamed, stating he should have listened to the therapist all along and filed a complaint with Child Protection and the Medical Board, and suggested they do so immediately during that session. The therapist responded by cautioning against impulsive decisions, and recommended that a few sessions be spent discussing complaint routes and what they meant to Bill before taking any action. The therapist also rejected Bill's harsh assessment of his failure, and commented that although his particular plan of handling the situation had not proven effective, Bill's general tendency to take charge of his life and decisions had been a hard-won fight for him given his history, and was a valuable trait, even if his rendering of it was too inflexible. Bill had gotten in over his head in this situation, and the most positive response would be to learn from his errors, not to attack himself, act impulsively, or surrender his judgement to the therapist's.

In the next 2 months, a number of issues were processed. The pros and cons of various complaint routes were explored, the need to temper but not eliminate Bill's stubbornness and rigidity were discussed, and his episodic impulsiveness, particularly in the face of anxiety and perceived failure, were explicated. Although Bill eventually decided to pursue formal complaint routes against the pediatrician, the process afforded the opportunity to demonstrate to Bill that he was acceptable even when he erred, and to challenge his rigidity productively. Bill later commented that he appreciated the therapist not taking advantage of him when he was down by immediately contacting the authorities, and that this incident was pivotal in his being able to trust the therapist, because his initial motivation in complaining was to please the therapist, whom he feared might reject him because of his errors.

Selection of the assignments and a sense of what might be coming during the affective responses are crucial to the success of this process. A clear sense of timing about when to "let up" is also important. A therapist who is dogmatic, unforgiving, or insensitive will fare poorly. This process, when done well, accomplishes a number of things. The client can see from his own experience that he can make significant behavioral changes; that he can make errors and recover from them; and that he can experience strong affective responses and weather them without disruption of his behavioral progress.

The therapist derives from this process a clearer understanding of the client's coping patterns, strengths and weaknesses, areas of resistance, and typical ways of defending against change. Behavioral assignments are goal oriented, even though the emotional impact on the client is pervasive and sometimes profound. Not uncommonly, as this process requires numerous judgement calls, the therapist may miscalculate by not pushing the client enough, pushing the client too hard, being judgmental about mistakes, not being sufficiently challenging, or being too challenging about possible distortions in the client's understanding. This process works best when the therapist is relatively transparent about what occurs in therapy and why. Similarly, the therapist is straightforward about errors, admits them, and reformulates accordingly.

Case Example

Tom, 25, was sexually abused by a priest in his pre-adolescent years, by an older male sibling in early adolescence, and by a female high school teacher in mid-adolescence. In addition to sexual abuse, there was a history of emotional deprivation. Both parents were highly career oriented, and Tom spent much of his childhood growing up in different cities where his parents were assigned for employment. Most of his care was provided by his older male sibling, and Tom himself provided a great deal of care for younger siblings. Not surprisingly, he presented with considerable pseudo-maturity and had little recognition of the degree to which his own emotional needs were not met.

Therapy initially progressed very well. Tom effectively addressed a long-standing, self-defeating pattern of not finishing school work and was quite elated when he received a B.A. after finishing up a large number of incompletes. Next, he made an effective and articulate complaint to the diocese that employed the priest. Even though the minister was deceased, Tom found considerable resolution in having his complaint heard and acknowledged by church authorities. Tom attempted to track down the high school teacher, who had in the meantime changed school districts. He contacted Child Protective Services in the teacher's new county, who told him that the case was too

old to prosecute but assured him that they would open a file on her
and monitor her closely.

Tom's next goal was to confront his brother, but he became somewhat hesitant and self-doubting, which had been uncharacteristic of
him in the therapy. The therapist encouraged Tom to press on and did
not attend to Tom's hesitations. Tom made a reasonable plan to confront his brother and rendered it well. However, the brother's response
was demeaning. Tom became extremely depressed, hopeless, and
had serious feelings of worthlessness. He believed that he was a failure. He was sophisticated enough to appreciate that his brother was
very difficult, and did not blame himself for the brother's poor response, but instead felt worthless because of his severe, and to him
inexplicable, depression. At that point, Tom's therapist decided to
obtain a consultation.

The consultant suggested to Tom's therapist that he had been inattentive to Tom's suggestions of wanting to slow down before tackling
his brother. Tom had had the role of a parentified child in raising his
younger siblings, and the consultant suggested that Tom had slipped
into the role of being a "super client" and the therapist had unwittingly
encouraged this and had been insufficiently attentive to the striking
lack of distress and difficulty Tom experienced as he progressed
through one therapeutic success after another. The consultant suggested further that Tom's depression might be related to a feeling
that his therapist, like his parents and brother, was inattentive to his
emotional needs; this depression was partly historically related and
partly related to an error on the therapist's part.

The therapist, in exploring this further, also recognized a countertransference issue. The therapist himself had been sexually abused
by an older cousin. Part of the therapist's inattentiveness to Tom's suggestions of slowing down before tackling his brother was perhaps related to the therapist's eagerness to have Tom confront his older
brother, something the therapist had never done with his older cousin.

As suggested by the consultant, the therapist in the next session
discussed the idea that he had been insufficiently attentive to Tom's
hints of wanting to slow down before tackling his brother, and this
might be related to his depression in that it was another neglect of
Tom's emotional needs as he tried to please an authority figure. The
therapist also let Tom know that this blind spot was due to the thera-

pist's own countertransference, which he planned to pursue and resolve in his own supervision. As suggested by the consultant, the
therapist did not disclose the nature of the countertransference.

Tom's depression significantly resolved over the next two sessions
and he described that for the first time, he felt that he could "be a mess"
and be acceptable and that someone else could take care of him. It
appeared that the consultant's view of the dynamics of the situation
was reasonably accurate.

In this manner, not only does the client see he can manage a trial-
and-error process, but he observes the therapist doing so. The point
is not to create errors on the part of the therapist but to recognize
that in this active, directive strategy there is some likelihood that
errors will occur, and the therapist should respond to them in a way
congruent with the way the therapy is conducted.

It is important to note that transparency about the therapy does
not mean transparency about the therapist. In the example above,
detailing the nature of the therapist's countertransference would
have been a strain on the therapeutic boundary. Rather, the client is
kept informed about what is going on and why but not about the
therapist's personal issues. Hence the client was informed that the
therapist made an error because of his own background and that the
problem was being addressed in supervision, but not what these
issues were. This way of doing therapy shares a cognitive-behavioral
bias that the most effective treatment is nonmysterious: The client
understands what transpires and why. Therapeutic progress and the
means by which it is achieved are the client's to keep while boundaries are maintained and modeled.

Later Stages

After the client has accumulated some experience in making
positive behavioral changes in the present and emotionally integrating them, this model is applied in situations that have more historical
import. Specifically, the therapist and the client begin to plan how
to address parts of the abuse history directly using these strategies.

An effective tool is the use of letters directed toward the perpetrating individuals or others who enabled the perpetration. These

letters are not vehicles of communication to those individuals but
rather a journal process in which the client can record various feelings
he experiences in imagining communication with these individuals.
The intent of this exercise is to give the client a more full and complete understanding of his affective response to the individuals in
question and also to clarify what he wishes to say to them.

With these issues clarified, the therapist and the client can begin
to explore a variety of options to obtain some resolution of the historical abuse situation. The therapist does not a priori assume that any
one solution is better than others. Solutions range along a continuum
from directly interacting with the perpetrator, with or without the
therapist present, or with other family members or support people,
to interacting with other individuals in the system in which the
perpetration occurred, to having the story be heard and acknowledged by significant others, to writing a final unsent letter in which
the reaction of the client to the abusive behavior is described. In
other words, the options range from the most direct to the purely
symbolic. The goal of this procedure is to assist the client in having
emotional resolution in a context in which his experience is acknowledged, where he receives support and validation, and where emotional integration can occur.

This part of therapy can be particularly tricky. The intent is to help
the client have the optimal experience for resolving the abuse. As
this is an adult client who is removed in time from the abusive situation, and the abusive individuals or enablers are not part of the
therapy process, it can be difficult to judge the most efficacious
options. Corroborative interviews with spouses, significant others,
friends, siblings, or other family members can assist in planning this
and should be utilized when appropriate. At this point in the therapy,
many clients are sophisticated enough to do their own corroborative
interviews and data gathering about the options. Whenever this more
empowering option is available, it is generally preferred. It is important to make certain that the client does not make an impulsive
decision but an informed one about which option is the best.

In situations of doubt, the recommended strategy is to choose the
option with the highest likelihood of success, carry it through to its
resolution, and process it in therapy; if this has not been sufficient,
then move to more risky options. Options that seem high risk and

prone to failure are generally not encouraged in this model; although if the client is intent on pursuing them, the therapist might outline the pros and cons and help the client process this. In other words, the client might choose to pursue an option with which the therapist disagrees. In keeping with the stance of empowering the client, the therapist should not interfere with this, although the therapist can insist it be discussed before and after action and can offer his or her opinions and cautions prior to the choice.

Case Example

Ted, 25, had been sexually abused by a stepfather. He found the initial behavioral assignments difficult and was resistant but followed through and made a degree of progress in his primary relationship and his work situation that exceeded his expectations. Ted became hopeful for the first time that he could manage himself.

Ted outlined to his therapist a plan to confront his stepfather. The therapist was cautious and not encouraging of this plan because of Ted's three siblings; his younger brother refused to discuss the sexual abuse (and Ted strongly suspected that he too had been abused by the stepfather), his older sister was openly supportive of the step-father and hostile toward Ted, and his younger sister, with whom Ted had the closest relationship, appeared to very passive and dependent and vacillated between supporting Ted and supporting the older sister, depending on who talked to her the most at any point in time. The therapist commented that Ted's plan warranted caution because Ted had little clear indication of support within the family, and the family history suggested that both the stepfather and the older sister could be explosive in their behavior and affect. Ted's mother, with whom he had had a strong relationship, was deceased.

Ted's only support in the family was an aunt in whom Ted had confided about the abuse as an adolescent and who contacted Child Protection. This aunt then took Ted in. Child Protection did not intervene because Ted "was too old and a male anyway." As the therapist and Ted discussed the pros and cons of the situation, they continued to disagree. The therapist told Ted that although she remained uncomfortable with the plan, it was Ted's prerogative to pursue it and she would be there to support Ted and process the situation should Ted decide to implement it.

On the surface, the meeting between Ted and the stepfather was disastrous. Ted, who was gay, was vilified by his stepfather, who told him that the sexual abuse was another example of his "sick faggot imagination" and refused to discuss it further unless Ted agreed to undergo counseling at an organization affiliated with the fundamentalist church where the stepfather was a deacon. His older sister sided with their stepfather, verbally abused Ted, and pressured the younger sister to side with the stepfather and shun Ted. A tense situation persisted for a few weeks until the younger brother, who had been brought into the family dispute by the older sister, announced to everyone that he too had been sexually abused by the stepfather, at which point, the younger sister clearly threw her support behind Ted and his younger brother. The stepfather and older sister announced that they would disown all three of them for being "perverts and liars."

These events required a few months in therapy for processing and integrating. However, at the end, the therapist came to the conclusion that Ted's course of action was reasonable and told Ted that. Ted had correctly assessed that his older sister was intractable, his younger sister unpredictable, and his younger brother inscrutable; and that his strategy, although high risk, was the only one available if he wished to deal directly with the abuse history, which he did. Later, Ted told the therapist that the therapist's acknowledgement of the reasonableness of Ted's judgement had been a major boost to his self-confidence.

Throughout this process the client has the option of disregarding or delaying certain options. It can sometimes be useful to take a break from therapy before pursuing certain options. Sometimes, as clients feel more effective and powerful and have a growing sense of themselves as competent and worthwhile, they begin to tackle behavioral changes in their lives during their therapy but without input from the therapist.

Case Example

Matthew, 18, had considerable confusion about his sexual orientation, and discussed early in therapy the pros and cons of exploring same-sex relationships, which he had never before had. He opted to delay this exploration. After a series of successes in handling school-related challenges, assertive situations with friends and family members, and a confrontation with his abuser, his previous therapist, Matthew announced that one night he had gone to a gay bar and had his first sexual experience with a man, none of which had been discussed in therapy.

This situation presented an important therapeutic decision point. The style of the therapy had been one of mutuality and enhancement of Matthew's personal choices and power. Spontaneously applying concepts learned in therapy was consistent with the therapeutic style, and welcome. The therapist's challenge was to strike a balance between affirming and encouraging Matthew's self-directed choices, yet raising appropriate questions. These included whether Matthew's choices were well planned or impulsive, whether Matthew emotionally integrated the experience, whether these experiences were self-defeating, or whether Matthew used them to deflect anxiety or create a crisis that distracted from other, more pressing situations.

The therapist's response to Matthew was to inquire about his planning process and why he had not discussed it in therapy. The therapist learned Matthew had planned this situation well, including obtaining information on and implementing safe-sex procedures, but did not mention it in therapy beforehand because of his shame regarding same-sex desires. With this clarified, the therapist commended Matthew for his sound planning, particularly about safe sex, and suggested that Matthew's shame about same-sex feelings interfered with emotionally integrating them, which then became a therapeutic focus.

One of the long-term goals of therapy is to assist the client in making the bridge between skills learned in therapy and their application in the outside world. At times, when the behavioral change process starts "cascading," the therapist's role is to help the client become better at mastering his own change process by helping him attend to issues of pacing, emotional integration, sound decision making, and the like.

Matthew had done well in most of these areas, requiring only a nudge to begin to integrate emotionally his same-sex experience and desires. His way of offering a *fait accompli* in therapy, but nondefensively, suggests a level of initiative, autonomy, and trust that signalled he was nearing termination. (There also may have also been age-typical issues of establishing autonomy with an authority figure.)

Throughout these processes, the therapist must tend to the symptomatology, affective state, and trust level of the client. The goal is to push the client to make significant behavioral changes and to integrate emotionally—but not too hard. Mild distress or slight increases of symptomatology are acceptable in this model, but when there is any significant drop in the client's functioning level, the therapist should pull back from more difficult material and move into a supportive role. The therapist can be relatively transparent about this process, working cooperatively with the client to ascertain when the stress has become too much and making joint decisions about this. For many sexual abuse victims, the levels of coping they have achieved, however flawed or incomplete, are an important accomplishment. Therapy should not undermine them. The intent of this model of therapy is to build on what the client has already achieved, not eradicate and replace it. Whenever possible, some forward momentum on behavioral change is maintained, even if only symbolic.

Case Example

Steve, 23, had been abused by an uncle and aunt who raised him; the uncle physically and sexually, the aunt physically. Both had been alcoholic most of their adult lives and were deceased. Prior to living with the aunt and uncle, Steve had experienced considerable emotional deprivation; his biological father had abandoned the family and his mother had died when Steve was 3.

Steve made reasonable progress in therapy, reducing a persistent sexual dysfunction, retarded ejaculation, which troubled his current same-sex relationship. His next goal in therapy was to speak with a number of his relatives about the abuse. Steve was particularly ashamed about the sexual abuse because it occurred from ages 11 through 17. He spent time processing that the sexual abuse was not his fault and addressing his concerns that his poorly educated relatives might blame him, as the uncle was viewed within the family as being a saint for putting up with his abusive wife. Steve was planning a rare visit to his home state in the coming month to talk to his family.

Suddenly, Steve's company was acquired by another and he was laid off without warning a month before he had been promised a highly desired promotion. Steve was devastated, because he had worked hard and had no warning.

Steve and the therapist discussed the pros and cons of delaying his talk with his family. The therapist was particularly concerned because Steve tended to be overresponsible and unaware of the emotional impact of stress on him. Steve agreed that the sudden changes in employment were very stressful, but felt he had worked hard in therapy to prepare for this visit and he needed to "do something" to address the history of the abuse directly.

The therapist hit on a compromise solution. A long-time dream of Steve's was to learn to play the flute. His aunt and uncle had forbid him to learn music because they viewed it as "unmanly." Learning the flute had, for a long time, been a symbol for Steve of something he might do when he was free from the constricting influence of his family. Steve and the therapist discussed this as a symbolic but nevertheless powerful action that might satisfy Steve's need to "do something" while he delayed interacting with his family to a less stressful time in his life. Steve took flute lessons. These served as a useful bridge until his employment situation improved and became a symbol for Steve that he was autonomous and independent of his family.

Termination and Continuation

Therapy can end at varying points in this model. The change process for clients is conceptualized as one in which they simultaneously come to greater understanding of the effects of the abuse in their lives, learn behavioral change strategies to alter these effects, take appropriate steps to address directly historical material as it becomes manifest in their lives, and continue this process in an ongoing fashion. The point of ending is not a point of cure nor a remaking of the client but a process of setting in motion a more or less stable parallel track of functioning in which the self is enhanced and affirmed. As a result, there can be different points of ending. In the words of Arendt (1955), "We can no more master the past than we can undo it. But we can reconcile ourselves to it" (p. 21).

Some clients end therapy when they have made simple behavioral changes in their lives. They may be feeling better than before and do not want to "risk it" by pursuing more volatile material directly related to the abuse. If the therapist has an opinion about the advisability of pursuing or not pursuing this material, he or she is free to offer it. In any case, the recommended therapeutic stance is to congratulate the client on the progress made and to welcome him to return later if needed. This is true whether or not the therapist and the client disagree about the advisability of pursuing historical material.

Other clients continue therapy through behavioral changes, and continuing through emotional integration of certain aspects of the abuse. It is important for such clients to understand that even though they have done impressive work, they are not "cured," but have addressed the known issues at hand. It is important for such clients to realize that ramifications of the abuse undetected by both the client and the therapist may emerge at a later date. The client is free to return without any implication that therapy failed. Rather, the new material is understood as exemplifying the complex nature of abuse effects. The past therapy would be conceptualized as having been successful given what was known by the client and therapist at that time. New issues can be addressed building on the success of the earlier therapy.

Case Example

Ed, 22, had been in 10 months of therapy 2 years previously addressing chronic unassertiveness, sexual acting out, episodic alcohol abuse, a history of sexual abuse by his biological father, and considerable emotional deprivation. It was not easy for him, as he was prone to panic attacks, but he made reasonable progress and felt confident and competent in ending therapy.

Ed returned when he developed his first long-term relationship with a man. He had done a good job asserting his needs early in the relationship, but as intimacy increased he became fearful of abandonment and worried that if he asserted himself, his partner might abandon him. He became increasingly unassertive and resentful, which peaked when he and his partner began discussing living together and could not agree on a neighborhood, type of apartment, and the like. Ed also felt dejected, believing that he had undone his earlier therapeutic progress.

The therapist disagreed, reminding Ed that his progress had been real. The therapist explained that it was unlikely that Ed's fears of abandonment and difficulties managing intimacy and autonomy could have occurred earlier because he had never had an ongoing relationship before. The recent problems were consistent and understandable from Ed's history. The therapist suggested to Ed that the earlier progress was his to keep, as he had maintained his other improvements; the new situation reflected problems that were earlier unknown. The therapist suggested Ed continue in therapy to address these, which he did.

The client may wish to return to therapy at a later date to address issues truly or seemingly unrelated to the abuse; returning to the original therapist is safe and relatively efficient, as there was a positive relationship and is a shared understanding about the client's history. These are examples of the dental model of therapy described above.

This is not to suggest that all points of ending are necessarily sound. Situations in which the client is avoiding important material in either the behavior change process or the exploratory part of the therapy, situations where the client appears to be acting out or experiencing poor behavioral controls, or situations where the client abruptly stops for no apparent reason are undesirable. The recommended therapeutic style remains respectful, transparent, mutual, and flexible.

The therapist can describe his or her observations and understanding of the current situation, and suggest to the client what he or she considers the best course of action. The client's input is solicited and discussed. If the situation is resolved to agreement, then the termination proceeds or the therapy continues. If the client and the therapist remain in disagreement and the therapist has attempted to understand the client's view but the client continues to want to terminate, then the therapist can state that even though he or she believes it inadvisable to terminate, the client is welcome to come back at a later date for any number of reasons, including to process this disagreement further, to address new areas that have arisen, or to continue the treatment plan as recommended by the therapist.

This therapy model is not one in which the client primarily identifies, expresses, and catharts affect related to the abuse experience. Simply emotionally reliving the abuse experience is viewed as an irresponsible therapeutic goal. There is significant danger of regression; such catharsis does not necessarily lead to improvement in functioning level or increased behavioral skills; and there is no guarantee that catharsis will result in integration. Therapeutic approaches that posit affective experience as primary, we believe, run the risk of not only causing regression in the client and eroding functioning level but inculcating in the client a counterproductive sense of being a helpless victim—a rationalized version of the negative sense of self that is a core problem of the client.

The effects of the abuse and deprivation on the sense of self are considered primary and central as the focus of therapeutic efforts. The underlying affect is not considered central but more as a series of cues. An assumption is made in this model that affect is useful only to the extent that it is informative, integrated, and utilized effectively for behavioral change. Affective expression in and of itself is neither therapeutic nor untherapeutic. It can be either depending on the context and circumstances; however, it can be volatile, and requires careful management because of its "regressive pull."

THE ROLE OF OTHER THERAPY MODALITIES

Many clinicians who treat male victims of sexual abuse primarily utilize group therapy. The individual therapy model described here does not typically make use of group therapy, although it could in some circumstances. These include when the group is run by a professional leader; when the goals of the group and individual therapy are congruent; and when the client is in need of what group therapy can offer.

It is our view that group therapy is most effective as a way to educate clients about sexual abuse, to provide support, and, to a limited extent, to function as a "social laboratory" to address interpersonal deficits. Other than for these goals, we are not enthusiastic about group therapy as the primary treatment for a number of reasons.

The individual therapy relationship described earlier, although goal oriented and directed, is nevertheless a deeply intimate one. Both the therapist and the client, especially the client, are vulnerable, and the trustworthiness of the therapist in periods of success and failure is a central therapeutic tool. For clients who have experienced the violation of trust that is central to sexual abuse, this interaction is uniquely powerful, cannot be duplicated in a group process, and is more akin to the kinds of intimate relationships the client will face in the real world. Group therapy diffuses the intensity of the interaction; on the other hand, a highly distrustful client too fragile for individual therapy might find a group with a strong leader and a focus on education about sexual abuse a more tolerable first step.

It is our observation that much group therapy tends to be more dogmatic than our model, in that particular goals and ways of achieving the goals are assumed best for those who have been sexually abused. The model presented here is more individually tailored and nondogmatic.

Although the intensity of support and group structure can be powerful in making certain kinds of therapeutic gains, they can also freeze the client into a relatively low level of functioning in which the role of victim is perpetuated. Clients may not learn to become independent centers of initiative but may remain on some levels passive and dependent on group approval. It is also our observation that only the most skilled group leaders are unable to prevent a group, particularly a long-term group, from functioning at the least common denominator of group members' functioning and affective levels. In other words, those clients who are most damaged and un- able to get beyond chronic feelings of anger, self-attack, disappointment, and rage are often unwilling to let others move on to other levels.

Given the historical self-help emphasis of many sexual abuse treatment programs, this may not be a popular perspective. We believe, nevertheless, it is a sound one. We view it as unwise for professionally trained therapists to abdicate their responsibility to assess accurately and thoroughly and to develop individualized treatment plans for their clients because of the pressures of self-help movements. If a therapist has nothing more to offer a client than a duplicate of what a self-help movement can offer, such a therapist should direct their clients to self-help groups, where they can get comparable services for free.

Some high-functioning individuals can partake of self-help approaches; obtain the support, education, and feedback that such approaches are best at offering; and proceed, without therapy or continued dependence on the self-help organization, to make effective changes. We are objecting, rather, to "therapy" that gives little more than the offerings of self-help movements or that suggests that clients who have been sexually abused are intrinsically unable to lead their lives without therapy or self-help movements. The model proposed here can accommodate the limited and purposeful use of self-help groups, although not in a random or primary fashion. It can also accommodate individuals who need little more than what self-help groups offer and individuals who need no therapy.

Couples and family therapy can occur congruently with the individual therapy model described here, although clearly in an auxiliary manner in serving to corroborate information or focus on limited goals of change within the system. These types of therapy tend to diffuse the intensity of the therapeutic style described here.

We suggest that therapists be deliberate and judicious and plan well in utilizing therapeutic modalities. This model assumes that individual therapy is central, with group, couples, or family components as auxiliary and selected for congruence with the individual therapy goals and style. Other models suggest different choices. If treatment plans are carefully and individually rendered and congruent, then a variety of viable and helpful approaches can be used to treat male sexual abuse victims and, sometimes, even the same client.

THEORETICAL IMPLICATIONS OF THIS MODEL

Having outlined a clinical model that draws on self-psychology, we now suggest some areas of theoretical synthesis between certain aspects of self-psychology and current understandings of sexual abuse, especially the effects of sexual abuse. We think this is important for a number of reasons. The field of childhood sexual abuse risks becoming a clinical backwater by its lack of integration with more general theoretical structures available in mental health. An example illustrates this point.

There have been some attempts to create a specific sexual abuse trauma syndrome. These efforts have generally not been successful nor accepted broadly, partly due to their lack of specificity. Most of these attempts utilize overinclusive symptom lists with an additional requirement of a historical factor of sexual abuse; this, however, does not change the lack of specificity in the symptoms.

Other attempts have involved the application of posttraumatic stress disorder (PTSD) to childhood sexual abuse. The concept of PTSD may have some merit, as it could bring conceptualization about the effects of childhood sexual abuse closer to mainstream conceptualizations; however, it appears this particular syndrome may be a poor candidate in relation to sexual abuse.

Although PTSD has been applied to a number of situations such as spouse battering (Walker, 1989), it is a concept developed on Vietnam-era veterans; to a certain extent, it still bears the marks of its relationship to that specific group. If the conceptualization of PTSD is generalized to capture more fully the experience of other groups, it may be useful. At the current time, it seems somewhat off-track with the experience of sexual abuse victims.

Finkelhor (1990b) criticizes the use of the PTSD diagnosis on a number of counts: It does not fully capture the experience of sexual abuse victims, it has a misplaced emphasis on the affective realm, and it ignores cognitive effects. A PTSD diagnosis incorrectly suggests that sexual abuse victims who do not have PTSD are somehow less traumatized. There have been some attempts (Conte & Schuerman, 1988) to structure symptoms presented by victims using symptom check lists. Although these approaches can be helpful in summarizing what is known, they are essentially atheoretical and simply rearrange or cluster the data.

A core problem in these conceptualizations is that they are not sufficiently psychological in their approach. The sexual abuse experience is not only central to these concepts, it predominates. Sexual abuse happens to individuals who have histories of other experiences, personality characteristics, cognitive styles, and important historical events that may or may not resonate with the sexual abuse experience. Put another way, most conceptualizations pay insufficient attention to the fact that the experience of sexual abuse is filtered through individuals who have other characteristics unrelated to the abuse.

Finkelhor and Browne (1986) suggest a conceptual model for understanding abuse effects that effectively describes social environmental factors in abuse. Their model could be enriched by intrapsychic understandings of the abuse experience for victims, as much as the more intrapsychic ideas outlined here require understanding of social environmental factors to place the individual in context.

Wedding these two perspectives can provide a framework for understanding some anomalies in research on sexual abuse. For example, Finkelhor (1990b) discusses the fact that most studies on the impact of sexual abuse have found that varying percentages of victims are symptom free. These percentages generally run from 20% to 30% of abused children. Although some researchers have theorized that effects are delayed, there is no empirical support for this idea. Finkelhor concludes, "a final conjecture, and the one that seems the most plausible, is that the asymptomatic children are the ones who have suffered less serious abuse and have adequate psychological and social resources to cope with the stress of abuse" (p. 328).

Browne and Finkelhor (1986) note that asymptomatic children are abused for a shorter period of time, receive support from adults, come from well-functioning families, do not experience violence, and are not abused by a father figure. Such findings can serve as a bridge to developing theoretical explication and clinical integration of their meaning. We suggest that a developmental psychological perspective is necessary to round out a social environmental, abuse-centric perspective.

Theoreticians have not fully addressed the specific effects of sexual abuse. Sexually abused children have characteristics prior to the abuse, some of which may be conducive to symptomatology or psychological distress, and some of which may immunize against distress. A good theory about the effects of sexual abuse must differentiate specific effects of sexual abuse from factors prior to the abuse.

In addition to the theoretical need for such theory, there are pragmatic needs. In civil law, in which sexual abuse victims attempt to obtain financial compensation for damages received from the abuse situation, a crucial legal concept is that of proximate cause. Legal counsel for the victim must show to a reasonable degree of scientific certainty that not only do symptoms and areas of distress exist in the abused individual, but they were likely caused specifically by the abuse and not by other factors before, during, or after the abuse experience. A good theory, then, must be able to take into account preabuse historical factors, the specific nature of the abuse experience, and experiences after the abuse to create a model that can predict a range of different outcomes.

We offer in the remainder of this chapter some theoretical suggestions to that end, using the self-psychology perspective of Kohut. We outline relevant features of Kohut's theory, apply them to sexual abuse experiences, and test the theory on some current conundrums in the research on effects of sexual abuse. We offer this particular theory as an example of the more broad-ranging theoretical integration we believe needs to occur. Abuse-centric/sociological and intrapsychically oriented/psychological perspectives are both needed.

A Self-Psychology Perspective

Simply put, a narcissistic injury is a profound blow to one's self-esteem. For the majority of sexually abused children, sexual abuse is an experience in narcissistic injury. Sexual abuse is a wounding both by commission and omission. The abusive acts are damaging in a variety of ways (Finkelhor, 1990b; Tharinger, 1990); the failure of a perpetrating adult figure to respond in the best interests of the child and the typically confused or inadequate response from other adults to the abuse are damaging by what does not occur. The result of this neglect and devaluation is a loss, in many cases drastic, of self-esteem, initiative, and legitimate entitlement. The self is prone to fragmentation, enfeeblement, and disharmony.

Provided the child arrives at the point of sexual abuse not otherwise psychologically crippled or severely traumatized (e.g., from prolonged involvement with pathological parents or other toxic childhood experiences), the narcissistic injury (if it is brief) can be a temporary, albeit nontrivial, wound—a developmental challenge to be mastered. Because this wounding occurs relatively late in childhood compared to other critical developmental events, its effects are likely to be less damaging. As sexual abuse continues over time, has violent or other damaging features, or is associated with other varieties of abuse or neglect, its ability to damage increases.

The child who has been chronically narcissistically injured through-out childhood by events prior to and separate from those described here, however, reaches the abuse experience in a different and highly vulnerable state. To these victims, the narcissistic injuries of sexual abuse are met not as a developmental challenge to be surmounted but rather as another danger that threatens to shatter an already tenuous psychological constitution. These fragile children and youth make up a majority of the most severely disturbed casualties of sexual abuse, those for whom a resilient response is beyond their personal resources, and for whom the narcissistic injury of sexual abuse is a *coup de grace* leaving them emotionally debilitated. We theorize that these individuals make up most of those whose postabuse histories are characterized by the worst symptomatology.

Kohut (1971, 1977, 1984) writes extensively on narcissistic injury and develops an analytical psychotherapy for the healing of narcis-sistic injuries, or self-deficits. Although he writes generically of the narcissistic injuries in children as a function of unresponsive, unem-pathetic, and unavailable parents, his theoretical model can be applied, if not exactly then heuristically, to the narcissistic injuries of sexually abused children and youth.

This discussion simplifies Kohut's theory of self-psychology, and the theory's application to the narcissistic injuries of sexual abuse is inexact. We apply Kohut's concepts to a later developmental period than that on which he developed his theory. Nonetheless, we believe these ideas can help create a better understanding of the complex effects of sexual abuse on a full range of children and youth.

Self-Psychology Applied to Sexual Abuse

From a self-psychology perspective, sexual abuse is seen as a narcissistic injury that can create distortions ranging from mild to severe in the sense of self. The degree of narcissistic injury is likely to be a function of both characteristics of the abuse and character-istics of the abused child. The length of time the abuse took place, the degree of violence, the sadism of the abuse, and the amount of violation of trust and personal boundaries are all likely to be impor-tant factors that will predict a range of severity, from mild to devastat-ing, of the specific effects of the abuse experience.

There is also a range of postabuse effects. These are related to the response of family and other adults to the abuse experience, psychotherapy to remediate the abuse experience, and positive or adverse experiences with the child welfare system and the courts. These also range over a broad continuum. The cumulative effect of the postabuse experiences may eventually be sufficient to reverse the negative effects of the abuse, if the abuse is mild enough and the postabuse experience is positive enough. Whether or not this desirable state of affairs is common, it is possible.

Our model can take into account a third factor, the preabuse history. As a number of research studies have shown, children who are abused are not a random group. Rather, children who come from dysfunctional families and who have experienced other and earlier narcissistic injuries are overrepresented in the group of children who become sexually abused. We are not suggesting that all sexually abused children have had previously narcissistic injury. We are suggesting some sexual abuse perpetrators, usually the more planning, chronic and cunning ones, ascertain the vulnerability of their intended victims and choose accordingly.

Such individuals have relatively well-developed abilities to determine which children are likely to be vulnerable based on the degree to which they have been narcissistically injured. Other groups of offenders who may be more situational, less planful, and more clumsy may select previously narcissistically injured children less effectively or may select intended victims in a random manner with no attempt to pick the more vulnerable victims.

Therefore, depending on perpetrator characteristics, a range of intended victims is chosen, from most damaged to nondamaged. The net effect of the choices of the different perpetrator types, however, is that children who are narcissistically injured are overrepresented among children who are sexually abused.

Further, this theory predicts that preabuse history is an important, but not sole, predictor of the effects of the abuse. In other words, given a predictable level of abuse, preabuse history produces a range of effects from mild to severe. This can occasionally be seen in situations of a repetitive, fixated sexual perpetrator with multiple victims in which the perpetrator performs essentially the same acts in the same manner with a variety of victims. Because the specifics of the abuse in this situation are more or less constant, preabuse history is the most precise predictor of the ultimate outcome and gives the widest range of outcome predictions.

When sexual abuse cases are summed together, however, it is difficult to pick out the preabuse, postabuse, or abuse factors as a group because of their high variability within each category. It is for this reason that much of the research literature is so hard to interpret. Other than situations of repetitive, fixated offenders with multiple victims (providing consistency in the abuse effects) or a sexual abuse advocacy system in a particular locale that provides a comprehensive set of services in a predictable fashion to abuse victims (providing consistency in the postabuse effects), preabuse, postabuse, and abuse history vary widely in most situations. This results in masking differential effects.

Application of This Perspective to Some Conundrums

This theory can also be helpful in explaining certain anomalies in the literature. For example, Finkelhor (1984) and Johnson and Shrier (1985) found that sexually abused males engage in more homosexual behavior than nonsexually abused males. This effect is considerable. In the Finkelhor study, there is a four times greater likelihood of homosexual activity; in the Johnson and Shrier study, males who were sexually abused identified themselves as homosexual seven times more often and bisexual six times more often than the non–sexually abused control group. This has led some researchers to speculate about the validity of the stereotype that sexual abuse causes homosexuality.

However, an understanding of the literature on homosexuality contradicts this. Although the causes of different sexual orientations remain unclear, it is clear that whatever its causes, sexual orientation appears to be set in place by early childhood, definitely before latency. Most sexual abuse occurs in latency or after. This suggests that sexual abuse is not causative of homosexuality; rather, that sexual orientation is likely to have been in place prior to most instances of abuse.

But a conundrum remains. What then can explain these findings? This conceptualization of narcissistic injury has been applied to the coming-out and identity development experiences of gay men and lesbians (Gonsiorek & Rudolph, 1991). Using a similar framework to the one presented here, Gonsiorek and Rudolph suggest that the disparagement of homosexuality extant in the culture and its internalization in children who eventually become gay, bisexual, or lesbian produces a kind of narcissistic injury, occurring later than most and therefore generally less severe, but that poses certain developmental challenges that are played out during the coming-out process of gay men and lesbians.

Returning to the data of Finkelhor (1984) and Johnson and Shrier (1985), the following explanatory mechanism can be derived. A class of sexual abuse perpetrators more or less carefully selects children who are most vulnerable. In the rubric described here, that is likely to mean children with the greatest degree of narcissistic injury. It is already clear from the literature that children from dysfunctional families, with alcoholic parents, and the like are overrepresented among children who become sexually abused; that is, they are selected by certain sexual abuse perpetrators. We suggest that if the disparagement of same-sex feelings in the culture produces a kind of narcissistic injury for youth who become gay, lesbian, or bisexual, then certain sexual abuse perpetrators can read this as a vulnerability and select pregay youth as victims. In other words, perpetrators who operate in this manner consistently select for vulnerability no matter what its cause, whether toxic families or the damaging effects of societal bigotry.

Earlier chapters of this book speak of the need for information on child sexual abuse to work effectively across the ranges of diversity. As Wyatt (1990) notes, "Although initial reactions to sexual abuse may not reveal ethnic differences especially when black-white comparisons are made, there may be some aspects of ethnic minority children's lives that affect long term adjustment to these traumatic experiences and prevalence rates as well" (p. 338).

Wyatt (1990) describes how racism has particular effects on black children. She recounts the stereotypes of many researchers that black children are more sexual, and notes that black children experience the effects of racial discrimination as much as their parents in their social environments and schools. Furthermore, racial and ethnic minority children observe the disempowerment of their parents and as a result have the normative idealization of parents disappointed. Although Wyatt does not conceptualize her descriptions in a self-psychology framework, much of her discussion can be reconceptualized in this manner. Namely, racial and ethnic minority children endure narcissistic injuries in childhood and later as they begin to perceive and experience the effects of racism and ensuing economic oppression.

This conceptualization is akin to the one by Gonsiorek and Rudolph (1991) on gay and lesbian youth as it posits narcissistic injuries that occur later in the developmental sequence. The effect may be to increase the vulnerability of those racial and ethnic minority children to those sexual perpetrators who seek signs of such vulnerability in their victims. More importantly, this conceptualization can serve as a vehicle to understand interactions between the effects of external societal bigotry, preexisting personality variables, and sexual abuse.

This model can also serve as a guide to treatment. Once a careful assessment is made of the injuries endured at the three levels (preabuse, postabuse, and during abuse), then a treatment plan can be made accordingly. For example, treatment of an adolescent sexual abuse victim who has suffered significant narcissistic damage prior to the sexual abuse is likely to be more long term than an adolescent victim whose preabuse experiences were benign.

The effects of these three levels of narcissistic injury are not simply additive. For example, one would theoretically expect that the experience of narcissistic injury and toxic parenting prior to sexual abuse experiences might produce a general deficit in coping skills and sense of self. An adolescent with such a history would have not only quantitatively more damage but also an impairment of coping abilities that makes specific effects of sexual abuse more overwhelming than they might otherwise be. Further, a damaging family might be more likely to respond poorly in the postabuse period and be less able and thoughtful about mobilizing appropriate resources for the victim. In reality, the effects are more complex than an additive model can accommodate.

Similarly, an adolescent coming from a high functioning family who experiences abuse from a randomly selecting impulsive perpetrator might have a positive outcome, particularly if this high functioning family is adept at mobilizing quality resources in the post-abuse period.

To return to the legal considerations noted earlier, although the legal system would like to make relatively simple distinctions between the damage caused before and during the abuse, these effects are not so simple. However, the model based on self-psychology outlined here does allow a framework for beginning to differentiate damages from causes. It might also serve as a vehicle to educate the courts that simple either/or determination of percentages of damages is not always psychologically meaningful or sensible.

SUMMARY

The model presented in this chapter is client driven, not theory or politically driven. The model is informed by theory specific to sexual abuse but is not driven by it. This model can accommodate variation along gender, racial, ethnic, sexual orientation, class and other lines. To utilize this model effectively, careful assessment and history taking are crucial. The treatment recommendations that derive from this model have a high probability of being individually tailored. This model taps into a in-more depth psychological approach that can function as a complement to more abuse-centric, sociological perspectives.

We appreciate that our suggestion of preabuse history as an equal partner in understanding abuse effects runs counter to current theory and practice in the field. We anticipate that this perspective will be misconstrued by some as "blaming the victim." We reject this criticism.

Our view is that abuse-centric perspectives that posit that sexual abuse is reliably a more powerful event in the lives of victims than any, or even all, other events in the individual's life are thoroughly implausible. There is no evidence to warrant subsuming all other events in an individual's developmental history to these relatively late-occurring events. In fact, there is no known developmental, psychological, or behavioral event as powerfully predictive of later functioning and psychological structure as sexual abuse is alleged to be by some abuse-centric theoreticians and practitioners. Further, such an atomized, fragmented view of sexual abuse victims is not conducive to a therapeutic process of rendering the person whole again.

Such abuse-centric perspectives, because of their psychological barrenness, produce little direction for clinical treatment.

The horror of sexual abuse is precisely that it "gets under the skin" psychologically and can elicit powerful interactions with preexisting issues in the victim. Clinical theory and practice have the obligation to grapple with these complex issues.

PART II

Family Systems Therapy for Adolescent Male Sex Offenders

WALTER H. BERA

5

Clinical Review of
Adolescent Male Sex Offenders

THIS CHAPTER BRIEFLY REVIEWS the common clinical issues observed in adolescent sex offenders, focusing on the prevalence of family issues reported in the literature. Adolescent sex offenders are defined and demonstrated to account for a significant percentage of sex crimes. Family issues are theorized by many clinicians as a major factor in adolescent sex offender development. A general model of the adolescent sex offender etiology is presented in an attempt to organize the clinical literature in a logical manner. The chapter ends with the explication of a descriptive adolescent offender typology that connects the individual, victim, and family factors reviewed.

This chapter should be read in the context of the historical and background information on sexual abuse and critique of certain models provided in chapter 2. Chapter 3, on adolescent sexual abuse victims, is also useful with regard to a number of clinical issues shared by both populations.

Definitions of Juvenile Sex Offenders

Sexual abuse can include all forms of forced, tricked, or manipulated sexual contact. Such behaviors include sexual intercourse, cunnilingus, fellatio, anal intercourse, and digital or other intrusions into the victim's orifices. They can also include the intentional touching of a victim's private parts by the offender. There are also "nontouch" forms of sexual abuse such as obscene phone calls, messages or drawings, sexual exposure, voyeurism, and fetish-associated burglary, such as stealing female underwear.

A juvenile sex offender can be defined as a youth from puberty to the age of majority who has committed one or more of the above-mentioned acts (Ryan, 1986). The clinical literature on this population uses the terms *juvenile*, *teenage*, and *adolescent* interchangeably. Recently, preteen sexual perpetrators have been identified and are sometimes included in references to "juvenile sex offenders." These younger offenders are not, however, the focus of this chapter or book.

Groth and Loredo (1981) suggest criteria for defining the juvenile sex offender. They include the age relationship and social relationship between the persons involved, the type of sexual activity, and the types of coercion used in the offense.

Case Example

Larry is a 13-year-old who had been reported for "playing doctor" with a 5-year-old neighbor girl he had been baby-sitting. On investigation, it was discovered that the doctor game involved fondling and oral sex. It was ascertained from interviews with the girl that the events had begun 5 months previously, when Larry began baby-sitting. She reported that the abuse occurred on almost every one of Larry's biweekly baby-sitting visits. Larry told the girl not to tell anyone, because these were "secret examinations" and they would both get in trouble. He always rewarded her for being a good "patient" by playing whatever other games she wanted and giving her a lollipop—just like the real doctor.

Juvenile sexual abuse is legally defined by the statutes of the state in which the abuse occurs. These codes typically define a juvenile offender as someone who is below the age of majority, usually age 18, who has committed a sexual offense. The sexual offense statutes are variously titled: criminal sexual conduct (e.g., rape, child molestation), intrafamilial sexual abuse (e.g., incest), lewd and lascivious communication (e.g., obscene phone calls).

A contact-type sexual offense is often defined by criteria such as a power differential between offender and victim (e.g., age difference, greater physical size or mental capacity, position of authority), sexual contact between family members, or use of force, intimidation, or trickery to manipulate a victim to perform a sexual act to which he or she would not otherwise consent. Noncontact sex crimes are legally defined under a variety of statutes, some of which may not be "sex" related (e.g., fetish burglary may be tried as a burglary charge, or window peeping as a trespassing charge).

Increased Awareness of Adolescent Sex Offenders

Increased reporting of sexual abuse has led to a significant increase in the number of sex offenders arrested and adjudicated. The U.S. Department of Justice (1993) reports a number of important statistics. In 1992, 97,761 rapes were reported in the United States, with 51.5% cleared by arrests. There were 83,997 other sex crimes, such as child molestation, reported. From 1988 to 1992, the number of rape arrests increased 4.9%, and arrests for other sex crimes increased 9.5%. Of the 1991 U.S. prison population, 3.5% were incarcerated for rape and 5.9% were incarcerated for other sex crimes.

The percentage of people imprisoned for sex crimes is high in certain states. For example, the Minnesota Department of Corrections (1993) shows that sex offenses make up the leading index crime, accounting for 21% of the prison population. The U.S. Department of Justice (1993) shows that sex offenders are among the highest recidivists of all criminal types.

Simple imprisonment has not been an effective deterrent, with recidivism rates for sexual offenders averaging 19.5% and ranging from 6% to 35% in one survey of 11 studies (Finkelhor, 1986). As a result, prison-based programs have been developed across the country to treat sex offenders and are showing some success (Knopp, 1984). Prentky (1989) makes a case for treatment as an ultimate cost reduction by estimating the expense of investigating one offense and treating one victim at about $80,000. Nevertheless, the cost of incarceration and treatment for such a large population of inmates is substantial, and new approaches for early intervention are clearly indicated.

This awareness of the need for early intervention has led concerned clinicians and researchers to focus attention on the juvenile sex offender. Previously, juvenile sexual misconduct was minimized or ignored by supervising adults as naive experimentation or clumsy exploration. As a result, sexual offenses committed by juveniles were severely underreported (Knopp, 1985).

That has been changing. U.S. Department of Justice (1993) juvenile arrest statistics show a 17% increase in U.S. forcible rape arrests and a 28% increase in other sex offense arrests (e.g., child molestation) from 1988 to 1992. In 1992, 5,369 forcible rape arrests and 16,632 other sex arrests were reported for juveniles. Juveniles make up 16% of all arrested rapists and 19% of those arrested for other sex crimes.

Child sexual abuse reports demonstrate that more than 50% of the molestation of boys and 15% to 20% or more of the sexual abuse of girls is perpetrated by adolescents (Rogers & Terry, 1984; Showers, Farber, Joseph, Oshins, & Johnson, 1983). Based on surveys of victims, 20% to 30% of all rapes and 30% to 56% of all cases of child molestation can be attributed to adolescent sex offenders (Brown, Hill, & Panesis, 1984; Deisher et al., 1982; Fehrenbach et al., 1986).

The importance of intervening with the juvenile sex offender is demonstrated in a study by Abel, Rouleau, and Cunningham-Rathner (1986) in which adult sex offenders reported an average of 380 sexual crimes. On average, adolescents currently being evaluated report substantially fewer victims. Several studies (Abel et al., 1986; Gebhard, Gagnon, Pomeroy, & Christenson, 1965; Smith, 1984) report that approximately 50% of all adult sex offenders admit that their first sexual offense occurred during adolescence.

Knopp (1985) suggests the following advantages of early interventions with juveniles:

1. Deviant patterns are less deeply ingrained and are therefore easier to disrupt.
2. Youth are still experimenting with a variety of patterns of sexual satisfaction that offer alternatives to consistent deviant patterns.
3. Distorted thinking patterns are less deeply entrenched and can be redirected.
4. Youth are good candidates for learning new and acceptable social skills.

5. Public safety is improved by preventing further victimization.
6. Fiscal economy is enhanced.

As a result of the increased awareness of adolescent sexual offenses, there are now more than 700 specialized juvenile sex offender treatment programs in the U.S.; approximately 20 were identified in 1982 (Knopp, 1985; Knopp, Freeman-Longo, & Stevenson, 1992).

Adolescent Developmental Issues

The clinical understanding of juvenile offenders can be complicated by the fact that normal adolescence is often a stressful time in the development of sexuality (Leaman, 1980). Puberty usually begins around age 11 in boys and girls, and major physiological changes are usually completed by the late teens. Production of sperm begins. Boys often experience "wet dreams," which may be psychologically disturbing. During these years, body configuration changes and an increase in hormone production arouses strong sexual feelings in adolescents. Sexually oriented dreams and fantasies may be frequent and intrusive. Masturbation may be an activity that the adolescent views as shameful.

Adolescents often begin to assume rigid gender roles—roles that are strongly influenced by their peers and society (Berger, 1974). Opposite-sex friendships, dating, romantic attachments, and sexual experimentation become increasingly important. Normal adolescent conflicts over independence and separation from the family may also be expressed in a sexual mode. Teenagers may use sexual relationships to put distance between themselves and their families.

There is evidence with regard to sexual abuse, adolescent pregnancy, abortion, and sexually transmitted diseases to indicate that teenagers frequently become involved in sexual activity without adequate information about birth control, sexual relations, and other sex-related concerns. Parents report that they provide little or no information on sexuality and sexual abuse—often because they did not receive such information themselves as adolescents. This reflects society's general erotophobia or discomfort with sexual issues, especially regarding teenagers. When teenagers are successful in achieving developmental milestones, they are able to enter young adulthood with a secure self-image and feelings of self-worth. A failure of healthy adolescent maturation is the development of sexually victimizing behavior (Strong & DeVault, 1992).

HISTORICAL OVERVIEW OF THE ADOLESCENT SEX OFFENDER

The majority of studies and publications concerning sex offenders pertain to adults. Adolescent sex offenders have received less empirical study; however, a growing body of literature does exist and is worthy of review for the practitioner or researcher who is serious about becoming acquainted with this arena of sexual deviancy. Due to limitations of space, a lengthy review is not attempted here. Instead, a brief historical review is designed as an introduction to this literature base. The reader is encouraged to pursue further exploration using the sources cited here as well as the bibliographies of these sources.

In the earliest references to adolescent sexual deviance, criminally victimizing behaviors are not distinguished from "sexual misbehavior," which includes status offenses or socially unacceptable behavior. These early studies reflect the cultural erotophobia and homophobia discussed in chapter 2. For example, in 1943, Doshay studied 256 juvenile sex offenders treated in New York Court Clinic and found little recidivism as adults. However, many of the referral problems of his sample were behaviors that adults at that time believed were problematic for youth (such as a peer-age consenting sexual contact) but would not be termed *offenses* or *abusive* today. Markey (1950) examined 25 boys and 25 girls referred to a juvenile court for "immorality." The age range was 13 to 17, with an average age of 15.2. From extensive testing and interviews, he concludes that sexual symptoms are not in themselves evidence of morbid sexual development but represent poor personality integration. He describes family trauma as the primary source of sexual maladjustment. Maclay (1960) describes 29 boys who committed sexual misdemeanors. He concludes that boys who indulge in sexual delinquencies come from homes that fail to give them adequate emotional support.

Research began to gain greater specificity in the late 1960s and 1970s. Shoor, Speed, and Bartelt (1966) describe 80 adolescent child molesters. They conclude that such offenders are loners, have minimal social peer group activities with boys or girls, and prefer playing with younger children; their main work experience is baby-sitting younger children. They typically have little sex education, are socially and sexually immature, and have distorted family relations and personality patterns.

In one of the first studies to report on behavior clearly defined as illegal and abusive, Groth and Loredo (1981) studied 26 male offenders between the ages of 15 and 17. Fourteen of these boys were convicted of rape and 12 of child assault. A modal description of the convicted adolescent offenders in this study is a 16-year-old boy of average intelligence. He usually carried out his assault alone, and the victim was usually a female a year younger than he. Weapons were used in about one third of the offenses. Drugs and alcohol played a minor role. About three fourths of the offenders had committed a previous offense. The average educational level was 8th to 9th grade.

The 1980s saw a huge increase in the number of programs for adolescent sex offenders. The decade began with a handful of known adolescent sex offender treatment programs, a number that grew to more than 700 in 1992 (Knopp et al., 1992). The quantity and quality of the clinical literature increased as well. Davis and Leitenberg's (1987) review of this literature highlights some consistent findings:

1. Adolescents account for a large share of the sex offenses committed in the United States, with the most conservative estimates being about 20% of all cases.
2. Nearly two thirds of victims are younger children, with the vast majority being acquaintances or relatives of the offender.
3. In general, victims are more frequently female than male, with the proportion of female victims lower in cases of child sexual abuse and greater in cases of noncontact offenses such as exhibitionism.
4. More than 95% of reported adolescent offenders are male. (Note that the in-depth study of female sex offenders only began at the end of the 1980s—Mathews et al., 1989.)
5. Adolescent sex offenders more frequently present a history of being physically abused and probably sexually abused when compared with other groups of adolescents,.
6. Adolescent sex offenders, compared to other delinquent youth, have similar current and past signs of behavioral and school disturbances.

7. Adolescent sex offenders claim to have had more sexual experiences, including consenting ones, than comparison groups of adolescents.

8. Preliminary relapse statistics and uncontrolled treatment outcome statistics are encouraging, with typical rates of less than 10%.

9. The research on adolescent sex offenders, behavior, and victims is still in an early stage. Studies involving matched comparison groups are lacking.

The Adolescent Victim/Offender

For some time, the "sex abuse victim turned sex offender" theory of sex offender etiology enjoyed widespread popularity, perhaps because of its simplistic, intuitive appeal. However, the rates of offenders with sexual victimization backgrounds are not high enough to justify this as the only etiology, and in cases when the offender is a former victim, it is probably not a complete explanation (Becker & Kaplan, 1988; O'Brien, 1989). Physical and emotional abuse are also common in the lives of young sexual perpetrators but have not been adequately reported. Such abuse may be a significant contributor to sexual abuse. Furthermore, there are no good studies on the percentage of victims who become offenders, though it is clear that most do not. Nevertheless, the study of the victim/offender adolescent is important for both its treatment and its prevention implications.

Reported rates of sexual victimization among adolescent sex offenders vary greatly. Brannon, Larson, and Doggett (1989) reviewed the incidence of sexual abuse among 63 incarcerated male juvenile offenders. The average age was 16.1 and only 11 were officially charged with a sexually related offense. Seventy percent reported sexual abuse; females accounted for 58% of the perpetrators and males for 42%. The reported abuse included fondling, intercourse, fellatio, and sodomy, with some of the abuse being brutal. Petrovich and Templer (1984) found that of 83 adult rapists studied, 59% were abused by a female prior to age 16.

Fehrenbach et al. (1986) found a 19% prior sexual victimization rate among the sex offenders they studied. The authors suggest this is an underestimate because it is the result of the intake interview, and admission of abuse increases as trust grows in therapy. Gomes-Schwartz, Horowitz, and Carderelli (1990) found a 38% victimization rate among sexual offenders, whereas Becker et al. (1986) found a 23% victimization rate. O'Brien (1989), in a study of 170 adolescent offenders, found a 37% rate, with approximately one third reporting victimization by a female.

Allen (1991) suggests that barriers to recognizing child sexual abuse by women are the result of the cultural norms and deep-seated beliefs held by professionals and society in general. These barriers include overestimating the strength of the incest taboo in women, overextending feminist explanations of child sexual abuse, and over-generalizing the lack of reports of child sexual abuse by women.

Gilbert (1989) reviewed the limited clinical literature on sexual abuse among siblings. Sister-brother incest is the most reported form of sibling sexual abuse and typically occurs in dysfunctional families in which parents are physically or emotionally unavailable. Many of these homes are highly sexualized (e.g., children witness adults engaging in sexual intercourse).

These statistics indicate that a significant percentage, and even the majority, of perpetrators were female, but only recently have researchers begun to study female perpetrator populations (Mathews, 1987; Mathews et al., 1989; McCarty, 1986).

In O'Brien's 1989 study, although 37% of adolescent offenders reported direct sexual victimization, the highest rates are among incest offenders (42%). Extrafamilial child molesters or those who molest children who are not in the family, as in a baby-sitting or playground situation (40%), report victimization as a child, as do non-child molesters, such as the acquaintance rapist, exposer, and window peepers (29%). O'Brien also found that adolescent incest offenders tend to come from families judged much more severely disturbed than other offender types as determined by a clinician's rating.

Significant Family Systems Issues

Many clinicians and researchers working with juvenile sexual offenders see dysfunctional family systems as significant in the etiology or maintenance of sexual misconduct. Chaotic family systems with role confusion are common. Father-son relationships in particular are strained or nonexistent.

When reviewing the literature on dysfunctional family dynamics associated with many juvenile perpetrators, the danger of backward causality and inappropriate overgeneralization from captive clinical, residential, or prison populations must be kept in mind—there is a need for research from general population samples and nondysfunctional family samples or controls. The following overview is presented as an aid for clinical mapping of juvenile offenders and their families.

Knopp (1982) surveyed nine model treatment programs for adolescent sex offenders. Based on therapist observations, dysfunctional or chaotic family systems often played a significant role in contributing to the offender's pathology, fathers were emotionally and physically distant, and father/son relationships were inadequate. Family resistance to acknowledging sexual victimization and exploitation, minimization of the significance of the child's offenses, and blaming the victim were common.

Awad, Saunders, and Lavene (1979) discovered significant family issues in the 24 male juvenile sexual offenders compared to 24 other delinquents matched for age and social class. Family instability, psychiatric disturbances, and unsatisfactory parent-child relationships were common characteristics in the sex offenders. Seventy-nine percent of the sexual offenders experienced long-term separations from at least one parent. Clinical ratings of the juveniles' relationships with their families reported that 36% of the mothers and 63% of the fathers were seen as rejecting, and 26% of the mothers and 50% of the fathers were seen as emotionally detached.

Burgess and Holmstrom (1975) and DeFrances (1969) report that at least 50% and possibly as many as 80% of all child victims are sexually abused by people known to them. Parents, stepparents, brothers, sisters, or other relatives are responsible for 30% to 50% of all sexual abuse cases reported. These researchers conclude that, because of a child's trusting relationship with the offender, the use of physical force is rarely necessary to engage a child in sexual activity. Such cooperation can be obtained through the offender's position of dominance, a bribe or reward, a threat of physical violence, or other pressure or persuasion.

DeFrances (1969) estimates that poor supervision by parents and failure to set proper controls for a child or adolescent's behavior is a contributing factor in over 70% of all cases of sexual abuse, whether perpetrated by adolescents or adults. One third of these families have a history of a prior sexual offense involving a family member. Eleven percent of the mothers stated they had been child victims themselves. DeFrances concludes that for an adolescent growing up in such families, the sexual abuse behavior in which he or she engages may be an attempt to fulfill needs that are normally met in other ways; for example, the abuse may be motivated by a need for love, affection, or attention that the adolescent cannot find in family relationships. Conversely, a need to defy a parental figure, express anger about a chaotic home life, or act out sexual conflicts may lead an adolescent to become sexually exploitative.

A parent's difficulties with past personal issues of sexual abuse is also associated with teen incest perpetrators. For example, in a study conducted by Kaplan, Becker, and Martinez (1990), mothers of adolescent incest perpetrators were compared with mothers of nonincest perpetrators. Significantly more of the incest group mothers reported a history of physical and sexual abuse, sexual dysfunction, and prior psychotherapy.

Prentky and Cerce (1989) studied 81 adult sex offenders in an attempt to determine the severity of both sexual and nonsexual aggression. They examined four areas of developmental pathology during childhood and adolescence: caregiver instability, institutional history, sexual abuse, and physical abuse. They found that the severity of sexual aggression is predicted by caregiver instability and sexual abuse; however, the severity of nonsexual aggression is predicted by institutional history and physical abuse. People who experience frequent changes in caregivers and grow up in sexually deviant or abusive contexts are more likely to become sexually aggressive. Conversely, those who spend long periods of time in institutions, frequently change institutions, and experience physical abuse and neglect in childhood are likely to become nonsexually aggressive.

To summarize, experts on juvenile sex offenders state:

The family and environment are essential influences in the development of sexuality and, therefore, family trauma, physical and sexual abuse, neglect, scapegoating, undefined family relations, and exposure to sexually traumatic material in the environment may contribute to the development of sexually offending behavior. (National Task Force on Juvenile Sexual Offending, 1993, p. 31)

A MODEL OF THE ETIOLOGY AND
MAINTENANCE OF ADOLESCENT SEX OFFENDERS

Becker and Kaplan (1988) note that, at the present time, there is no empirically validated model that explains the development of deviant adolescent sexual behavior.

This section presents a model of the etiology and maintenance of the adolescent sex offender (see Figure 5.1). This model, the etiology and maintenance of adolescent sex offenders (EMASO) model, shares elements of adolescent and adult sex offender models.

O'Brien (1986) develops the general schema for laying out social factors, individual factors, and the abuse cycle related to adolescent sex offenders that were adopted for the EMASO model. In his four factor model, Finkelhor (1986) suggests that the offender must overcome internal inhibitors and victim resistance for child abuse to occur. These notions are extended to victims of all ages. Ryan, Lane, Davis, and Isaac (1987) inspired the abuse cycle paradigm.

The EMASO model attempts to organize in a logical manner the many social, family, individual, and situational factors suggested in the literature. These factors contribute to adolescent sexual offender development and maintenance of the abuse behavior. As such, the EMASO model summarizes historical and current factors in abuse behavior.

The model is based on clinical and research data and designed to be a conceptual tool for organizing assessment and treatment issues. The clinical use of the EMASO model is presented in chapter 6. Caution is needed in applying the model because, like other models, it is not empirically validated.

The following sections define each element of the model.

Social Factors

Factors pertaining to society and its organization include gender stereotyping of male and female roles and relationships, values of

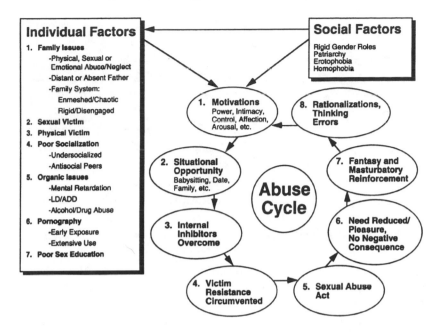

Figure 5.1. Etiology and Maintenance of Adolescent Sex Offenders
SOURCE: Adapted from O'Brien (1986).

patriarchy, homophobia, and erotophobia. Such social attitudes may set the social or cultural context in which sexual abuse behavior develops (Finkelhor, 1986). (See chapter 1 for discussion of these factors.)

These factors contribute to the development and maintenance of the individual factors and offender abuse cycle.

Individual Factors

Following is a list factors, some of which contribute to an individual's development of offender behavior and contribute to or help maintain the abuse cycle.

Family Issues

Family issues include physically, sexually, or emotionally abusive parenting, emotional abuse/neglect, and a distant or absent father (Steele, 1986). Smith (1984) reports that in his sample of juvenile sex offenders, 41% experienced intrafamilial violence or neglect during childhood, compared to only 15% of the non-sex-offender sample.

Family systems can appear as "enmeshed and chaotic" when poor emotional boundaries, chaotic role boundaries, or reversals exist among members. Such a family system tends to be in the backgrounds of people who commit incest and child molesters (Bera, 1985; Olson, Sprenkle, & Russell, 1979; Trepper & Sprenkle, 1988). Another pattern is the "rigidly disengaged" family system, where there are very rigid role boundaries between members and members are emotionally distant. This family system is more often associated with sexually aggressive, sexually compulsive, and disturbed impulsive behavior (Bera, 1985).

Other forms of family dysfunction seen with some adolescent sex offenders are homes where the adolescent has witnessed violence, such as husband/wife battery, or abuse among siblings of a physical or sexual nature (Longo, 1982). Such a history of witnessing violence is associated with violent behavior in the juvenile (Smith, 1988).

Lewis, Shankok, and Pincus (1979) studied extremely violent and less violent incarcerated boys. In addition to a higher reported history of physical abuse, 79% of the more violent children had witnessed extreme violence directed at others, usually in the home, compared with 20% of the less violent children.

Marshall, Hudson, and Hodkinson (1993) argue that such troubled familial history, particularly the failure of the parents to ensure secure attachment bonds between them and their children during infancy and childhood, creates developmental issues for those who will become sex offenders. Secure attachments provide children with an affectionate and empathic view of others that instills the skills, desire, and confidence to achieve intimacy with peers in adolescence. The failure to establish secure attachments results in problematic relationships that can lead to sexual misconduct.

Although further research is needed to confirm that aspects of the family environment differ for juvenile sex offenders as compared to other juvenile populations, the question remains how this contributes to a juvenile becoming sexually abusive. Davis and Leitenberg (1987) offer some possible explanations. For example, when a family tolerates physical abuse and neglect, the adolescent may learn this as acceptable behavior, may seek revenge on substitute targets, may offend to restore self-esteem, and may socialize with and then sexualize relationships with much younger children. Sex is then used as an expression of power, anger, and control.

Sexual Victim

Experiencing sexual victimization is reported in a significant percentage of adolescent sex offenders (Groth & Birnbaum, 1979; Ryan & Lane, 1991). As previously noted, it is not a complete explanation for perpetrator development.

Physical Victim

The experience of being physically abused may lead to physical aggression that, at times, is acted out in a sexual manner (Lane & Zamora, 1985).

Poor Socialization

Membership in a delinquent peer group may lead to becoming a sexually aggressive or a peer-group-influenced type sex offender. Fehrenbach et al. (1986) show that 65% of adolescent sex offenders evidence serious social isolation. Davis and Leitenberg (1987) reviewed the literature on juvenile sex offenders and found consistent reports that these perpetrators have little skills establishing and maintaining close friendships. Undersocialized adolescents may gravitate toward younger children, providing opportunities for child molestation or incest (Bera, 1985; Groth & Birnbaum, 1978).

Organic Issues

Attention deficit disorder, mental retardation, or alcohol/drug abuse contributes to sexual acting out when the individual overcomes the normal inhibitory mechanism or judgment for sexual impulses (Haaven, Little, & Petre-Miller, 1990; Lightfoot & Barbaree, 1993; Stermac & Sheridan, 1993). These issues have an organic or psychophysical impact on the adolescent.

Pornography

For a young adolescent who is sexually naive and lacks a clear and comprehensive knowledge of sexuality versus sexual abuse issues, exposure to pornography may lead to mimicking the behavior seen in the pictures. For others who have extensive exposure to pornography, it may act as a disinhibitor, rehearsal, or rationale to sexually aggress. (See Rosenberg, 1990, and Kutchinsky, 1991, for extensive inquiries on pornography and sexual aggression from varied perspectives.)

It has been clinically observed that when asked where he got the idea to commit the abusive act, a juvenile may mention having been exposed to explicit or pornographic material through magazines, cable TV, or videotapes. At other times he will say that peers had talked about sexual behaviors in very graphic and intriguing ways.

Poor Sex Education

Some adolescents may be vulnerable to abusive "experiments" with sexual behavior due to a combination of inadequate sex education, nonawareness of sexual abuse and its effects, cultural erotophobia, and the onset of hormonal changes in adolescence that increase normal sexual drives (Becker & Kaplan, 1988; Goldman & Goldman, 1982).

The Abuse Cycle

The social factors and individual factors reviewed above can begin a cycle of events that leads to the initiation and repetition of sexually abusive behavior (Lane, 1991). The cycle of behavior often occurs in the following stages.

Motivations

As a result of learned social attitudes and the predisposing factors in an individual's history, a number of motivations may develop such as the need for intimacy, affection, power, control, affiliation, or arousal. The adolescent may attempt to fill this void through victimizing sexual behavior (Lane & Zamora, 1985; O'Brien, 1983).

Situational Opportunity

An opportunity can arise where an adolescent has access to a vulnerable and available potential sexual victim. In these situations, the objectification of the victim is supported by the individual's social attitudes and individual history. A baby-sitting situation can be the site for the first incident of child molestation. A dating situation can be the site for acquaintance rape. After repeated success at perpetration, the offender may plan to put himself or herself in situations where abuse opportunities exist (Ryan et al., 1987).

Internal Inhibitors Overcome

The offender must overcome or rationalize internal deterrents to begin to offend sexually. Various "thinking errors," minimizations, or excuses can act as disinhibitors (Finkelhor, 1986; Yochelson & Samenow, 1977). Failure to predict or to hold oneself accountable for a negative impact on the victim results in a lack of empathy.

Victim Resistance Circumvented

The offender can "groom" the victim by winning a position of trust or authority in a child molestation or acquaintance rape (Finkelhor, 1986). In window peeping, the victim may not know the abuse is occurring. Shock, surprise, or threat overcome the victim in exhibitionism and stranger rape. Coercion may be covert to achieve compliance, or may be excessive and violent.

Sexual Abuse Act

A sexual perpetration occurs with a child, peer, or adult.

Need Reduction/Physiological Pleasure and No Negative Consequence

As a result of the sexual misconduct, the adolescent can experience a feeling of psychological need reduction and physiological pleasure. If there are no negative consequences such as an abuse report, arrest,

or confrontation, the experience may become the basis for continued rehearsal and fantasy of abusive scenarios (Becker, Kaplan, &
Temke, 1992).

Fantasy and Masturbatory Reinforcement

Aspects of the abuse can be replayed through fantasy and reinforced through masturbation (Abel, Barlow, Blanchard, & Guild, 1977;
Becker et al., 1992).

Rationalizations/Thinking Errors

The offender will rationalize his behavior in a number of thinking
errors: "it was no big deal," "he or she asked for it," "they didn't resist
much and therefore must have liked it," "it won't happen again."
Such rationales are needed to allow continued fantasizing or to overcome internal inhibitions for future abuse (Yochelson & Samenow,
1977).

Without intervention, the offender can return to the beginning of
the cycle at "motivations"—motivations that could continue to be met
in abusive ways. If this abuse cycle is repeated enough, the offender
may develop a deviant arousal pattern that necessitates considerable
intervention to modify (Becker & Kaplan, 1988; Groth, 1979).

Case Example

Bill was a 15-year-old with learning disabilities and general social
immaturity. As a result, he often played at the park with younger children with whom he felt comfortable and authoritative. He developed
a club for his 9- and 10-year-old friends. Membership soon required
certain "secret rituals." One day Bill convinced a 10-year-old boy in the
club to allow Bill to fondle him. Bill found this to be extremely arousing. He replayed the fondling scenario in his mind while masturbating that evening and again at subsequent times. He considered the
touching "harmless." This increased the erotic power of the child
abuse scenario and led to planning additional abuse on that child, as
well as grooming future victims.

The adolescent can repeatedly replay the sexually abusive act and
reenforce it through masturbation. This process of cognitive rehears-

al paired with physiological arousal can strongly predispose the adolescent to seek another abuse opportunity. The sequence of motivations, situational opportunity, internal inhibitors overcome, victim resistance circumvented, sexual abuse act, need reduction/pleasure, no negative consequence experienced, pleasure experienced or need reduced, fantasy and masturbatory reinforcement, and misattributions/thinking errors becomes a repetitive cycle that can repeat many times until intervention occurs.

TYPOLOGIES OF ADOLESCENT SEX OFFENDERS

Various typologies of adolescent offenders have been used over the years to help organize clinical and research studies. These typologies have arisen because the heterogeneity of offenders is evident and combining the whole pool of offender data can readily undermine the usefulness of the results (Finkelhor, 1986). Such typologies can help in developing a meaningful explanation of a particular offender type's dynamics as compared with other types, and in suggesting more specific and appropriate intervention strategies (Knight & Prentky, 1993).

Most typologies of adolescent offenders are general classifications with two or three categories. Atcheson & Williams (1954) conducted a 10-year longitudinal study of 2,516 male and 596 female juvenile delinquents. One-hundred-sixteen boys were convicted of sexual misbehavior and classified in the following three categories:

1. Specific sexual offenses (includes exhibitionism, indecent assault, immorality, rape, and indecent acts)
2. Nonspecific charges (includes vagrancy, incorrigibility, and sexual promiscuity)
3. Unrelated charges

Groth and Loredo (1981) differentiated 26 older adolescent males into those who raped ($n = 14$) and those who molested children ($n = 12$). The rapist was slightly older and had a higher incidence of interracial assaults, and the victims were more likely to be strangers. A weapon was more likely to be used and sexual intercourse was more likely involved. The child molesters had the highest percentage of victims who were friends and relatives. Eighty-six percent of child molesters had prior peer-age sexual experience, which discredited the idea of child molestation as naive sexual exploration.

Lewis, Shankok, and Pincus (1979) studied 17 violent boys (with an average age of 15) who had been convicted of sexual assault. Eight were convicted of rape or attempted rape of females, and two were convicted of assaulting women and younger males. Seven were convicted of other forms of sexual assault on females such as grabbing breasts and/or buttocks or beating women. The comparison sample was 61 boys who had been convicted of committing other serious violent acts such as murder, assault, armed robbery, and arson.

Of the 17 sexual assaulters, 10 had committed two or more sexual offenses. Victims ranged in age from 4 to 60. The study attempted to determine whether this violent subgroup of juvenile sexual assaulters differed psychiatrically or psychoeducationally from other violent juveniles. The author found that the violent juvenile sexual assaulters suffer from significant psychological problems more often than other violent juveniles, usually commit other types of violent acts, and have had serious behavioral disorders since early childhood. Sexual assaulters are characterized by violent childhoods, and their behavior throughout childhood and adolescence resembles that of violent nonsexually assaultive boys. Both the violent and the sexually assaultive groups function far below their expected reading grade, had been abused physically and/or sexually by their parents, and are likely to have witnessed extreme violence.

Deisher, Robinson, and Boyer (1982) studied 83 male adolescent sex offenders 12 to 17 years of age (mean age = 15). They used a classification system of three distinct types.

The first group included adolescents who sexually victimized young children (n = 31). Male teenage child molesters typically have a long history of underdeveloped peer relationships and social isolation. They are often scapegoated in their own families. A combination of poor social skills, isolation from peers, and conflicting family relationships contributes to low self-esteem and attraction to younger, more submissive children with whom they are more comfortable. The offenses against children usually take the form of forced mutual fondling of genitals or other sexual contacts of penetration.

The second group committed violent assaultive sexual behavior against a peer or adult (*n* = 23). The teenager referred for rape or indecent liberties with a peer or adult is more likely to use physical force or a weapon. Superficially, such forceful offenders may be involved in peer group activities, yet unable to identify one or more friends. Despite appearances, these teenagers are usually disturbed, as shown by their severely limited ability to empathize with the victim and their unwillingness to see their behavior as problematic. To protect the community, residential treatment must be considered for this group of offenders because they generally do not engage in outpatient treatment.

These teenagers are usually manipulative and attempt to avoid incarceration or therapy. Court-ordered therapy is crucial for outpatient treatment of the assaultive sexual offender because of the otherwise high attrition. Professionals are often fooled and manipulated by the smooth and articulate interpersonal style of the adolescent rapist. It is precisely this smooth, personable style that allows the youth to negotiate the sexual situation that results in an assault. The behavior toward the victim apparently has little to do with sexual needs but rather with violent aggression and reflects serious conflicts about anger and personal power.

A third category of sexual offenders included adolescents whose crimes did not involve physical contact with their victims; their crimes included stealing women's underwear, exposing themselves, and compulsively peering in windows. Although physical harm is not a factor, this activity is not in accord with normal adolescent sexual development. It can cause significant psychological distress and trauma to the victim. Teenagers in this category report feelings of inadequacy, are often unable to develop dating relationships, and have significant difficulties managing feelings of anger and frustration. These behaviors may precede more serious, hands-on offenses.

There has been a notable recent effort toward developing a typography of the sexual offense behavior and the inferred motivation of the offense behavior of sex offenders. Knight and Prentky (1990) have devised two separate typologies: one for child molesters and another for rapists.

These classifications are complex multiple-factor arrays or decision trees of dichotomous variables that represent important features of the offender groups. This is a research-oriented typology based on an incarcerated adult population at the Massachusetts Treatment Center in Bridgewater, Massachusetts. This typology was recently used to classify juvenile onset sex offenders (Knight & Prentky, 1993).

Knight and Prentky (1990) classify child sexual molesters on two separate axes. Axis 1 uses two independent dichotomist decisions that result in four types. The first classifies the offenders as either high or low in fixation on children, with highly fixated subjects as those whose thoughts and social interactions focus primarily on children. Offenders low in fixation do not show the same focus on children. The second decision judges social competencies high or low, depending on the offender's success in employment, adult relationships, and social responsibilities.

Child molesters are classified on Axis 2 according to the nature of their contact with children using a series of decisions that result in six separate types. The first decision classifies the offender according to the amount of contact he or she has with children with those who have high contact, further divided into whether the meaning of the contact for the offender is "interpersonal" or "narcissistic." Interpersonal contact with children means contact over a broad range of activities (not simply sexual interactions), and sexual interactions are not primarily directed toward orgasm. Narcissistic contact is directed primarily toward achieving sexual orgasm. Offenders who do not have significant contact with children are further subdivided into four subtypes: high or low degree of physical injury to victims, and those who do or do not have sadistic fantasies or behaviors.

The Knight and Prentky (1990) rapist taxonomy classifies subjects according to four primary motivations for raping: opportunistic, pervasively angry, sexually motivated, or vindictive. These types are well described by their title. The authors further subdivide the opportunistic, sexual nonsadistic, and vindictive rapists into two subgroups according to levels of social competence, as defined for their child molester typology in terms of success in employment, adult relationships, and social responsibilities.

This typology was applied to 564 adult male sex offenders who had been committed as sexually dangerous to the Massachusetts Treatment Center, a locked treatment facility. This group was divided between those who had been abusive as juveniles and those whose onset of abuse behavior was in adulthood. This division resulted in 61 rapists with juvenile onset and 55 child molesters with juvenile onset.

The result of the taxonomic analysis of group differences between adult and juvenile onset perpetrators was that only a subset of the types found in the adult onset samples was appropriate to the juvenile onset samples. Specifically, for both the rapist and the child molester typologies, the low social competence, high antisocial types appear to be most prevalent among juvenile onset sex offenders. Interrater reliability was .80 to .98. Abstracts of the subjects' files were used for classification purposes.

The study further corroborated the hypothesis that juvenile sexual offenders are heterogeneous and that the development of cohesive subtypes is possible. Although not yet applied to juvenile sex offenders in a clinical setting or for treatment planning, important and sound methodological procedures in chart review for developing research and clinical typologies have been demonstrated by Knight and Prentky (1993).

The PHASE Typology

As of 1993, more than 1,000 teenagers and their families had been assessed and/or treated in the Minnesota-based Program for Healthy Adolescent Sexual Expression (PHASE), which began in 1981. (Also known as the O'Brien-Bera PHASE typology, it is usually cited as the PHASE typology.) As a result of the large number of clients and the pressing need to diagnose and develop disposition or treatment plans, a rudimentary clinical typology of adolescent sex offenders and their family systems was developed.

A typology was originally proposed by O'Brien in 1983 and presented as a paper in 1984 (O'Brien, 1984). In 1984 and 1985, Bera elaborated and refined the typology. In developing such a typology from clinical experience, it was hoped that the typology would be heuristic and parsimonious—that is, it would help in decision making with different clients, developing a clearer explanation of overall offender dynamics, and suggesting the appropriate treatment strategy.

Bera (1985) investigated the validity and reliability of this typology of adolescent sex offenders, and began analyzing their corresponding family systems. The present version of the PHASE typology (O'Brien & Bera, 1986) has become a widely used adolescent sex offender typology. This typology of offenders and their family systems can help organize clinical impressions and is a classification system that can guide practitioners through ethical and therapeutic decision making. The typology is clinically based, however, and future empirical research is needed.

Type 1: The Naive Experimenter/Abuser

Case Example

> Johnny was a 13-year-old boy who had been asked to baby-sit a 5-year-old neighbor girl named Nicky. Johnny had been baby-sitting for only a short time and the situation was new to him. While there, he discovered a *Playboy* magazine hidden under the couch; Johnny found the explicit photographs arousing. While helping Nicky change into her pajamas, he wanted to see what it was like to kiss her and touch her in the way that had been depicted in the photographs. After a short time he felt guilty and stopped. Later that week, Nicky told her mother and Johnny was arrested for criminal sexual conduct.

Based on clinical experience, the naive experimenter/abuser is generally a younger male, age 11 to 14, who has little previous history of acting out. He usually has adequate social skills and peer relationships. He tends to be sexually naive and the abuse event appears to have been situationally determined (e.g., baby-sitting, family gathering, camping). Psychological testing and family history tend to be unremarkable. He typically engages in a single or a few isolated events of opportunistic sexual exploration with a victim who is usually a young child between the ages of 2 and 6. There is usually no recourse to any force or threats. His primary motivation for the abuse is to explore and experiment with his newly developing sexual feelings. The DSM-III-R psychological diagnosis is often an adjustment disorder.

Type 2: Undersocialized Child Molester

Case Example

Jerry, 15, had no close peer relationships and only a few school acquaintances. He could be considered a loner, and he spent a good portion of his time watching television or playing video games at home. He was well liked by his parents and was no trouble at home or at school. When playing outside he often was by himself or with considerably younger children. In the course of playing with the younger children, he became sexually involved with them and required fondling and oral-genital contact as a necessary part of being a member of a club he had formed. There were no threats or force used, but he did maintain secrecy with the children by telling them not to tell their parents. One of the children broke the secret to a teacher at school and Jerry was arrested for criminal sexual conduct.

The undersocialized child molester is clinically observed to suffer from chronic social isolation and has little peer acceptance. He gravitates toward younger children who admire or accept him, and is internally dominated by feelings of inadequacy and insecurity. Psychological testing often reflects social isolation, insecurity, and low self-esteem. He has little history of acting out socially and the family often has a distant or absent father figure. The sexual abuse behavior can reflect a chronic pattern of sexual behaviors with children that includes the use of manipulation, trickery, enticement, and rewards. The victim is usually a young and available child in either incest, baby-sitting, neighborhood play, or family situations. The molester's motivation for the abuse typically is an attempt to achieve intimacy or a sense of self-importance, self-esteem, self-identity, or autonomy. The DSM-III-R diagnosis of the offender is often conduct disorder-undersocialized aggressive, or paraphilia.

Type 3: Pseudosocialized Child Molester

Case Example

Norm was a 17-year-old boy, the youngest of six children. He was an exceptional achiever: an A student in school, a member of the theater department, and in the top bracket of students completing the SAT.

This religious and college-bound youth had engaged in kissing, oral-genital sex, and penis-vaginal rubbing with a niece 6 years younger. The abuse events occurred regularly over a 3-year period, and it appeared he had trained her into her victim role and coaxed her to remain silent. Vaginal redness led to questions by the girl's physician and the final disclosure. The entire family was shocked when Norm was arrested for criminal sexual conduct.

The clinical impression of the pseudosocialized child molester is of an older adolescent in the 16- to 18-year-old bracket. He has good social skills and is comfortable, but not intimate, in peer settings. There is little or no history of acting out socially, and he usually expresses confidence and security in most arenas. Psychologically he tests as "normal" on the Minnesota Multiphasic Personality Inventory (MMPI) and the Millon Adolescent Personality Inventory (MAPI). He is often a victim of some early childhood abuse such as physical, sexual, or emotional abuse or neglect. A "parentified child" family role is apparent. He is often intellectually gifted and a hard worker at home and in school.

The pseudosocialized child molester's abuse behavior reflects a more chronic pattern that can last years. The sexual abuse behavior is highly rationalized by the offender and little remorse or guilt is clearly demonstrated. The abuse events are characterized by the offender as mutual, intimate, and noncoercive. His motivation appears to be the narcissistic exploitation of a vulnerable child to meet his own sexual needs.

This type is often underdiagnosed during assessment because of his social skills and intellect. But this type has the greatest potential of achieving significant social status as a result of these intellectual gifts and coping mechanisms that can help place him in a position of trust and authority over children or adolescents: minister, school teacher, or youth leader. The DSM-III-R diagnosis can include pedophilia, conduct disorder, or personality disorder.

Type 4: Sexual Aggressive

Case Example

Troy, 15, was a victim of severe physical abuse at the hands of his stepfather, his mother's third husband. The mother often suffered from physical beatings from her husband as well. Troy had a history of fire-setting, theft, vandalism, and truancy. Very social and flamboyant, he took a 14-year-old girl out on a date and when she refused to "go all the way," Troy slapped her and forced her to perform oral sex on him, threatening to use a screwdriver if she didn't. Afterwards, she stumbled home and told her mother what happened, and Troy was arrested that evening by police for first-degree criminal sexual conduct.

Sexual aggressives are clinically observed as products of disorganized and abusive families. They have good peer-age social skills and are often charming and gregarious. Often having a long history of antisocial behaviors and poor impulse control problems, they typically fight with family members and friends and are likely to abuse chemicals. The sexual abuse usually involves the use of force, threats, or violence, and the victims can be peers, adults, or children.

Psychological testing often reveals an antisocial and character-disordered teenager. The offender's motivation for abuse is the use of sex to experience personal power or express anger when his desires have been frustrated. DSM-III-R diagnosis is often conduct disorder, socialized, aggressive.

Type 5: Sexual Compulsive

Case Example

David, 16, was an enthusiastic football player and good student at school. His mother was a traditional homemaker and his father was generally absent, working two shifts in a hospital. David committed a series of exposing incidents in front of high school girls near his school, and was identified and arrested by the police. In the course of therapy, it was discovered that he had exposed himself numerous times to his older sister, who kept it a secret and just yelled at him. The total abuse history spanned a 2-year period.

The family of the sexual compulsive is usually clinically observed as having rigid role boundaries and being emotionally disengaged. The parents are often emotionally repressed and have difficulty expressing intimacy. The offender has an inability to express negative emotions in a clear and straightforward manner. This type of offender typically engages in a repetitive, sexually arousing behavior of a compulsive nature. Such offenses often include nontouch behaviors like window peeping, obscene phone calls, exhibitionism, and fetish burglary (e.g., stealing women's underwear). A minority of this type are compulsive child molesters.

This behavior is generally seen as an autoerotic with no clearly apparent relationship to the victim. The offender is self-controlled, self-determined, and narcissistically absorbed. The offender appears to experience relief of anxiety or mood elevation by the behavior. DSM-III-R diagnosis can include one of the paraphilias, conduct disorder, or identity disorder.

Type 6: Disturbed Impulsive

Case Example

> Bill, 15, was living with his father, who had been awarded custody of him and his sister following an acrimonious divorce. Bill had grown up in a house where tension and anxiety were present as a result of the marital discord, and he generally learned to keep to himself. One day while retrieving the vacuum cleaner from his sister's closet, he turned to his sister, who was sitting in her underwear, and grabbed her, tore off her underwear, and attempted to mount her while she yelled "Stop! Stop!" Finally she pushed him off and he seemed to "come to his senses," grabbed the vacuum cleaner, and left to complete his chores. Because of the family tension, the sister kept the event quiet. A second incident occurred with a girlfriend of his sister, whom Bill suddenly accosted while ice skating with her, grabbing her breast and buttocks. This incident was reported to the police and Bill was questioned and left in the custody of his father. He was finally arrested after accosting an adult female in the laundry room of his mother's apartment building. Again, the assault was sudden and unpredictable. Bill was subsequently placed in a psychiatric hospital.

Disturbed impulsives may have a history of psychological problems, severe family problems, substance abuse problems, or significant learning problems. Thorough history and psychological testing are imperative. The sexual abuse is characterized as impulsive or reflecting a disturbance of reality. It can be a single, unpredictable, uncharacteristic act, or may be one among a pattern of sexual abuse acts. The offense may reflect a malfunction of normal inhibitory mechanisms due to organicity or thought disorder, or as a result of chemical abuse. The motivation is complex and individually determined. DSM-III-R diagnoses are varied.

Type 7: Group Influenced

Case Example

> Greg, 12, was a lonely boy whose only friend was Travis, 14. One evening they went to a neighbor's house after the parents had left. While there, Travis encouraged a group that included Greg and a 12-year-old boy and his 11-year-old sister to engage in a game of strip poker. During the game, when her brother went to the bathroom, the girl was accosted by Travis and Greg, who kissed and fondled her. The whole group told her not to tell, but the next morning she told her parents, and Travis and Greg were arrested for criminal sexual conduct.

The group-influenced offender is usually a younger teen who is not likely to have past contact with the juvenile justice system. The sexual abuse occurs within a peer group and the victim tends to be known by the offenders. The offender tends to defer responsibility for the sexual offense to the victim and/or other offenders in the group. The motivation for the sexual abuse can be the result of peer pressure or expectations—a "follower" dynamic; or an attempt to gain peer attention, approval, or leadership—a "leader" dynamic. DSM-III-R diagnosis is usually one of the conduct disorders.

Preliminary PHASE Typology Research Support and Application

The PHASE typology is generally supported in preliminary research (Bera, 1985). The PHASE typology is clinically supported by a high interrater agreement of 81%. The typology is also supported by statistically significant findings on empirical variables, which provide an empirical base for the PHASE typology; significant differences exist among the seven types.

In the Bera (1985) study, the 51 adolescent subjects were placed into the following offender types:

- Type 1: Naive experimenter/abuser (n = 8)—15.7%
- Type 2: Undersocialized child molester (n = 6)—11.8%
- Type 3: Pseudosocialized child molester (n = 5)—9.8%
- Type 4: Sexual aggressive (n = 6)—11.8%
- Type 5: Sexual compulsive (n = 5)—9.8%
- Type 6: Disturbed impulsive (n = 7)—13.7%
- Type 7: Group influenced (n = 9)—17.6%
- Not sure (n = 5)—9.8%

The undersocialized child molesters and the pseudosocialized child molesters tend to view their family as "high cohesion/high adaptability types" on Olson's circumplex model as measured by the FACES-II test, a measure of family systems (Olson et al., 1983). They generally view their families as emotionally very close, loyal, dependent on each other, connected, spending time with each other, making decisions based on family needs, focused, and sharing interests. Members of this group also generally see their family roles as fluid, changing, unclear, lenient, flexible in decision making, and inconsistent.

The majority of sexual aggressive, sexual compulsive, and disturbed impulsive types see their families in the low cohesion/low adaptability quadrant of Olson's circumplex model. They see their families as emotionally separated, independent, open to outside people and ideas, having fluid generational boundaries, valuing time alone, preferring separate space, having few family friends, making most decisions individually, and supporting individual activities.

The PHASE typology has been applied usefully in the prevention, triage, and research of adolescent sex offenders. The SHARP program is the first video-based adolescent perpetrator prevention education curriculum available for middle school and high school students (Minnesota Department of Human Services, 1986). The PHASE typology is the basis of the offender types portrayed and interventions recommended. It is now used in hundreds of school violence prevention programs.

The Oregon Department of Family Services (1986) used the PHASE typology as the basis of its matrix of treatment interventions for juvenile offenders, and the typology continues to be used as a clinical and research tool in PHASE.

Rasmussen, Burton, and Christopherson (1990) modified the PHASE typology for sexually aggressive children into six types: sexually curious, reenacting trauma, socially motivated, egocentric, behaviorally disordered, and group influenced.

Some Reservations About Offender Typologies

Offender typologies, like the PHASE typology, are an improvement over undifferentiated categorization of all sex offenders. Although the PHASE typology differentiates seven types, the differentiation should be understood as preliminary. Continued clinical experience, theory development, and research are needed to confirm the model, and more types and subtypes probably will develop. For example, Knight and Prentky (1990, 1993) suggest an adult offender typology of as many as 24 different types.

The PHASE typology was derived on a large outpatient population. It does not appropriately describe a residential population. For a residential population, the typology should be considered a starting point, in combination with Knight and Prentky's (1990, 1993) typology. Professionals should not be blinded from seeing offenders who do not fit the model or falsely label those who share a type's characteristics and are not offenders.

Meyers, Bays, Becker, Berliner, Corwin, and Saywitz (1989) caution about the dangerous temptation of having behavioral scientists appear as expert witnesses in child sexual abuse cases to testify that an individual fits a particular offender profile or type. No offender typology, including the PHASE typology, can be used to differentiate offenders from nonoffenders and should not be used to support guilt or innocence.

The PHASE typology is developmentally sensitive, recognizing age differences, motivations, contexts, and peer influences. Still, as with all typologies, it does not account well for individuals who may cross multiple categories.

Summary

   This chapter briefly reviews common clinical issues observed in adolescent sex offenders with a focus on the prevalence of family dysfunction reported in the literature. Family issues are demonstrated as significant factors in adolescent sex offender development and maintenance. A model of the adolescent sex offender, the EMASO model, is presented to organize the clinical literature logically, and the PHASE typology of adolescent offenders connects the individual and family factors reviewed. Chapter 6 builds on the EMASO model and PHASE typology as they apply in clinical intervention.

   Research on models of etiology and maintenance of juvenile offenders and offender typologies with the inclusion of involved family members could provide relevant context and meaning to the numbers generated. The models presented here are an attempt to create such a context and to be useful tools for clinicians and researchers working within the sexual abuse domain. These models also attempt to overcome the limits of the models critiqued in chapter 2.

   As sexual abuse research continues to broaden and deepen in scope, the EMASO model, the PHASE typology, and other models and typologies will change or be elaborated. Although such research on multiple, interacting individual, family, and social variables is complex, the task can be simplified by such theoretical models (Finkelhor, 1986; Gurman & Kniskern, 1981, 1992). The potential rewards of addressing the serious issues that juvenile sex offenders present is significant.

6

Treatment Approaches for Adolescent Male Sex Offenders

CHAPTER 5 REVIEWS the behavioral and cognitive-behavioral treatment techniques that currently dominate the adolescent sex offender treatment field;this chapter focuses on the adolescent offender's family as a primary resource for assessment and therapy. The PHASE typology's treatment implications are explicated. A model outpatient adolescent offender program structure is summarized, and a seven-stage model for family-based adolescent offender therapy is provided. Levels of family-based involvement are presented to help guide clinicians wishing to augment their current family therapy approaches.

OVERVIEW OF TREATMENT METHODS AND TECHNIQUES FOR JUVENILE SEX OFFENDERS

Knopp, Freeman-Longo, and Stevenson (1992) conducted a national survey of sex offender programs and received responses from 755 juvenile sex offender services. This section uses that survey as a base from which to structure a brief overview of the present major treatment methods and techniques used with adolescent sex offenders. Results of the survey are included for each method, and the percentages used in this chapter are from this survey.

Settings and Modalities

Juvenile sex offenders are treated primarily in community-based outpatient programs, which account for 75% of all services surveyed. Sixty percent of these outpatient services are private services and 40% are public services. Residential services account for 25% of all services, with 55% public and 45% private.

When asked "Do you use family treatment with offenders?" 92% of the community-based services and 86% of the residential-based services said "yes." No differences were found between low-level family information or education sessions rather than regularly scheduled family therapy.

Eighty-four percent of respondents identified peer group therapy as the preferred juvenile sex offender treatment method. This type of therapy utilizes the developmentally typical peer group social orientation of teenagers for therapeutic support and confrontation.

Cognitive-behavioral and behavioral methods were identified in some form in 65% of the services. The most important example of a cognitive-behavioral technique is a clear definition of the offender's "sexual abuse cycle" (Lane & Zamora, 1984). Elaborating on Lane and Zamora's original "rape cycle," Ryan et al. (1987) state:

> In order to prevent further sexual offending behaviors, the offender must understand the cognitive, behavioral, situational and psychological events which contributed to the offense. The cycle concept provides a framework in which the offenders can attach their individual feelings, thoughts, and behaviors, seeing themselves as unique individuals while identifying what they have in common with each other. After mastering their understanding of the cycle and seeing how it applies to them as individuals, the offenders then practice identifying the times in their past in which they responded similarly and situations in their present life which trigger the beginning of the cycle or signal that they are at the early stages of the cycle. They must identify the areas in their thinking which enabled them to progress through the cycle, and practice new ways to respond which will interrupt the cycle before the offending behaviors occur. (pp. 386-387)

Lane (1991), Lane and Zamora (1984), and Ryan et al. (1987) identify the following points from the beginning of the cycle to the sexual offense.

1. Negative self-image
2. Predicting rejection
3. Isolation
4. Fantasies
5. Planning the offense
6. The sexual offense
7. Return to negative self-image as a result

Various exercises are used to define the cycle in individual, group, and family therapy: paper-and-pencil exercises, use of a tape recorder, negative and positive consequences, and other cognitive behavioral techniques. Workbooks are available to help define these offense cycles and develop prevention strategies (Kahn, 1990).

Relapse Prevention

The offender can develop abuse prevention strategies by building a series of internal interventions or self-management skills to break this abuse cycle. A modified "relapse prevention" model, with an external supervisory component (Gray & Pithers, 1993; Pithers, Martin, & Cumming, 1989), is a systematic approach to teaching these strategies to the offender. Families, friends, probation officers, school officials, and employers are educated on how to assist the offender's process of avoiding relapse. Pithers, Martin, and Cumming (1989) explain:

The external, supervisory dimension serves three functions:

> 1. Enhancing efficacy of probation or parole supervision by the monitoring of specific offense precursors.
> 2. Increasing efficacy of supervision by creating an informed network of collateral contacts to assist the probation officer in monitoring the offender's behaviors.
> 3. Creating a collaborative relationship between the probation officer and mental health professionals conducting therapy with the offender. (p. 23)

The importance of aftercare issues, community safety, and community supervision is emphasized through the modified or expanded relapse prevention model (Freeman-Longo & Knopp, 1992). (For a detailed review of relapse prevention models, see Laws, 1989.)

Cognitive-Behavioral and Behavioral Approaches

Yochelson and Samenow (1977) developed a cognitive-behavioral approach now used in some form in most programs. The original model suggests that sex offenses may be one outcome of irrational thinking patterns and an antisocial way of looking at life. The approach generally consists of helping the offender define and then confront the "thinking errors" that lead to criminal behavior. Examples of common thinking errors of sex offenders are "she/he asked for it"; "my life's so bad, I deserved a little fun"; and "it's not that big a deal."

Among the most widely used techniques is a combined cognitive-behavioral exercise called "covert sensitization" that pairs thoughts of negative consequences with thoughts of offending.

A controversial behavioral technique is masturbatory satiation, which "attempts to reduce (deviant) arousal by boring the patient with his own deviant sexual fantasies" (Barnard, Fuller, Robins, & Shaw, 1989, p. 819). The offender masturbates to a healthy sexual fantasy then switches to a part of his abuse fantasy for a long period without ejaculation. This is often done while talking into a tape recorder. The goal of this procedure is to have the offender associate abusive fantasy with boredom and frustration. An example of a protocol for masturbatory satiation tapes can be found in Steen and Monnette (1989).

In practice, this technique can be difficult to evaluate because it relies on the offender's self-report. If the offender lies about the nature of his fantasies, this technique can reinforce a sexual compulsive's victimizing arousal pattern. Some clinicians try to control this through use of plethysmography. Because of resistance to the use of directed masturbation in the course of treatment, the principles of this technique can be translated into a cognitive-behavior exercise called "verbal satiation," in which the "boring" process depends on repetition of fantasy material.

An even more controversial technique is aversive conditioning, which is used in 29% of the community-based services and 16% of the residential services. Aversive conditioning is the use of an aversive stimulus, such as a sharply snapped rubber band, noxious odors, or electrical shock, to stop sexually abusive thoughts. An example of one procedure is for the client to make an audiotape that describes the initial stages of approaching a potential victim. The client can then train himself in a behavioral lab by employing a noxious odor to stop the negative sexual thoughts.

Another method rarely used with juveniles is for the client to indicate to a behavioral trainer the arousal of the negative thought and then receive a semipainful electrical shock. This "thought stopping" can continue outside of the lab by using a rubber band on the wrist to be snapped with the arousal of negative sexual thoughts (Steen & Monnette, 1989). Typically, the procedure also employs complementary training for positive, nonabusive sexual thoughts during masturbation, often called "masturbatory reconditioning."

For motivated adolescents with compulsive or distressing sexually deviant thoughts, these procedures can be effective and offer a sense of control and rapid relief. For others, emotional distress has been observed. These forms of aversive conditioning are often used in conjunction with a penile transducer (Knopp, 1984).

Finally, an example of an extreme aversive technique is Smith and Wolf's (1988) report of an "aversive behavioral rehearsal" technique primarily developed by Wickramasekera (1980). No published reports of this technique as used with adolescents were found, although there are anecdotal reports of similar techniques being used in some adolescent programs.

This technique involves the use of male and female mannequins and other props with which the client rehearses the entire abuse scenario eventually in front of a video camera, therapist, treatment group, spouse, relatives, and friends. Out of 154 cases using the technique, only 5% of those completing the procedure are known to have reoffended over a mean 2-year follow-up period (Smith & Wolf, 1988). A small control group of 10 who refused the procedure or went through other components of the program are reported to have a 20% rate of known reoffense over a shorter period of time.

Exhibitionism encompasses the bulk of the reoffensive behaviors. The authors note that clients can experience this powerful technique as humiliating and state that careful preparation is important.

Psychophysical and Psychopharmacological Approaches

Penile Transducer

The penile transducer is used in 22% of juvenile sex offender programs. A sexual arousal assessment using the penile transducer is conducted in a private laboratory. A transducer is a small rubber gauge that the client is directed to place around his penis while he is alone in the lab. This transducer is connected to instruments that measure the degree of erection the adolescent gets while watching slides and videos or listening to audiotapes that depict various appropriate and inappropriate or abusive forms of sexual interactions. The procedure attempts to get direct measures of deviant arousal versus nondeviant arousal.

The penile transducer has been used in individual cases where there is the likelihood of recidivism based on a high degree of denial, minimization, or lack of awareness of arousal cues. This is a special concern for the adolescent who has a considerable history of sex abuse. This method can be useful in breaking through therapeutic impasses and measuring progress.

However, there is also evidence that oppositional, denying, or unmotivated offenders are able to suppress arousal and "fake" the exam. There are also concerns that behavioral arousal changes may not generalize outside of the lab. For example, Becker et al. (1992) found that 58% of the juveniles who denied their sex offense were "nonresponders," and concluded that plethysmography is of limited use with this subgroup of perpetrators because it does not differentiate between cues. They believe that the deniers have the ability to suppress arousal in the laboratory.

The early hope that penile transducers could be used to "prove someone is a sex offender" has been thoroughly discredited; today it is used primarily for research or therapy. (For a recent review of the major methodological issues concerning the validity of phal-lometric tests, see Schouten & Simon, 1992.)

The benefits of laboratory assessments include a measurement of arousal patterns that informs both the client and the therapist regarding the role of arousal and/or preference in the offending behavior, a measurement of change over time, and the offender's conscious or unconscious ability to avoid deviant arousal. Posttreatment change is affected by the offender's application of cognitive change (i.e., motivation to avoid deviant thoughts and employ treatment tools).

Polygraph

The polygraph ("lie detector") is used in 25% of the community-based services and 19% of the residential services. It can be used to support more accurate self-report histories by the offender and as a progress check in therapy (Barbaree, Marshall, & Hudson, 1993; Steen & Monette, 1989).

The clinician should be aware that the polygraph has significant limitations and is prone to abuse, especially for assessment (Lykken, 1981). The polygraph is an instrument that shows general, nonspecific, somatic arousal responses. It is prone to having significant false positive errors that can lead to condemning an innocent party (Gale, 1988).

Depo-Provera

Depo-provera is used in 11% of the community-based programs and 8% of the residential services. Depo-provera is a form of medroxyprogesterone that lowers the testosterone level in the blood stream. There is some evidence that a lower testosterone level decreases the frequency and degree of sexual thoughts and behavior, as well as overall aggression (Barnard et al., 1989). However, such anti-testosterones are rarely used with adolescents except for those who are extremely aggressive or compulsive. Side effects can include interference with bone growth, a decrease in testicle size, weight gain, increased lethargy, and decreased sperm count. (For an excellent review of pharmacological treatments of the adolescent sex offender, see Bradford, 1993.)

CRITIQUE OF CURRENT METHODS AND RATIONALE
FOR A FAMILY-BASED ASSESSMENT AND TREATMENT APPROACH

The major treatment approaches currently in use are predominantly individual or group focused in therapy format and behavioral and cognitive-behavioral in technique. Family therapy is infrequently emphasized. This is probably the result of the application of adult sex offender methods to adolescents. Based on learning theory, adult methods treat sexually offending behavior as negative thinking or learning in the individual, the basic theory is that if you change a person's thoughts and behaviors in treatment, the person will change his thoughts and behaviors in the community (Greer & Stuart, 1983).

Unfortunately, individual-focused therapies and behavioral methods may suffer from generalization; that is, the behavioral changes displayed during the treatment process may not continue to be displayed over time in the family and community. Reliance on the client's self-report of change in the home and community is particularly problematic. Strategies currently used to minimize these problems have a strong emphasis on confrontational group therapy approaches, plethysmography and polygraph monitoring, and teaching relapse prevention strategies (Knopp, Freeman-Longo, & Stevenson, 1992).

Although there is much consensus in this field regarding intervention with the juvenile sex offender, not all experts in the field support the same techniques (National Adolescent Perpetrator Network, 1993). The use of intrusive behavioral methods such as olfactory aversion therapy, satiation, aversive behavioral rehearsal, or depo-provera for changing juvenile arousal patterns is still experimental. Many clinicians and experts, including this author, believe that teenagers, whether having been sexually abusive or not, should not be induced or "court ordered" into experimental therapies that include possibly dangerous or humiliating procedures until the long-term benefits and risks of these therapies are clearly known.

Although most clinicians acknowledge the benefits of family involvement, the field fails to employ family therapy to the extent possible with adolescents and often limits therapy to "fix the kid" strategies. To improve the effectiveness of adolescent sex offender treatment and to maximize generalization, further expansion of therapy utilizing a holistic, family systems approach and victim/family sensitivity throughout the process is important, along with expert application of the strategies already reviewed.

Chapter 5 describes family system issues that are significant to the etiology or maintenance of the abuse behavior. Given the importance of these family variables in the development or maintenance of an adolescent's sexually abusive behavior, the need for a family-based assessment for the juvenile sex offender is significant. Such an assessment can help develop abuse prevention strategies, diagnostic protocols in the assessment phase, family treatment goals, and strategies in the treatment of adolescent and family. With successful family therapy, the resources of the family members can be mobilized to maintain adolescent behavioral changes after termination of treatment (Gurman & Kniskern, 1981, 1991).

General Recidivism and Treatment Studies

Recidivism and treatment follow-up studies are noted for their methodological difficulties. Finkelhor (1986) notes that most studies use subsequent offenses that come to the attention of authorities or a follow-up sex crime as recidivism criteria only if a legal conviction occurred. Most studies only follow offenders over a short period of time (less than 5 years) and therefore probably underestimate true recidivism. Many early studies failed to distinguish between treated and untreated offenders, and others failed to distinguish between different types of offenders.

Of more value from the studies are results that distinguish offender variables most predictive of reoffense. Here there is general agreement. As summarized by Finkelhor (1986), adult child molesters of boys are about twice as likely to offend again as adult offenders of girls (27% to 40% versus 13% to 18%, depending on the study). Exhibitionists also have high reoffense rates (41% to 51%). Adult incest offenders appear to have lower recidivism rates (10% to 12% versus 18% to 24% for other sex offenders). These figures should be cautiously interpreted, given evidence that some also abuse outside the family or later in life with grandchildren.

Some preliminary adolescent recidivism studies are available. Smith and Monastersky (1986) found that a sample of 223 juvenile sex offenders (most of whom had been in some form of treatment) had a 7% reoffense rate over a 20-month follow-up. Bremmer (1992) found a similar low recidivism rate.

Lieker (1986) studied 154 adolescents in Utah convicted of a sex offense between 1974 and 1984. Records were searched for any sexual crimes committed after age 20. Of this sample population, almost 17% were known to have committed further sex-related crimes once they became adults. Fifty-six percent of these juveniles received no treatment. The recidivism rate of these adolescents is two to three times larger that the 5% to 7% rate mentioned in the previous studies. The lack of systematic sex abuse treatment can be speculated as the reason for the difference.

In a review of the recidivism literature, Davis and Leitenberg (1987) conclude that recidivism data provide "reason for some optimism about the long-term progress for most adolescent sex offenders" (p. 425). They also note that treated juveniles have lower recidivism rates than adults.

In summary, the evidence suggests that early intervention with a juvenile offender may reduce future victimization and lower the potential for continuing the deviant sexual abuse patterns into adulthood. Caution is still needed, because comprehensive recidivism studies find that the longer the follow-up the greater the recidivism, and the findings are dependent on how recidivism is measured. Well-designed, clearly controlled, empirical follow-up studies of treated and untreated adolescent offenders that span a number of years are needed to confirm these early impressions.

NEED FOR ASSESSMENT AND CLINICAL PROGRAM STRATEGIES AND TOOLS

Criminal justice and mental health professionals face increased numbers of juvenile offenders to assess, process, and treat, and a growing literature on offender assessment and treatment. They are called on to diagnose offenders regarding degree of dangerousness and potential for reoffending, decide whether treatment should be residential or outpatient, and face other complex and ethically troublesome decisions that may affect all involved: Should such treatment be behavioral, family systems based, individual or group therapy based, residential or hospital based? Should it include psychiatric drugs, focus on sexuality or other personal issues, be of short or long duration, and include what kinds of aftercare plans?

The problems are similar to diagnosis problems in teenage chemical abuse. When a juvenile is found abusing alcohol or drugs in a school, community, or home or when driving, he or she is ideally referred for chemical dependency assessment. The assessment results in a label of experimenter, chemical abuser, or chemically dependent. If judged an experimenter, he or she is often referred to a drug education program. If judged a chemical abuser, he or she is likely to be referred to an outpatient treatment program that may include groups in school or at a local center. If judged chemically dependent, he or she is may be referred to an inpatient treatment program, often followed by an aftercare plan. (Note that in practice there is often over- or underdiagnosis of chemical dependency in adolescents.)

Similarly, criminal justice and sexual abuse professionals attempt to triage the sexually offending teenager toward receiving the appropriate degree of intervention. In practice, such an assessment is much more difficult than chemical health assessments because of the greater emotional reaction to the topic, the newness and lack of sophistication of the field, and the often more complex individual and family dynamics. Broader issues such as treatment options, competing theoretical orientations, costs, and insurance are significant as well.

While similar factors lead to over- and underdiagnosis of chemical dependency in adolescents, such diagnostic errors have a greater consequence in the sexual abuse field. Underdiagnoses could lead to the sexual victimization of additional people. Overdiagnoses label adolescents as dangerous "sex offenders," at times for life. As a result, juvenile sex offender treatment recommendations place greater demand on professionals in a much younger field of inquiry.

This chapter attempts to provide some direction to criminal justice and sexual abuse professionals by outlining the Program for Healthy Adolescent Sexual Expression (PHASE), the PHASE typology, and the benefits of maximizing family involvement. Chapter 7 addresses broader system issues and the coordination of treatment with the victim and victim's family.

PHASE: A FAMILY-BASED OUTPATIENT TREATMENT MODEL

The Program for Healthy Adolescent Sexual Expression (PHASE) was created in 1981. PHASE is an outpatient, family-centered program in the Minneapolis/St. Paul metropolitan area for the assessment and treatment of adolescent males and females who have behaved in sexually abusive or victimizing ways. PHASE provides a comprehensive program of clinical services involving psychological assessment, sexuality education, and individual, family, and group therapy.

PHASE has a significant emphasis on family involvement and therapy. Some of the primary aspects of PHASE are reviewed below, followed by an overview of the PHASE typology and its treatment implications.

Eligibility

Client eligibility requirements for entrance into PHASE are as follows:

1. Adolescent males, age 12 to 17, who have committed a sexual offense
2. No chronic history of physical violence
3. No active chemical dependency
4. Referral by juvenile courts, social worker, probation officer, or parents
5. Requirement of ongoing family participation and/or the participation of other involved persons such as foster parents, social workers, or probation officers

PHASE clients' sexual offense histories range from a fairly isolated experience to multiple offenses extending over a number of years. Offenses include obscene phone calls, exposure, sexual fondling, child molesting, incest, fetish-burglary, and rape.

Intake and the Assessment/Education Program

At first, the adolescent offender and his parents or concerned persons meet with staff for a 2-hour intake interview. Program philosophy and content are discussed, and background information on the juvenile's offenses as well as family dynamics is gathered. A psychological test battery can include the MMPI for age 16 and older, or the MAPI for age 15 and younger to assess symptom and personality issues; a sexual attitude questionnaire to assess general sexual opinions; and a sentence completion test that provides a qualitative, projective assessment. Other tests may be based on the concerns of the intake staff. The theme of the intake and testing is to assist in the assessment process and to determine the family's appropriateness for the monthlong assessment/education portion.

If appropriate, the adolescent and his family next enter into a 1-month, structured assessment/education program. Here they join six to eight other families who are working on similar sexual concerns. Each young person is assigned an individual therapist who works with him and his family throughout the program. Meetings include a weekly 2-hour adolescent group, two to three scheduled individual sessions, and two designated family sessions.

The adolescent groups explore the laws concerning sexuality, attitudes regarding sex roles and sexual expression, and the differences between consensual touch and exploitative touch. The various nontouch offenses are defined. Discussion includes a variety of safe, responsible ways to express one's sexuality.

Parents and/or concerned persons attend four support groups that meet while the adolescents are in group. In these meetings, the parents and concerned individuals are provided the same information given to the adolescents, as well as an opportunity to share concerns and progress with each other and provide support.

Upon conclusion of this component, each case is presented to the treatment team, decisions are made, and a diagnostic conference is held where decisions about the need for further treatment or referral are discussed. Adolescent offenders whose abuse behavior was nonviolent, with incidents few in number, and whose behavior could be best characterized as naive or experimental may be terminated at this time, with or without recommendation for continuing non-sex-offender-specific therapy. The offender must write a letter of apology to the victim as therapeutic restitution and reconciliation.

Adolescents with a more severe or chronic history and dynamic of sexual acting out are referred to PHASE outpatient treatment or other outpatient treatment programs. Sibling incest perpetrators often continue to live out of the home while in an outpatient program. If an adolescent also poses a significant risk to the community, an intensive residential treatment program is recommended.

Treatment Program

Juveniles entering the treatment part of PHASE continue in individual, group, and family therapy under the direction of their personal therapist or case manager. The treatment program typically runs for 7 to 8 additional months, but may continue for as long as 1 year. Each adolescent, working with his therapist, develops an individually tailored treatment plan.

Family participation and family therapy are considered crucial in the treatment program. Parents, siblings, and extended family members are affected by the consequences of the adolescent's behavior. The focus of family therapy is to improve family relationships in order to maximize the family's strengths, to support the adolescent as he proceeds through treatment, and to maintain his nonabusive behavior after graduation.

Weekly group therapy helps the teenager develop a better understanding of others' values and beliefs, in addition to improving self-awareness, social skills, and self-esteem. One-on-one therapy sessions provide a psychologically safe environment in which to address personal issues.

General treatment goals include recognizing and accepting responsibility for sexually abusive behavior; understanding the consequences of sexual abuse actions on themselves and on others; developing healthier ways to meet sexual, emotional, and interpersonal needs; and integrating these new skills and insights. Treatment dura- tion of PHASE ranges from approximately 6 months to more than 1 year.

Staff

The PHASE staff consists of a director and a program coordinator who supervise clinical staff, and an intake worker who coordinates incoming referrals, the assessment/education program, and testing. A number of treatment therapists have psychology, social work, or family therapy backgrounds and provide long-term psychotherapy in the treatment program. Supervision is provided by a doctoral-level clinical psychologist with expertise in child and adolescent development and a psychiatrist certified in child and adolescent psychiatry.

The PHASE Typology and Its Treatment Implications

Based on the PHASE typology, differential treatment issues and strategies are suggested according to the offender type and dynamics outlined in chapter 5. The treatment addresses offender and family issues and offers brief suggestions for how to address these issues in a structured, family-based program such as PHASE. Offenders who are likely to benefit from short-term therapy rather than a longer-term outpatient program or who may need to be referred to an out-of-home placement or residential setting are defined.

Type 1: The Naive Experimenter/Abuser

The naive experimenter/abuser commits one or a few acts of naive, opportunistic sexual exploration with no recourse to force or threats. A concrete education in adolescent sexuality versus sexual abuse is imperative for both the adolescent and his parents. This type appears to develop more open family communication on issues of sexuality in order to minimize future potential for problematic sexual behavior. The treatment of the naive experimenter/abuser typically ends at the conclusion of a short-term yet intensive assessment/education program of about 2 months.

Type 2: The Undersocialized Child Molester

The undersocialized child molester tends to be a younger teen with abuse that typically spans a number of months demonstrating a chronic sexual abuse pattern involving one or more child victims. Typical therapy issues include helping the family become a less enmeshed-chaotic system in which the offender is very family centered. Role reversals usually need to be addressed as well. The communication pattern of such families requires change, as do the peer communication and socialization skills of the offender.

Typical referrals are for outpatient adolescent sex offender treatment including individual, peer group, and family therapy.

Type 3: The Pseudosocialized Child Molester

Typically bright and social, the pseudosocialized child molester tends to be an older teen with a more chronic abuse history of a year or more. Therapy goals include breaking through the offender's denial and minimization, which are well defended because of his facile social skills. The offender often lacks genuine motivation for therapeutic change because his ability to compartmentalize his life is an effective defense.

This type of offender poses a significant danger of developing into a lifelong pedophile or personality disorder. This is the type that has the potential to evolve into the professionally successful minister, teacher, or youth leader who shocks the community by his unexpected arrest for years of child molestation.

These offenders are usually referred to an outpatient sex offender treatment program that includes individual, peer group, and family therapy. If a lack of compliance or heavy denial is demonstrated through the initial assessment/education program, an out-of-home placement or a residential program may be necessary.

Type 4: The Sexual Aggressive

Most rapists and violent sadistic child molesters are placed in this PHASE type. The offender is often antisocial and character-disordered with a significantly dysfunctional and abusive family system. Therapy includes effectively addressing the disorganized family system and abusive family members' tendency to undermine the adolescent's constructive therapy goals. The offender must develop more appropriate ways to express his anger and ways to satisfy his needs in a nonexploitative way. It is difficult to maintain the character-disordered offender's motivation in treatment.

The usual referral is to a residential adolescent sex offender treatment program or a trial attempt in an outpatient adolescent sex offender treatment program with a high level of supervision. All treatments should include intensive individual, peer group, and, where possible, family therapy.

Type 5: The Sexual Compulsive

The sexual compulsive engages in repetitive, sexually arousing acts such as window peeping, obscene phone calls, exhibitionism, and fetish burglary, or may also have a history of compulsive hands-on offenses. As a result, this type is considered a high recidivism risk.

Therapy typically focuses on the need to understand the behavioral sequence that led to the abusive events and to develop numerous interventions in that sequence that could be practiced in individual, group, and family therapy. Such therapy is done with the other PHASE types, but the sexual compulsive requires an intense focus on "relapse prevention" therapy.

The typical referral is to an outpatient adolescent sex offender treatment program with the option of out-of-home placement or residential treatment if the behavior is so compulsive that the offender cannot remain nonabusive in an outpatient setting.

Type 6: The Disturbed Impulsive

This is the most heterogeneous of the PHASE types in terms of abuse behaviors. The disturbed impulsive's offenses, whether a few or many in number, tend to reflect a malfunction of normal inhibitory mechanisms due to thought disorder, organic brain syndrome, intellectual or developmental disability, or chemical abuse. Therefore, the motivation is complex and individually determined, which makes effective assessment time consuming.

The therapist must complete in-depth psychological testing and a complete family and individual history in order to develop a concrete treatment plan. The families are often very dysfunctional and difficult to engage in therapy. Because of the complexity and impulsive nature of this type, it also has a high reoffense potential.

Depending on the results, referral could be to an inpatient psychiatric unit, a residential adolescent sex offender treatment unit, or a trial treatment in an outpatient adolescent sex offender program.

Type 7: The Group Influenced

The group influenced offender is typically a younger teen whose abuse occurs in concert with other peer offenders. Offenders should be split into separate therapy groups if referred at the same time, and the various offense stories should be compared and contrasted with the victim's testimony in order to develop a clear picture of what really happened. The offenders must be confronted about inconsistencies, rationalizations, projections, and blame. Each offender then must own his fair share of responsibility for the abuse and its effects on the victim. The usual referral is to an outpatient adolescent sex offender program unless the "leader" is actually a member of one of the more severe offender typologies.

The PHASE Typology:
Discussion

The PHASE typology is widely used in training and increasing awareness of those who must detect, assess, or treat juveniles with sexual misconduct behaviors: teachers, police investigators, juvenile probation officers, therapists, and social workers.

The PHASE typology is helpful in emphasizing that adolescent sex offenders are an aggregate of several distinct and discontinuous types. These types do not lie on a "continuum" and are not amenable to treatment by one particular therapy theory. For example, it may be inappropriate to use an "addiction" model on any type except perhaps the sexual compulsive. A "psychodynamic" approach may be inappropriate for the naive experimenter/abuser, who warrants a more direct and efficient psychoeducational approach.

Differentiating types helps "sort" those who are appropriate for a particular setting and model and address individual characteristics. The following factors determine the treatment a certain type will receive.

Setting. Is the adolescent a danger to himself or the community and therefore in need of inpatient treatment or residential treatment versus outpatient treatment? Are his victims or potential victims present in the home, requiring some period of separation?

Duration. What is the appropriate length of treatment? For example, it can be short for the naive experimenter/abuser and the followers in the group-influenced types, and medium or long for the more severe offender types such as the child molester, sexual compulsives, and sexual aggressives.

Therapeutic Strategies. What therapy and combinations of therapy are judged most appropriate? What therapists and therapeutic settings and orientations might be most appropriate for a particular client?

The PHASE typology can help guide individual/family assessment, suggest criminal justice restrictions, and differentiate therapeutic needs relevant to the issues of the particular client types.

A FAMILY SYSTEMS APPROACH: PERSPECTIVES AND EARLY STRUCTURING

Juveniles presenting to treatment nearly always have a parent or parent figure involved and present at intake. Bera (1985) found that out of 51 adolescent offenders studied in an outpatient program, all but one had a mother or stepmother and all but 12 had a father or stepfather involved in the current family constellation.

Early involvement of family members in therapy helps mobilize and maintain their commitment to the process, thereby maximizing the potential for comprehensive, effective assessment and treatment of the juvenile offender while in the program and after discharge. Significant family members provide important data in order to make a comprehensive assessment. An assessment is incomplete without the family to confirm and contextualize the adolescent's self-report and police, victim, or probation reports.

Early family involvement serves two key functions: it maintains the family members' awareness of and lowers the denial of the sexual abuse and it maintains the family's responsibility for abuse prevention and support of treatment strategies. The therapist frames his or her role as a "temporary consultant" to the caregivers, who bear the long-term responsibility. This critical early structuring enjoins the responsible caregivers as the "most important part of the treatment team" from the beginning of the assessment and therapy process. This encourages, maintains, and respects the family hierarchy (Minuchin & Fishman, 1981).

Such a therapeutic frame helps minimize the "abdication dynamic" by which temporarily overwhelmed caregivers attempt to give over responsibility for the care of the troubled adolescent to "professionals." The therapist hired to treat the adolescent can be triangulated to the point of suffering blame by parents, the adolescent, or both when inevitable difficulties occur.

A family-based intake assessment and therapy perspective also makes it possible to assess unrecognized victims and offenders in the family, extended family, and community. It allows these victims to get help early in the offender's therapy process.

Many practitioners agree that family involvement is potentially very useful. However, as many therapists are aware, a variety of roadblocks can appear when trying to recruit family members to take part in the treatment process. Many of these roadblocks are rooted in resistance on the part of the family. The following section offers strategies to deal with some of these potential roadblocks.

STRATEGIES TO INCREASE FAMILY INVOLVEMENT

Therapists can use a number of strategies to increase family involvement, especially before and during the intake session, when the critical early structuring of the therapy process occurs (Gelinas, 1988). The program should encourage parents, stepparents, and other family members to attend the intake assessment. This should include significant extended family members as well as the adolescent's siblings.

The intake assessment is an excellent opportunity to frame the sexual abuse in a nonshaming manner that emphasizes its effect on the whole family. For example, the therapist might state, "We're aware that Tony's behavior has affected everyone in the family, and it is important that they get some information and a chance to address their concerns as well." Such a statement helps the family feel their connection to the sexual misconduct without feeling blamed, thereby establishing a foundation for their participation in the treatment process.

Scheduling

Scheduling is one of the biggest headaches therapists encounter in their daily work. Most therapists are quite familiar with the emergence of resistance symptoms at this stage in the treatment process. Therefore, scheduling should be flexible in order to maximize the caregivers' involvement and to minimize potential schedule conflict excuses. A good way to respond to a parent's schedule conflict is simply by saying, "Well then we will schedule some other time" and offer alternative times and dates.

Missing Family Members

A strategy developed by Whitaker (1982) is to refuse to see any member of the family unless the whole family comes. The therapist can make himself or herself available by phone to answer resistant family members' concerns, which in turn help structure the first session.

Similarly, intake staff can make themselves available by phone to clarify and explain the intake and therapy process. This can be especially important to fathers who are often not "psychologically minded" or feel "dragged into therapy" or blamed. It is important to provide clear information and reassurances in a cordial and non-shaming manner. Some parents are concerned about what siblings, especially younger siblings, might hear. It can be clarified that the younger siblings will be in another room during the graphic descriptive portions of the intake.

Parents who are strongly resistant to involvement can be pressed to attend by the referring agency, usually the court system. This situation allows the intake therapist to avoid being the "bad guy," and frames the intake as an opportunity to address the entire family's concerns and develop support for an ongoing therapy process.

The Intake Session:
Structuring the Therapist/Family Relationship

In the intake session, it is useful for a therapist to maintain the role of "family consultant" or "advisor" to the parents, and to provide information that can help the family now, during the program, and after the program.

The therapist's personal limitations of time, knowledge, and power to change the presenting problem can be emphasized while the therapist provides general structure and leadership. Taking a personal "one-down approach" with such statements as "You know your child better than anyone could and you know clearly the problems he has" can help convey to the family a sense of safety, authority, and esteem. This frames the family as the crucial part of the treatment team. Treatment can be described as an opportunity to learn about how the sexual abuse began and develop ways to prevent it so that everyone can "pull together" to avoid being "dragged through this whole thing again."

The involvement of significant siblings and extended family members is especially important in minority and ethnic families. Martin and Martin (1978) state that the African American extended family provides a myriad of services such as informal adoption of children whose parents cannot care for them, financial support for unemployed members, childcare for working single parents, food, and shelter. The therapist's openness, respect and sensitivity to ethnic and minority differences can help increase significant family members' involvement and distinguish the program from past negative experiences with the majority "establishment."

A SYSTEMIC APPROACH
TO ADOLESCENT SEXUAL ABUSE

Treating the sexual abuse behavior is necessary but not sufficient in complete treatment of the conditions that allowed the development or maintenance of the problem. To reduce the risk of future sexual abuse, the systems to which the adolescent is connected in relationship to his sexual abuse must be dealt with. Relationship

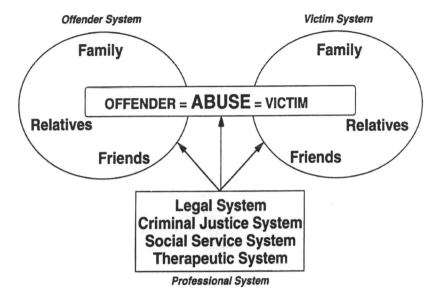

Figure 6.1. Systems and Perspectives Involved in a Sexual Abuse Case

dysfunctions often precede the sexual abuse behavior and are exacerbated by the abuse behavior. They can be dealt with most effectively in a family therapy context. The previous sections develop strategies to increase family involvement, "get them in the door." This section describes the development of a coherent systemic approach or "what to do once they're here."

In addition to family systems concerns, there are the "ecosystemic" issues of the social, racial, class, ethnic, and community contexts in which the abuse occurred (see Figure 6.1). As chapter 2 describes, these issues have a significant impact on how sexual abuse is defined and responded to. There are also the concerns of the other involved parties or stakeholders. The safety and needs of the victim and the victim's family are of first concern, whether the abuse occurred inside or outside of the family. In the initial stage of treatment of incest cases, the offending sibling is usually placed outside the home with a relative or in a foster home. Managing and coordinating the victim's issues are necessary aspects of a complete treatment plan. Criminal justice, social service, and therapeutic professionals are also involved, as may be extended family, community, school, and church figures.

STAGES OF FAMILY THERAPY
FOR ADOLESCENT SEX OFFENDERS

The therapy of adolescent sex offenders can be viewed in a series of stages. Each stage addresses particular goals that can be met using specific processes and techniques. Accomplishment of the goals at the preceding stage sets the foundation for the following stage. A stage approach helps demarcate therapeutic progress for the client, family, and involved professionals, and provides an orderly and structured plan to deal with the numerous issues present in adolescent offender treatment.

Therapeutic Context

The stages that occur in individual, group, and family therapy settings form the therapeutic focus for the treatment modalities of each stage. The therapeutic goal for a particular stage is introduced in individual therapy. Individual concerns and fears can be dealt with in this context of privacy, intimacy, and support.

An example is the abuse biography that is part of Stage 2; the individual writes the abuse biography detailing his history of sexual/ physical/emotional abuse victimization and experience that led to and maintained the perpetration. He then shares the biography with his individual therapist, who provides feedback to help fill in gaps and clarify language in the biography. When an abuse biography is done, it can then be brought to group therapy.

In group therapy, the client can read his abuse biography and receive feedback and support from other group members. The sharing of this very personal history with others who have similar problems is an important part of developing group cohesion, overcoming shame, and giving up the secrecy associated with the sexual abuse.

Finally, the abuse biography is shared in family therapy. The family members ask questions concerning aspects of the abuse biography, because they often know the time frames and individuals involved, and therefore have a contextual grasp of the client's behavior. The therapist helps the family members ask questions that they previously may have been afraid to ask. This is an important stage in increasing family cohesion and breaking through denial, secrecy, and misattributions.

In this model, a therapeutic goal is first introduced and developed in individual therapy and then brought to group and finally to family therapy. Individual therapy is then used to help process the reactions of the group and family to the therapeutic task, setting the foundation for the next stage.

Structured family-based outpatient treatment programs such as PHASE coordinate individual, group, and family treatment modalities and can safely treat some fairly severe offender types by appropriately coordinating services. For example, a sibling incest offender can be placed in a relative's home, foster home, or group home setting where there are no vulnerable children present, thereby providing the victim safety and the offender therapeutic motivation. This allows the offender to be treated in or near his community, and it is easier to coordinate with the other therapists or caregivers involved, such as the victim's therapist or social worker. Many of the adolescent sex offenders and families served by PHASE receive primary treatment in a 6-month to more than a year time frame, with follow-up therapy as needed afterward. (Note that average length of treatment is longer nationally, reflecting possible differences in offender population served and program philosophy.)

Roles of the Therapist

In helping adolescent sex offenders and their families face juvenile sexual abuse, it is useful for the therapist to have a particular vision of his or her roles with the client, family, and other involved professionals through the stages of therapy. These roles change when the therapist is acting as an "individual therapist" versus a "family therapist" versus a "group therapist" versus an "organizational consultant." It is important for the therapist to clarify his or her role in each context.

Primarily, the therapist frames the problem; provides leadership, information, and support; and helps set direction for the troubled families and concerned persons who have enlisted this "expert's" help in dealing with the sexual abuse behavior.

It is useful to analyze the problem of sexual abuse therapy by levels of interaction. Individual therapy can deal with intrapsychic issues such as the individual's thoughts and feelings surrounding the abuse, the consequential misattribution or thinking errors, and the learning of the sexual abuse sequence. Another level of interaction is between family members and the family systems from which the offender came or in which the abuse occurred.

Another level involves the issues surrounding the victim/offender dyad explicated in chapter 7. Another level is peer interaction as demonstrated in group therapy and in reports from the school, community, or foster home. Finally, there is the professional level of involved social workers, therapists, attorneys, probation officers, and the like. Failure to look at the systemic and ecosystemic issues with which adolescent offenders present can lead to incomplete or abortive therapy results.

The therapist must consciously interrupt dysfunctional communication and interaction patterns demonstrated by the client and family and work toward changing the family structure. At each stage, the intervention is also diagnostic, as the therapist observes how the client and family respond. The response clarifies the issues to struggle with in the next stage. For example, as the parents read the teenager's abuse biography, it is not unusual that one or the other will recall personal abuse experiences. Such repressed experiences can explain a mother's protectiveness or a father's distance. With such issues uncovered, the family can more freely change in the desired direction.

The effective therapist working with adolescent offenders and their families plays a variety of roles and assumes leadership to provide complete treatment. The therapist, therefore, needs supervisory support to provide role clarity and share decision making. A sensitive and supportive team of treatment professionals and staff with good clinical direction can help therapists work with challenging families while minimizing professional "burn out."

Overview of Stages

The stages of therapy are as follows:

1. Assessment, education, and admission
2. Abuse biography: facts and behaviors
3. Abuse biography: thoughts and feelings
4. Abuse cycles defined
5. Relapse prevention training
6. Letters of apology and restitution/closure where possible
7. Graduation/aftercare

Each stage is defined and then illustrated by the case example of Peter and Jenny.

Case Example

Peter is a 14-year-old white male referred by the county probation service for a sexual health assessment. He had reluctantly admitted during a police investigation that he had sexually fondled a 4-year-old neighbor girl named Jenny while baby-sitting.

During the 2-hour intake interview with his family, Peter presented as a serious, responsible boy from an upper-class and very religious family. The youngest of four siblings, his brothers and sister were not involved because they lived out of the home. Peter and his parents were ashamed and did not know how to explain his sexual abuse. The family demonstrated strong discomfort and difficulty discussing any issues of sexuality.

Despite their reticence in informing the rest of the family of the abuse, Peter and his parents were open to signing a release-of-information form so the therapist could contact Jenny's parents. The two families had known each other for several years and attended the same church. Peter had baby-sat Jenny for 2 years, and all expressed concern about how Jenny and her family were doing. The two families had not talked to each other since the police investigation demanded that no contact occur between the two families. The victim and her family completed release-of-information forms, as did past and current therapists. Psychological and family tests were given to Peter and his family to complete.

As a result of Peter and his parents' motivation and Peter presenting as able to be nonabusive in an outpatient setting, they were accepted in the PHASE assessment/education program.

Stage 1: Assessment, Education, and Admission

Stage 1 frames and develops the treatment plan. The three initial
major goals—assessment, education, and admission—work together
synergistically.

Assessment involves interviewing and collecting data from the
individual, family, involved professionals, and the victim or victim's
family. Private sessions are held with the client, family, and siblings.
One goal is to obtain individual and family reports on sexuality and
sexual abuse history.

In the course of this assessment, individual and relationship dynamics are clarified. In addition, a review of chemical health, mental
health, and other issues is performed. Psychological testing is scored
and interpreted.

Ongoing education on the terminology, concepts, and differences
between healthy sexuality and sexual abuse are presented in group
sessions. This provides the words and concepts necessary to describe experiences the offender and family may have had but were
unable to articulate fully.

Because therapy is primarily a verbal activity, the provision of
concrete sexual information and terms is critical. This occurs in a
four session assessment/education group that includes peers who
are at the same stage as the offender. The parents benefit from a
parent education/support group because they are frequently unfamiliar with fundamental sexuality/sexual abuse knowledge. The combination of individual, group and family education with the ongoing
assessment provides the foundation for an initial or more complete
disclosure of sexual behaviors.

During these initial assessment/education sessions, the client and
family develop more comfort and ability to talk about sexuality and
sexual abuse. At the same time, the therapist is contacting other
involved professionals and the victim or victim's parents. The collat-
eral information is used to confront the offender and family appropriately and tactfully regarding discrepancies, denial, minimiza-

tion, and projection, which are typically a part of the defensive mechanisms used. Without a clear admission of sexual abuse, it is inappropriate to refer the client to an ongoing sex offender treatment program because there is no clearly defined basis for a therapy contract.

The assessment, education, and admission stage provides data to share with other involved professionals. It is important for the therapist to share this information with the other involved professionals either over the phone or in a face-to-face "treatment planning session" in order to develop a unified treatment plan. This also creates a network to prevent relapse during outpatient treatment.

Dynamics common in sexual abuse can triangulate professionals against each other. These triangulations should be confronted early to develop a unified treatment plan to maximize the likelihood of complete success. Without a cohesive plan and early resolution of differences, therapy may be aborted when the issues between professionals reoccur. Without a unified plan and clear mandate from the "stakeholders" in the case, treatment should not proceed.

Case Example

For Peter and his parents, the assessment/education groups for Peter as well as the parents support groups proved important in their development of sexuality and sexual abuse information and appropriate language. Over the course of Stage 1, Peter's parents became noticeably more able to talk about sexuality, sexual abuse, and the abuse Peter had perpetrated on Jenny.

In the last group, Peter was able to state for the first time that he abused Jenny many times, not just the one time that he had previously admitted. He admitted the abuse continued over a 3-month period during his weekly Friday night baby-sitting. The abuse included fondling Jenny and encouraging her to fondle him. Peter made Jenny promise not to tell or he would not be her "friend."

Peter denied a history of physical or sexual abuse. He said the idea to touch Jenny came about because of his own curiosity with some peers' frequent discussion of sexuality and sexual exploits. Peter's initial experimentation became a patterned sexual abuse cycle that included masturbating after the sexual contact.

During Stage 1, Jenny's parents were contacted by phone. They were relieved to know what was going on with Peter and his family, since their information was at least 3 months old. They were also gratified to learn that Peter had made a full admission that concurred with what their daughter had told them. The victim-sensitive offender therapy process was outlined for them.

When asked what they would like at this time, Jenny's parents asked if Peter could attend Sunday church service at another time. Jenny and her parents often saw Peter there. She was also reminded of the incident by seeing him when he rode his bike past their house. Peter and his parents were happy to comply with these requests to attend another service and not to have Peter ride by the house.

Jenny's parents said that Jenny had been to therapy and that she was no longer having nightmares or other symptoms. As a result, Jenny was presently not seeing her therapist. Her parents agreed to sign a release-of-information form and have her therapist contact PHASE to share information and coordinate future therapy.

The PHASE number was provided to the parents for future reference if needed. The therapist promised to contact the family later in the course of therapy to provide other information, options, closure, and restitution. The probation officer was called and agreed with the treatment plan that Peter should begin the long-term outpatient adolescent sex offender treatment at PHASE. Jenny's therapist was also called and agreed to coordinate therapy as needed.

Stage 2: Abuse Biography: Facts and Behaviors

After there has been a clear admission of the sexual offense by the offender, he is ready to enter an ongoing adolescent sex offender treatment program. The focus of this stage is to develop a complete "abuse biography" that details in chronological order the adolescent's physical abuse, sexual abuse, and other abuse events he suffered or perpetrated.

In writing this abuse biography, the offender should segment the task in small steps; that is, write about the first five years of the client's life, followed by kindergarten, first, second, and third grade, and so on. Simultaneously, it is useful for the family to develop a family history that can parallel and place the adolescent's history in context. At this stage, the therapist generally "restrains" the client and his family from too great a focus on the emotional aspects of their histories. This helps protect the client and his family from being flooded with emotion, which increases resistance and slows this recollection and fact-gathering stage.

During this stage there is clarification of the exact details of the abuse and the language or meaning the client uses to understand these details. In this phase, the therapy is more supportive than confrontational. In individual, group, and family sessions, the therapist uses Rogerian-style active listening skills and positive reframing. These individually and family-generated abuse biographies are then shared by reading them aloud (if possible) in individual, group, and family therapy.

Case Example

After settling into the adolescent treatment group, Peter began working on his abuse biography. He was the youngest of four, with very active older siblings, and frequently felt powerless and left out of significant sibling and family events. The family's rigid religious beliefs and discomfort in discussing personal matters seemed to result in little discussion of sexuality, much less sexual abuse issues. The parents' own recalling of Peter's early development confirmed Peter's impressions. The parents had learned a lot that they "should have" known before about sexuality and sexual abuse.

As a result of his lack of information on sexuality, Peter had been extremely intrigued by his peers' graphic information about sexuality and sexual experience. Peter was jealous and again felt insignificant and powerless. He saw a ready opportunity while baby-sitting one Friday night.

Peter's writing of his abuse biography went very slowly. In a halting fashion, he tried to describe in detail each of the sexual abuse incidents that occurred over the 3-month abuse period. The therapist was very supportive and encouraging. At times, when Peter was barely able to get the words out, the therapist even helped write down Peter's words. If Peter became emotional and felt overwhelmed, the therapist would back off, acknowledging and appreciating Peter's guilt and remorse, at times saying, "It is a very good sign of health that you feel this bad for what you did." After a few minutes, Peter would feel settled and the therapist would return to the task of having Peter describe "just the facts" of what occurred, stating that "We will deal with these feelings and emotional pains in the next stage." It was in this way that the abuse biography was completed over a 2-month period.

Stage 3: Abuse Biography: Thoughts and Feelings

With the facts and memories clearer, the effect of writing and then reading the biography aloud in individual, group, and family settings can be very powerful. At this point, the therapist elicits the feelings and rationales the offender experienced in order to keep perpetrating. Emotional consequences of the abuse and the effects on involved parties are clarified, as are the defenses and misattributions utilized by the individual and family. This process of working through feelings and developing insights from the abuse history is critical in later defining the sexual abuse cycle that the offender has developed.

Case Example

Peter shared the biography in group and in family therapy. The therapist wrote on a copy of the abuse biography, making notes of feelings, misattributions, and insights developed during the readings in group and family therapy. Peter read slowly, sometimes in a shaking voice, and the remorse and tears came out.

Peter was especially anguished sharing the abuse biography with his parents, which resulted in tears for all involved. The seriousness of Peter's molestation of Jenny and the shame and guilt for his behavior was clear.

Stage 4: Abuse Cycles Defined

The sexual abuse cycle is defined in individual, group, and family therapy until what happens cognitively, emotionally, and situationally before, during, and after an abuse event is clear (see Figure 5.1). Developing a detailed understanding of the cycle enables well-founded and effective interventions.

With a clear abuse biography, the abuse cycle is easily defined. Now the misattributions of fault, blame, denial, and other thinking errors can be directly addressed. Heretofore, the therapist has maintained a generally "neutral," nonjudgmental stance in order to elicit the offender's history, thoughts, and feelings. The defenses are now laid bare in the individual, group, and family sessions.

If necessary, the therapist can use a powerful technique of highlighting the misattributions that involves the offender writing a therapeutic letter of apology to the victim. Offenders who have been merely complying with the treatment to this point often find this task onerous, because the therapist has had contact with the victim, the victim's family, and/or the victim's therapist and incorrect self-reports are easily countered. The offender knows that attempts to attribute blame or minimize abuse effects would be fruitless. Such a letter forces the offender to face his responsibility for the sexually abusive behavior and to increase his understanding of the consequences on himself, his family, and the victim. Letters of apology to the victim's parents (if a child victim) and to the offender's own parents can also be helpful.

An exercise for offenders who have been victims of physical or sexual abuse is to write a letter to their offender. This step can be done before or after the letter of apology to the victim. Another exercise involves writing the abuse history as seen from the victim's eyes. This is an excellent means of developing empathy for the victim; lack of victim empathy is key to misattribution to overcome internal inhibitors in the abuse cycle.

If the offender has been displaying appropriate victim empathy, the letter of apology writing can be delayed to Stage 6.

Case Example

Peter's abuse cycle became evident as a result of the facts and feelings developed in Stages 2 and 3. This included the minimization of the seriousness of what he was doing ("just touching each other") and Jenny's apparent lack of resistance. Peter now realized Jenny had been obedient and compliant only because Peter had baby-sat her for a long time—not because she "wanted to do it." Because of the therapist's contact with the victim's family, concrete information of the effects of the abuse (e.g., nightmares and hypervigilance) allowed no room for minimization.

The therapist now used a large piece of paper to outline Peter's abuse cycle as developed from Stages 2 and 3. The cycle was defined as follows.

Motivation: Power, intimacy needs, and sexual experimentation, and after a time, the baby-sitting situation were combined with sexual arousal.

Situational opportunity: Regular Friday night baby-sitting of Jenny provided a consistent opportunity.

Internal inhibitors overcome: Peter denied to himself that what he was doing was really abuse, so he was able to believe it was OK.

Victim resistance circumvented: The long-term baby-sitting relationship created a situation of authority and trust. Peter called it a secret and special game, threatening that if the secret was broken, he and Jenny would never be friends again.

Sexual abuse act: Fondling Jenny's vagina; having her touch his penis.

No negative consequences and pleasure/need is reduced: Abuse remained a secret for 3 months. Pleasure was experienced, and Peter's power, intimacy, and sexual needs were reduced.

Fantasy and masturbatory reinforcement: Abuse events were replayed through fantasy and reinforced with masturbation between baby-sitting times.

Rationalization and thinking errors: To Peter it was "only" fondling. He rationalized that because Jenny did not actively protest, maybe she "liked it." When he felt sorry for himself, he thought he "deserved" what he "got" from Jenny.

Peter's motivation for power, intimacy, and arousal appeared to be met through sexual abuse, and the abuse cycle was reinforced and repeated over Peter's 3-month abuse career.

Peter wrote his therapeutic letters of apology to Jenny, her parents, and his own family. Despite his increased insight and awareness, three drafts were necessary before a final draft was approved in group. Rationalizations and thinking errors continued to creep in. The letters were an important step toward taking full responsibility for his sexual molestation of Jenny.

Stage 5: Relapse Prevention Training

Stage 5 develops effective interventions in the abuse cycle. The context and history has become clear and insights are present. Family members are developing new roles and relationships. The offender and his family have an increased awareness of the emotional, psychological, and situational processes that led to the offense. They are now able to develop appropriate alternative behaviors and interventions.

By identifying the stressors, arousal patterns, fantasies, and reinforcers involved in the abuse pattern, the offender and his family can identify the stressful "high risk" situations and accompanying effect. The offender can identify underlying needs for affection, power, competence, and acceptance that were precursors for sexual acting out. The roles of the family, social, and peer system in allowing the sexual abuse (covertly or overtly) are clarified. Nonabusive ways to meet these underlying needs, as well as healthy, nonabusive interventions in the abuse cycle, are practiced in individual, group, and family therapy. The probation officer is informed of the relapse prevention plan for court support and supervision.

Case Example

A number of interventions were developed to minimize Peter's potential for future abuse. He and his family agreed that Peter should never baby-sit again or be in situations where he had power over or responsibility for children. He practiced stopping his abusive thoughts whenever they arose. Peter's masturbation fantasies were restructured using masturbatory reconditioning. While masturbating, Peter practiced stopping inappropriate/abusive fantasies (e.g., thoughts of Jenny) and reinforced positive, age-appropriate and nonaggressive sexual fantasies (e.g., thoughts of romantic, caring interactions with consenting peer-age mates).

Peter's need for empowerment and intimacy was addressed in family therapy with the entire family, including the siblings. In addition, Peter became active in appropriate peer-age groups at school and the community such as the choir, athletics, and the Boy Scout program. The probation officer was informed of the relapse prevention plan.

Stage 6: Letters of Apology and Restitution/Closure Where Possible

The letters of apology can now be refined for actual use. The therapist attempts to set up a closure session between the victim and victim's family and the offender and the offender's family. (Details and outcomes of these sessions are contained in chapter 7.) If the victim and victim's family prefer, the letter of apology can be sent through the mail in lieu of a face-to-face meeting, and/or the no contact contract can continue.

In a subsequent session, the offender can make amends and closure with his own family concerning the abuse events. For this closure ritual, the offender is also asked to write a letter.

Case Example

Peter completed the final versions of his apology letters to Jenny, Jenny's parents, and his own parents and family. These letters were therapeutically refined to the point where it became clear that there was no misattribution of fault or blame to others. Peter's full acceptance of responsibility for the sexual abuse was evident.

The therapist called Jenny's therapist, informing her that the letters of apology had been completed and were appropriate. She called Jenny's parents and asked if they would like to receive the letters through the mail or in a face-to-face session or to continue with no contact between the two families.

Jenny's family chose to receive the letters in a face-to-face session. The session was scheduled to be held at Jenny's therapist's office, where Jenny's parents had a sense of control and power. A remorseful Peter read the letters of apology to Jenny and her parents. This session was later said to be healing by both the victim's and offender's families.

A family session was then held for Peter's parents and siblings in which he read his letters of apology to them. These sessions were emotionally powerful and significant therapeutic closure was evident.

Stage 7: Graduation/Aftercare

In this final stage of primary sex offense therapy, the individual and family can review what was learned in therapy. This review of the therapy and the changes that the offender and his family has experienced can refine intervention strategies for future risk situations. Therapeutic closure in the individual, group, and family sessions occurs when issues that have not been addressed in the sex abuse program are identified and aftercare therapy is facilitated. For example, for those clients who continue to have social skills deficits, an ongoing social skills group or activities are recommended. Another common referral is ongoing marital therapy for parents whose marriages are troubled.

The last session ends with a series of "predictions" that sexuality and/or sexual abuse issues can emerge at different points in the future. Sometimes called "developmental prescriptions," these points often occur at developmental transitions that remind the offender of some aspect of the sexuality/sexual abuse issues for which he had been treated. Examples include when the offender starts dating, marries, has children, or when his children reach the same age as when he was abused or abusing. It is emphasized to the offender and his parents that this is normal, and that he will have to separate current situations from the past in a positive way. It is recommended to the recovering offender and his family that it is best to inform those he becomes intimate with about his past history and to see a competent therapist at these points.

Case Example

Peter and his family completed their sex offense specific therapy. Ongoing recommendations included Peter's continued commitment to no future baby-sitting or supervision of children, and continuation of his peer-age activities in school and the community. Relapse prevention strategies were reviewed and developmental prescriptions were discussed.

The therapist, Peter, and his family predicted some of the future developmental transition points that may give difficulty. When Peter begins peer-age, consensual sexual relationships, he may experience some inhibitions resulting from confusion between the present positive sexual intimacy and his past negative sexual abuse. Or when he has his own children, concern about his past sexual behavior may be activated. Such concerns were addressed, with possible interventions and resources defined.

The parents felt they had learned so much in this difficult experience that they instituted a sexual abuse prevention education program at their church for the families and children in the congregation.

Follow-up check-in sessions were scheduled at 3 months and 6 months after graduation to confirm Peter's ongoing positive behavior.

FUTURE DIRECTIONS

This chapter argues for the family systems perspective in understanding and treating the adolescent sex offender—a critical point of intervention in sexual abuse. It offers a critique of the current state of clinical knowledge from a theoretical and clinical perspective. The family is suggested as a usually available, important, but underused clinical resource. Practical strategies for increasing family involvement in therapy are offered.

No attempt is made to review the many schools of family therapy that contribute to this clinical issue. However, two schools are suggested as examples of the rich possibilities available to clinicians. Structural family therapy has much to offer, especially due to its success with low socioeconomic families, juvenile misconduct, and ethnically/racially diverse families. Minuchin and Fishman (1981) demonstrate how to turn an institution for boys into a treatment for families—a lesson that many juvenile offender institutions could learn.

Strategic family therapies offer creative ways to deal with the resistance and persistence in families. Other models to consider are contextual family therapy and behavioral family therapy. (For an excellent overview of family therapy, see Gurman & Kinskern, 1981, 1991.)

Levels in Family-Centered Treatment

In a nationwide survey of juvenile sex offender treatment programs, Knopp, Freeman-Longo, and Stevenson (1992) state that family therapy is used in the vast majority of juvenile sex offender programs. The survey did inquire about the degree of intensity of family therapy. The literature suggests that more intensive family-centered therapy is underutilized for two probable reasons: the current dominance of cognitive behavioral methods in sex offender treatment, and the individual and group therapy modalities that are the focus of most psychology and social work clinical programs. The following material will help the clinician understand how to build increased awareness and skills in family-based adolescent sex offender therapy logically.

Figure 6.2 is a prototypical developmental sequence for family-centered treatment as developed by Doherty and Baird (1986). Though first used in training family physicians and in research, this model has also been applied to the development of family-centered school psychologists (Doherty & Peskay, 1992).

This model can be used to assess adolescent sex offender therapists' current skills in family therapy and to encourage them to build on these skills. The model provides a series of levels based on the therapist's interest and competence in negotiating the therapist, client, and family therapeutic triangle. A knowledge base, personal development level, and course skills are delineated for each level. The model is adapted to the adolescent sex offender therapist with permission from the authors and the Society of Teachers of Family Medicine.

Each level of involvement can stand on its own as a valuable way for therapists to interact with families. Each level represents a knowledge base and set of skills to be mastered, which should not be discarded when a therapist becomes more sophisticated and moves to the next level.

A sense of competency and safety at one level sets the stage for the next, such as knowing how to talk about the facts of sexual abuse before talking about feelings that result from sexual abuse before moving into systemic family therapy. This developmental level paradigm helps avoid inappropriate attempts to use sophisticated family therapy "prescriptions" before having a solid base of family information and interaction patterns.

Family therapy is a promising area for future scholarly and clinical development in the field of juvenile sex offender treatment.

Level 1: Minimal Emphasis on Family

In this baseline level of involvement, the therapist deals with the family only as necessary for practical and legal reasons; communicating with the family is not integral to the therapist's role. The therapist who concentrates on the individual cognition and behavior of the adolescent offender is characterized as the sole conscious focus of change.

Level 2: Ongoing Therapeutic Information and Advice

Therapist's Knowledge Base: This stage is primarily information based, plus requires an awareness of the triangular dimension of the therapist, client, family relationship.

Therapist's Personal Development: Openness to engage clients and families in a collaborative way.

Therapist's Skills

1. Literally and clearly communicates therapy findings and treatment options to family members.
2. Asks family members questions that elicit relevant diagnostic and treatment information.
3. Attentively listens to family members' questions/concerns.
4. Advises families about how to handle the therapeutic needs of the client.
5. For large or demanding families, knows how to channel communication through one or two key members.
6. Identifies gross family dysfunction that interferes with treatment and refers the family to a family therapist.

Level 3: Feelings and Support

Therapist's Knowledge Base: Normal family development and reactions to stress.
Therapist's Personal Development: Awareness of one's own feelings in relationship to the patient and family.

Therapist's Skills

1. Asks questions that elicit family members' expressions of concerns and feelings related to the patient's condition and its effect on the family.
2. Empathetically listens to family members' concerns and feelings, and normalizes them when appropriate.
3. Forms a preliminary assessment of a family's level of functioning as it relates to the patient's problem.
4. Encourages family members in their efforts to cope as a family with their situation.
5. Tailors therapeutic advice to the unique needs, concerns, and feelings of the family.
6. Identifies family dysfunction and fits a referral recommendation to the unique situation of the family.

Figure 6.2. Levels of Therapist's Involvement With the Family in the Treatment of Adolescent Sex Offenders

SOURCE: Adapted from Doherty and Baird (1986) with permission from the authors and the Society of Teachers and Family Medicine.

Level 4: Systematic Assessment and Planned Intervention

Therapist's Knowledge Base: Family systems.

Therapist's Personal Development: Awareness of one's own participation in the systems, including the therapeutic triangle, the treatment system, one's own family system, and larger community systems.

Therapist's Skills

1. Engages family members, including reluctant ones, in a planned family conference or series of conferences.
2. Structures a conference even with a poorly communicating family in such a way that all members have a chance to express themselves.
3. Systematically assesses the family's level of functioning.
4. Supports individual members while avoiding coalitions.
5. Reframes the family's definitions of its problem in a way that makes problem solving more achievable.
6. Helps family members view their difficulty as requiring new forms of collaborative efforts.
7. Helps family members generate alternative, mutually acceptable ways to cope with their difficulty.
8. Helps the family balance its coping skills by calibrating the various roles in a way that allows support without sacrificing anyone's autonomy.
9. Identifies family dysfunction that lies beyond primary care treatment and orchestrates a referral by educating the family about what to expect from the therapist.

Level 5: Family Therapy

Therapist's Knowledge Base: Family systems and patterns whereby dysfunctional families interact with a therapist and other involved professionals.

Therapist's Personal Development: Ability to handle intense emotions in family and self to maintain neutrality in the face of strong pressure from family members or other professionals.

Therapist's Skills

Following is not an exhaustive list of family therapy skills but rather a list of key skills that distinguish level 5 involvement with families.

1. Interviews family members who are quite difficult to engage.
2. Generates a testing hypothesis about the family's difficulties and interaction patterns.
3. Escalates conflict in the family in order to break a family impasse.
4. Temporarily sides with one family member against another.
5. Constructively deals with a family's strong resistance to change.
6. Negotiates collaborative relationships with other professionals in other systems who are working with the family even when these groups are at odds with one another.

Figure 6.2. Continued

7

Victim-Sensitive Offender Therapy:
A Systemic/Attributional Perspective

THIS CHAPTER PRESENTS a new paradigm for understanding interpersonal violence: the systemic and attributional model (Bera, 1990).
A systemic and attributional critique of society's current response to
sexual abuse is presented and a victim-sensitive offender therapy
(VSOT) model is proposed as an essential part of comprehensive treatment for both victims and offenders.

A system perspective emphasizes the whole of a problem rather
than its parts (Bateson, 1972; Whitchurch & Constantine, 1993). It
emphasizes the contextual and interactional dynamics of abuse, the
behaviors of the offender-victim dyad. This "system view" points out
that, although the vast majority of sexual abuse occurs within intimate
family and social systems (i.e., between family members, relatives,
friends, or acquaintances), victims and offenders are generally treated
in a fragmented, inadequate, and isolated manner, ignoring the
context in which the abuse occurred. Furthermore, because both
victims and offenders verbalize and act on misattributions of responsibility, they can be most completely treated by coordinated victim
and offender communication and intervention in a carefully prepared,
safe, and controlled manner.

The VSOT model is not the entirety of sex offender treatment but
one part of the processes outlined in previous chapters. Offender-
victim interactions potentially have the most positive impact on

victims and offenders of any contact with the legal or social service systems. But if such interactions are not utilized or if they are done primarily for the offender's benefit, they can have a profoundly negative impact on victims.

A primary goal of victim-sensitive offender-victim interactions is to empower victims while protecting their safety. A second goal is to enhance the offender's sense of responsibility for his or her actions while increasing the offender's awareness of the true impact of his or her actions on victims and others. A final goal is to maximize the potential for therapeutic closure between the offender and victim.

In VSOT, the treatment provider can carve out a role of being sensitive to the victim within the offender's social service, legal, psychological, and family milieu. That role involves using offender-oriented systems to address the victim's concerns about the offender's past, present, and possible future abusive behavior. The sex offender therapy provider clarifies his or her role by stating, "I'm your therapist, but I will also be sensitive to the victim's concerns in the course of therapy." Being sensitive to the victim's issues enables the therapist to maximize the potential positive outcomes for both parties.

In general, offenders and victims may get similar three-stage treatment: their treatment needs are assessed; individual and/or group therapy works toward confronting and correcting the clients' misattributions of responsibility (victim's self-blame or guilt, offender's victim or system blame); and clients write letters reflecting their new attributions and resulting feelings (confrontation letters by victims, apology letters by offenders).

The letters in many programs are not sent. The difference in this model is that the letters are sent. If the victim permits, the offender sends a letter of apology. If the victim and/or the parents choose to participate, meetings with the offender are held, enabling a real closure on the abuse experience rather than a symbolic one.

Further research is needed in the form of sensitively designed longitudinal studies on outcomes for both victims and offenders who participate in restorative offender-victim interactions. Early empirical studies on the positive impact of treatment strategies using victim-offender communication in the treatment of sexual abuse can be found in Yokley (1990). Outcome studies mediating other types of victim-offender conflict can be found in Umbreit and Coates (1992).

Although the model presented here is for juvenile sex offenders, it has also been used with adult sex offenders as well as juvenile and adult sexual abuse victims. The treatment stages are significantly longer for adult offenders than for juveniles. This three-stage model can be applied to the task of organizing the multiple issues in sexual abuse cases in general.

CONTEXT AND CRITIQUE OF CURRENT APPROACHES

Sexual Abuse Occurs Within the Victim's Family or Social System

The majority of victims of sexual abuse are assaulted by someone they know and should be able to trust: a family member, a relative, a neighbor, or an acquaintance. More than 80% of all child victims are sexually abused by people known to them. Parents, stepparents, or relatives are responsible for 30% to 50% of all cases, with neighbors, baby-sitters, or friends involved in most of the remainder (Finkelhor, 1986; Herman, 1992; Peters, 1976; Sgroi, 1975). In these studies, over one third of the assaults occurred in the child's home, whereas 20% occurred in the home of the offender. Adolescents and adult victims are more likely to encounter physical force or violence, usually in acquaintance or marital rape situations (Keller, 1980).

These studies demonstrate that incidents of forced, tricked, or manipulated sexual touch are usually committed by people who use their intimacy with the victim to perpetrate abusive behavior. Such incidents represent a fundamental breach of trust in society's most basic and precious relationships. These crimes of intimacy shake the victim's basic "faith in the world" and lead to the well-documented sequelae of abuse: victim guilt, shame, phobia, fear of risking intimacy, nightmares, and developmental disturbance (Briere, 1992a; Burgess & Holstrom, 1975; Finkelhor, 1986; Herman, 1992; Keller, 1980; Peters, 1976; Resick, 1993).

Treatment Is Often Fragmented,
Inadequate, and Isolated

The treatment perspective traditionally adopted by professionals working with victims or offenders focuses on the individual's personality or family background, thereby ascribing etiology and treatment strategies to individual psychological dynamics. Classic criminology suggests that the offender's personality develops from his or her sociocultural conditions and, indeed, ascribes the offender's criminal behavior to those conditions (Sutherland & Cressey, 1978). The sexual abuse event is divided into at least two parts—victim and offender—and leads to the kind of fragmented responses critiqued here.

Social service and criminal justice systems can respond to sex crimes in an inadequate, fragmented, and piecemeal fashion (Wilson & Pence, 1993). Typically, reports of child abuse are investigated by county child protection workers with the help of the police. If the offender is a family member (e.g., father), the offender is often removed from the home to avoid a traumatic and revictimizing experience for the victim.

In cases where the victims are adults, the police investigate the abuse while support may be provided by victim assistance programs or rape crisis center workers, where such programs are available.

Both child and adult victim cases are usually referred to the courts, where restraining orders and confidentiality laws (intended to protect the victim) and attorneys' strategic advice (intended to protect the alleged offender's rights) may further alienate the participants and exacerbate their trauma (Briere, 1992a).

"No talk" rules embodied in these legal devices increase the misattribution of responsibility: the victim assumes blame for the abuse and its consequences (often based on direct or indirect messages from the offender and/or other family members) while the offender (often aided by his or her lawyer) projects all blame onto the victim and paints him- or herself as the innocent victim of circumstance, a misunderstanding, or the system. Thus the adversarial legal process tends to cement countertherapeutic mindsets in victims and offenders (and often their therapists).

Although offenders may be ordered into treatment by the courts and may receive coordinated state- or county-funded services, a significant portion of sexual abuse victims receive no treatment for their abuse-related trauma (Sgroi, 1991). Officials often pay inadequate attention to the concerns of these victims. In cases where children are victims of extended family members or neighbors, the only help offered may be a pamphlet handed out after the evidentiary interview.

Although psychotherapy might help, often it is unavailable or too expensive. Many parents do not pursue professional help because of embittering experiences with the system and conflicted loyalties to the offender. Child sexual abuse forms the largest category of all reported sex crimes, yet of the offenders with whom we have worked, only a minority of victims has any contact with a professional therapist.

Although adult victims may receive help from rape crisis centers (available primarily in urban settings), the victim must actively search out the services and maintain therapy for complete treatment. For a number of reasons, however, rape crisis centers often fail to provide adequate support. In most cases they define their mission in terms of crisis management and advocacy rather than treatment. Although this constitutes a necessary first step, it is incomplete as a therapeutic process (Briere, 1992a).

After the abuse report and if there is a confession or legally "sufficient" evidence, sex offenders may be placed in a criminal "correctional" facility or residential treatment facility, or court ordered into outpatient treatment as a condition of probation. Usually some combination of the above is recommended. Prison and residential treatment facilities usually treat the offender in isolation from the community, using an individual and group therapy format (Swartz, 1989).

Even in incest cases there is often no sensitive opportunity for the victim to express his or her issues vis-à-vis the offender—no forum is offered for the victim to develop a therapeutic sense of power. Often, the next time the victim hears about the offender after the initial investigation or trial is through an announcement of the offender's impending release. "Untreated" victims may contact rape crisis centers or mental health clinics for help at this time.

Generally, victims and offenders are treated together in outpatient programs only if both are members of an intact nuclear family (Gelinas, 1988). If there has been a divorce or the victims arc outside the immediate family, attempts at achieving a therapeutic resolution of the abuse between the victim and offender are rarely made. In extra-familial pedophilia and rape, the victim is not considered a part of treatment and no attempts are made to confront the issues between the two people most involved.

In contrast to current fragmented isolated treatment modes, Gulotta and deCataldo-Neuberger (1983) argue for a very different, holistic perspective: a systemic and attributional approach to the whole field of criminology and victimology:

> It should be no longer concentrated only on the victim's [or offender's] personality and on his sociocultural condition, but should embrace the dyad, criminal-victim, a system which cannot be separated without inciting the same criticism aimed at all psychological currents of individualistic trend. (p. 5)

MISATTRIBUTION ISSUES FOR OFFENDERS AND VICTIMS

Offender Misattributions: Blaming Victims, Excusing Themselves

Attribution theory was developed within the field of social psychology and offers a useful perspective on sexual abuse. As Kelley and Thibaut (1969) define it, "Attribution theory describes the process by which the individual seeks and attains conceptions of the stable dispositions or attributes" (p. 5).

An action such as sexual abuse can be attributed to causes in the environment or in the situation, or to the underlying dispositions of the persons involved. The mainstay of the attributional process is that "intent" is imputed rather than observed. Heider (1958) was the first to call the attention of psychologists to the fact that actions are controlled more by how an event is perceived than by what actually happens.

Offender misattributions are well documented in the literature. Scully and Marolla (1984) interviewed 114 convicted male rapists to examine the motivations and attributions they used to explain their behavior. They report that these convicted rapists' attributions of blame or minimization to the victim fall into five major categories: women are seductresses, women mean "yes" and say "no," most women eventually relax and enjoy it, nice girls do not get raped, and the sexual assault is only a minor wrongdoing.

Similar attributions of fault to the victim are also found in various analog studies using male and female college undergraduates (Shotland & Goodstein, 1983) and medical students (Gilmartin, 1983). A possible explanation for the similarity of attribution to the victim by diverse subject pools is posited by Lerner (1980). He theorizes that people are inclined to believe in a "just world," a place where individuals "get what they deserve and deserve what they get."

According to this belief, the quality of "goodness" or "evil" is attributed to the personality or the behavior that brings about the good or the evil result. In order to maintain their view of the world as "just," people need such attributions of fault—or a negative disposition—to victims. If bad things can happen to good people, the same could happen to them. The "just world" view thus becomes "defensive attribution."

Study subjects attribute fault to sexual abuse victims regardless of age. Using scenarios involving child and adolescent victims with an adult offender, Waterman and Foss-Goodman (1984) replicated many of the adult and peer assault victim-blaming results. Regardless of the victim's age (7, 11, or 15 years) and the offender's adult status, respondents placed some responsibility for the sexual abuse on the victim. The major reason respondents gave for blaming child victims was, "The victims should have resisted." Significantly, subjects also blamed the nonparticipating parents of the victims because they "should have protected the victim" or they in some way contributed to the victimizing event.

Both subject characteristics and victim characteristics relate to how much victims are blamed. Respondents whose answers exhibit sexual conservatism and acceptance of interpersonal violence are more likely to find fault with the victim's behavior. Subjects who report histories as victims of molestation blame victims less than subjects who do not report such past incidents. Waterman and Foss-Goodman further suggest that "blaming the victims may contribute to a climate conducive to child-molesting" (1984, p. 347). A better understanding of the determinants of victim blaming may lead to strategies for changing these attitudes.

Scully and Marolla's (1984) findings also include rapists who admit responsibility for their behavior. These men developed excuses permitting them to view their behavior as idiosyncratic rather than typical; therefore they believe that they are not really rapists.

The men's self-attributions sort into three main categories: they were under the influence of alcohol or drugs and thereby had diminished responsibility for the rape; their act was a result of emotional problems that diminished their responsibility; and they painted an image of themselves as "nice guys" in an attempt to minimize the crime and negotiate a nonrapist identity.

Admitters project the image of someone who has made a serious mistake, but who in every other respect is a decent person. Their severe minimization of the effects of the abuse and their responsibility for them is readily apparent. Scully and Marolla (1984) note that this lack of personal acceptance of responsibility is fertile ground for the development of future sexual misconduct.

In Waterman and Foss-Goodman (1984), respondents attribute blame to the adult offender in child sexual abuse scenes for the following reasons (in descending frequency of report): the offender abused power, the offender was "sick," the offender was morally wrong, adults should know better, and the offender must have ignored the victim's protests.

In the same study, respondents attribute fault to the nonparticipating mother and father of the victim because the parents should not have left the child alone, the parents should have taught the child how to prevent abuse, and the parents did not elicit the child's ability to confide in them.

Furthermore, when the offender is the spouse of the parent, the nonabusive parent (usually the mother) is faulted for not sexually satisfying the offending spouse, not teaching the child how to prevent abuse, and not being the kind of parent in whom the child could confide.

Work continues on offender misattribution. Pollock and Hashmall (1991) focused on the themes and structures of the excuses of 86 child molesters and found similar results as the studies described above.

Misattributions by Victims:
Guilt and Self-Blame

Numerous studies (Burgess & Holmstrom, 1975; Herman, 1992; Landis, 1956; Peters, 1976; Sgroi, 1991) have found that child victims of sexual abuse tend to keep the secret from their parents because they feel the abuse is in some way their own fault and they fear rejection, blame, punishment, or abandonment for this confusing and often terrifying event.

The personal and psychological effects on the victim and family can be multiple: fear of safety at home, eating and/or sleeping disturbances, nightmares, learning disorders, and numerous other symptoms that are now suggested as constituting "post-sexual abuse trauma syndrome" (Briere, 1984, 1992b).

Because of the many attributional dynamics and their serious consequences, therapists who work with sexual abuse victims emphasize that the sexual abuse is never the victim's fault, that it is serious, and that victims may experience it as life threatening. Becoming angry about the abuse and going through a grieving process are therapeutic for the victim in "letting go" of the abuse events (Herman, 1992). Developing a sense of self-control and mastery over their own life situations is enhanced by such techniques as assertiveness training and self-defense classes (Bera, 1980).

These misattribution-laden mindsets on the part of both victims and offenders warrant coordinated assessment and treatment planning that benefits the clients, families, and professionals involved. Unfortunately, few current treatment approaches provide such a holistic approach. Most fail to offer any therapeutic closure options for the individuals most involved and affected by the abuse events: the victim and offender.

Systemic Perspectives
for Victim-Offender Issues

A systemic and contextually based process involving controlled interaction between the victim and offender is a common therapeutic strategy in incest treatment (Goodwin, 1982; Trepper & Barrett, 1986). This process is coordinated by the family therapist and provides critical information and therapeutic experiences for completing treatment in a systematic way. This process empowers the victim with additional information, a sense of safety and respect, and choices that can lead to a more satisfying and complete resolution of the abuse.

Gelinas (1988) emphasizes that individual and group therapy for trauma "is necessary but not sufficient to resolve the negative effects of incest on the victim's life. It is also therapeutically essential to work with the particular relational issues surrounding incestuous child sexual abuse" (p. 5). These issues are worked through with face-to-face family therapy that includes both the offender and the victim.

Another example of a systemic approach aimed at increasing appropriate avenues for therapeutic closure is the victim-offender reconciliation programs (VORPs) that have existed for a number of years (Knopp et al., 1976; Umbreit, 1985; Wright & Galaway, 1989). These programs bring victims and offenders together in a controlled, safe, and supervised process, and have been used successfully in robbery, assault, vandalism, and other crimes (Green, 1984). A body of literature and a number of professional associations have been developed within the VORP movement.

Concerns regarding the VORP approach focus on the inappropriateness of using a reconciliation or mediation model in crimes of interpersonal violence because of the significant power disparity between offender and victim. "Mediation" and "reconciliation" imply that two sides compromise and agree on some middle ground. The movement recognizes that such language is clearly inappropriate in cases of sexual abuse or physical violence.

This process is more accurately portrayed in new language and conceptual frames (most clearly developed by Zehr, 1990) as seeking "restorative justice" when injustice has occurred. Sexual and physical abuse is an abuse of power and authority, most often from a position of trust, over a vulnerable and available victim. The aim of VSOT is to empower the victim and restore justice by having the offender take responsibility for the offense and offer appropriate contrition, restitution, and apologies in a personal and meaningful way. (For a detailed history and discussions of these issues with illustrative cases, see Wright & Galaway, 1989.)

Victim-sensitive offender therapy attempts to be victim sensitive in both conceptualization and language. Ethically, it values the safety, rights, and needs of the victim as a primary aspect of offender treatment.

In workshops on the VSOT model, the traditional training of therapists, psychologists, and social workers is challenged because the issues of sexual abuse are outside the boundaries of discrete "disciplines" and demand a holistic or systemic view. Such a view helps overcome the dilemmas forced by "normally defined" disciplines while safely attempting a more complete therapeutic resolution of interpersonal violence.

An overview of those involved in many sexual abuse cases is presented in Figure 6.1. Sexual abuse connects the offender and victim and, as a result, their respective families.

The professional system includes the legal, criminal justice, social service, and therapeutic professionals connected to the victim or the offender. Because of the recognition of the involvement of these professionals in child sexual abuse, many counties have multidisciplinary child abuse teams to develop effective coordinated responses (Wilson & Pence, 1993). The VSOT model recognizes the need for coordinated treatment beyond simple investigation of the abuse.

Treatment Description

Systemic or multisystemic approaches represent today's most promising direction for sex offender treatment and control strategies (Freeman-Longo & Knopp, 1992). For example, Pithers et al.'s (1989) modified relapse prevention model integrates the offender system and professional system depicted in Figure 6.1. The model and its advantages are reviewed in chapter 6.

Victim-sensitive offender therapy was designed to overcome the aforementioned systemic dilemmas while redefining the VORP or mediation model from a victim-sensitive, ethical, safety, and rights position more appropriate for sexual offense treatment. It adds the victim system to the modified relapse prevention model.

To use this model, therapists working with sex offenders need to view the rights, feelings, and safety of the victim(s) (or potential victims) of their client's behavior as a primary concern. At the same time, therapists must avoid jeopardizing the rights of the offender. This ethical posture should guide every view, insight, and decision the therapist makes regarding the offender.

STRENGTHS OF THE VSOT MODEL AND VICTIM-OFFENDER COMMUNICATION MODELS IN GENERAL

Although the VSOT model runs counter to traditional, individually focused treatments, it is a logical consequence of a systemic, ethical, and attributional analysis of sexual abuse and has the following strengths.

1. The model keeps the offender fully responsible for his abusive behavior.
2. The model minimizes misattribution of fault to the victim.
3. The therapist is prevented from inadvertently colluding with the offender against the victim because of limited data, coming primarily from the offender.
4. The model keeps the offender out of trouble by confronting early on any malicious gossip and indirect "get-backs" directed against the victim or family.
5. The therapist maintains a clear ethical perspective throughout treatment, minimizing confusion at decision points.
6. The model maintains a victim-offender system view throughout that can maximize the degree of therapeutic closure for both victim and offender.
7. The model helps ensure completeness of treatment for the offender and thereby minimizes the potential for victimizing behavior.
8. The model gives the therapist more complete information at each stage to make sound treatment plans by supplementing traditional reliance on the offender's self-report with ongoing victim input.
9. The therapist is able to maintain a high level of credibility with other involved professionals (e.g., judge, child protection worker, social worker, probation/parole supervisor) by keeping the victim's interest at heart and soliciting the input of all concerned.

Yokley (1990), writing on sexual abuse victim-offender communication intervention models, summarizes a number of potential benefits for the victim:

1. The victim receives assurance of the reality of the abuse.
2. The victim feels relief of guilt/self-blame.
3. The victim has the means for appropriate expression of anger.
4. The victim can reconsider (misattributed) responsibility and empowerment through confrontation.

The offender can potentially benefit in the following ways (Yokley, 1990):

1. The offender accepts responsibility.
2. The offender develops victim empathy and awareness.
3. The victim earns emotional restitution.

Cautions and Guidelines

Yokley (1990) offers a number of guidelines for victim-offender communication interventions:

1. Victim safety and benefit is primary.
2. Victim-offender communication interventions should always be voluntary, at the victim's discretion, and in the victim's best interest.
3. Victim-offender communication interventions should involve only treated offenders who accept full responsibility and are remorseful.
4. The offender and the victim should be carefully prepared.
5. The offender should use responsible, victim-sensitive language.
6. The victim can be empowered and supported through early provision of information about the offender. This improves the victim's understanding of the offender's behavior.
7. Apology sessions should be timed prior to the end of offender therapy. It should be clear to the offender that further rehabilitation and supervision is often warranted.
8. Only trained sexual abuse professionals should be used.

THE VSOT PROCESS

The three-stage VSOT process was originally developed in the Program for Healthy Adolescent Sexual Expression (PHASE) and continues to be refined. Chapter 6 provides a description of concurrent clinical treatment of offenders' sexually abusive behavioral patterns. A brief description of the VSOT process follows.

Ideally, the VSOT process should be undertaken only after the offender has pled guilty and no lawsuits are contemplated by the involved parties. If either the victim or the offender has unusual life events or stresses, VSOT should be delayed to a more appropriate time. Examples of such stresses include significant thought disorder, psychiatric mental illness such as active schizophrenia, manic-depression, major depression, or unremitting rage or anger at the offender that precludes any chance of nonabusive communication. Such anger is most likely if a parent of the victim has been a victim himself or herself and has significant unresolved abuse, shame, and rage. There is no way to predict or guarantee the participants' behavior and foster reasonable expectations. Both the victim and the offender have the right to stop at any point in the process. Clinical judgment and the circumstances of each case should guide the application of this or any resolution model.

A summary of the VSOT process appears in Figure 7.1.

Stage 1: Communication Switchboard

The first stage sets the context and expectations for the assessment and VSOT process. At intake or shortly after the juvenile sex offender begins the assessment process, the therapist assumes a central role as communication coordinator or "switchboard" among all concerned participants, including the probation officer, previous therapists, the offender, and the victim (or parents of victims who are underage). The therapist explains the VSOT model, its stages and goals, and why certain information must be shared with other treatment personnel, agencies, the victim, his or her family, and their therapist.

The offender (or parents/guardian) signs release forms allowing the therapist to get the offender's police statements and to contact the victim(s) (or parents/guardian). This is the point at which the therapist clarifies to the client, "I'm your therapist, but I am also sensitive to the victim's concerns." Just as the family therapist is challenged to maintain multiple roles that must be clarified in the course of therapy, the VSOT therapist must openly clarify his or her roles with the victim and the offender.

Stage 1: "Switchboard" (intake to 2 months)
  A. Process for Offender
    1. Offender (or guardian) signs releases of information for:
       a. Victim and offender's police/child protection statements
       b. Permission to contact victim(s) (or parents/guardian)
  B. Process for Victim
    1. Therapist initiates contact with victim (or parents/guardian). Therapist answers questions, provides support for reporting, lets victim know disposition of case and offender's current status (i.e., on probation and in treatment).
    2. Therapist discusses victim's need for treatment of abuse effects and provides current information and therapy referral.
    3. Therapist solicits reports of offender's ongoing intrusive behaviors and responds with appropriate measures to curb them.
    4. Therapist explains the purpose of release-of-information forms, requests cooperation, and sends release form to victim (or parents/guardian).
  C. Goals
    1. To complete a contextually sensitive offender assessment.
    2. To ensure a complete and therapeutic exchange of all abuse-relevant information among involved systems and persons.
    3. To establish the identity of the VSOT therapist as the victim's advocate within the offender's milieu.
    4. To enlist victim's (et al.) involvement in the VSOT process.

Stage 2: Confront Misattributions and Check Progress (3-5 months)
  A. Process for Offender
    1. Therapist checks offender's misattributions toward victim(s) or system.
       a. Offender fully accepts blame/responsibility for acting on his decision to abuse.
       b. Offender clearly knows effects of abuse on victim.
       c. Offender owns full responsibility for abuse consequences to himself.
    2. Offender completes a sexual abuse biography and writes a clear letter of apology to the victim(s) (and victim's parents) for his abusive behavior.
  B. Process for Victim
    1. Therapist checks progress of victim therapy.
    2. Therapist provides needed information and a progress report of offender to victim and/or guardians.
  C. Goals
    1. To confront any continued sexual abuse misattributions.
    2. To complete a progress assessment of the offender and victim.
    3. To revise the treatment plan and closure expectations in preparation for Stage 3.

Stage 3: Closure Choices (6-12+ months)
  A. Process for Victim(s) (or Parents)
    1. Choose closure option.
       a. Offender continues a no contact contract with victim (and family).
       b. Offender mails a letter of apology to the victim.
       c. Offender attends a face-to-face closure meeting with the victim (and family), reads apology letter, answers questions.

Figure 7.1. Overview of the VSOT Process

2. Prepare for closure.
   a. Victim processes new questions and feelings.
   b. Victim clarifies expectations.
   c. Victim chooses ways to make the meeting room (if closure meeting is chosen)/home/neighborhood/school feel safe.
B. Process for Offender (and family)
   1. Offender understands and complies with the expressed choices of the victim(s) (or parents).
C. Goals
   1. Offender faces the personal effects of his abusive behavior and makes apology.
   2. Victim develops a sense of personal closure and control.

Figure 7.1. Continued

The communication switchboard stage allows the VSOT therapist to do a complete and contextually sensitive assessment of his or her client by getting all sides of the sexual abuse experience. Only a small minority of teenage sex offenders are completely honest about their sexual abuse or fully recognize the effects of the abuse on their victim(s), but they often are open to their therapist contacting the victim in hopes of making therapeutic progress and increasing the potential for achieving closure.

The VSOT therapist calls the victim(s) (or parents/guardian) to let them know the disposition of the case (e.g., "Frank pled guilty and is now on probation; he's in our outpatient treatment program."). It is not unusual for a long period of time to have passed since the abuse report, and victims may wonder about the results of the investigatory or legal process. This telephone call is often the first concrete information the victim has received about the offender since the investigation or trial.

In this phone call, the therapist supports the victim or parents for reporting the abuse, despite any frustrating or traumatizing interactions they may have had with the social service and/or legal systems. In our experience, only about 25% of the victims or their concerned persons who are contacted have been involved in any kind of therapy. Often they are embittered by the investigatory and legal process they have gone through, and do not trust asking for further "professional" help. During the time since the investigation, however, new thoughts or concerns may have come to mind that they may wish to share with a therapist.

The VSOT therapist educates parents about the need for victim treatment, where and from whom they can get it, and how it can be funded (victim-assistance programs, victim compensation, and/or restitution provisions in the offender's sentence). The VSOT therapist solicits any concerns the victim and/or parents have about the abuse, the victim's trauma-based behavior changes, or continued emotionally intrusive behavior by the offender. The therapist helps the parents sort out their primary concern (helping the victim heal) from their feelings of loss of relationship to the offender or the offender's family.

Because the offender is usually a neighbor or family member, some level of emotionally intrusive behavior may be continuing: The baby-sitter offender rides his bike past the victim's house every day; the two families encounter each other every Sunday at 9 o'clock Mass; gossip targeting the victim as "promiscuous" or "easy" haunts the victim at school. The VSOT therapist justifies the victim's trust and confidence in him or her by intervening whenever possible through alterations in the offender's behavior contract or amplified interpretations of existing court orders.

The VSOT therapist encourages the victim to ask any questions about the abuse he or she would like the offender to answer and to continue reporting any inappropriate offender behavior. By talking with the offender's therapist and seeing results, the victim may develop a sense of power and control of his or her situation. Ideally, the victim feels that what he or she went through then—and is currently experiencing—is important and is finally being heard.

The victim and/or parents have a direct impact on the offender's treat- ment by providing corroborating or contradictory evidence regarding the offender's disclosure of offense behaviors, and by exposing the offender's subsequent intimidation or power/control behaviors.

After explaining that the information will be used to confirm or confront information in the offender's disclosure, the VSOT therapist asks the victim or parents/guardian to sign releases of information for copies of the victim's police statement and interview with the child protection services worker. If the victim is in therapy, the family is asked to give permission for the victim's therapist to consult with the VSOT therapist.

In this initial stage, the VSOT therapist begins to enlist the victim(s) and his or her concerned persons in an ongoing information-sharing and therapy process. The victim learns that her or she will be provided with information, options, and choices as needed, and that the VSOT therapist is a significant supportive contact within the offender's milieu who will be at the victim's service in the months to come.

Stage 2: Confront Misattributions and Check Progress

Stage 2 occurs 3 to 4 months into the treatment program. The offender must complete a verbal or written abuse biography detailing his history of abusive sexual behavior. The VSOT therapist checks this document for misattributions the offender continues to hold against the victim and determines whether the offender fully accepts blame/responsibility for deciding to engage in his abusive behavior, whether the offender clearly knows the effects of the abuse on the victim, and whether the offender accepts full responsibility for the consequences of his behavior to himself (in other words, he does not blame the victim or "the system" for where he is now). All three conditions must be met before going on to Stage 3.

After the offender completes the abuse biography, he writes a letter of apology to the victim and victim's parents to begin making amends for his crime. The offender reads his biography and letter in individual, group, and family therapy sessions. The offender's therapist, family, and/or treatment group may reject the documents.

The offender rewrites and/or rereads these documents until they are accepted as both convincing and sincere. Sincerity is assessed by looking at omissions of fact or feeling, victim-blaming language, or incongruent affect while the offender is reading. Any inappropriate content or incongruent affect is confronted with feedback from the therapist, family, and group ("If the victim were here listening to this, I don't think she'd/he'd believe you").

Writing the letter (often only one or two paragraphs) is usually more stressful for adolescent offenders than writing several pages of abuse biography, perhaps because the letter is a more personal and direct admission of responsibility.

If the victim is in therapy and has given permission, the VSOT therapist consults with the victim's therapist to check on the progress the victim has made. The consultation provides two-way "reality checking." First, the VSOT therapist can compare the effects of the abuse and the victim's memory of events with the offender's self-reported abuse biography. Second, the victim's therapist (or parents/guardian) can gain access to the offender's abuse biography and police statements as a reality check for the victim (especially valuable when the victim has dissociated during the abuse). New information from the offender may help explain victim behaviors or phobias that were not thought to be abuse related.

The offender should not be allowed contact with the victim until his biography and letters are approved, he shows no tendency to blame the victim, and the victim does not blame himself or herself.

Finally, the VSOT therapist provides a progress report on the offender's readiness to continue the process, offers other information that may be useful, and again solicits any questions the victim may have regarding the abuse.

Stage 2 has three major goals: to confront any continued sexual abuse misattributions, to complete a progress assessment of the offender and the victim, and to revise the offender's treatment plan and expectations in preparation for Stage 3.

These goals are important in developing plans and expectations for the level of closure the victim chooses in Stage 3. Offenders and victims and their families may have high hopes that the closure session will "fix" everything so that their lives can go back to "normal." The therapist must clearly outline what can be accomplished at each level of closure to prevent the victim or the offender from being disappointed or having a sense of failure. The VSOT therapist helps the victim and his or her family plan what to expect so they do not feel "used" in the process and to save the offender from an inappropriate blast of rage that could be countertherapeutic.

Stage 3: Closure Choices

Stage 3 may occur when the adolescent sex offender has been in treatment for 5 to 12 or more months. Closure is the last major task in the VSOT process. The offender is nearing completion of his other treatment components: His abuse biography and letters of apology have been accepted by his therapist, family, and peer treatment group; he accepts full responsibility for all aspects of his abusive behavior; and he has some understanding of the effects of his behavior on his victim.

The VSOT therapist contacts the victim (or his or her therapist and parents) to discuss the closure process. The VSOT therapist outlines three levels of closure and gives the victim time to decide which one he or she will choose.

1. The offender will continue to comply with the no contact contract into the future. The VSOT therapist makes a commitment on behalf of the offender that the contract will be honored, backing up that commitment with a promise that the therapist will relay any breaches of the contract to the offender's probation officer.
2. The offender will mail a letter of apology to the victim. The VSOT therapist offers (with the offender's informed consent) whatever closing information about the offender's process that the victim asks for or that might be helpful to him or her.
3. The offender (and his family, if appropriate) attend a face-to-face meeting in a setting the victim chooses with any support people the victim chooses. At the meeting, the offender reads his apology letter(s) to the victim and his or her family and answers their questions.

After hearing these choices and processing the ramifications of each, the victim chooses a route. In the process of choosing, the victim may develop new questions he or she wants the offender to answer and may experience new feelings and emotions to work through with his or her therapist.

Among the victim's options is changing his or her mind about closure choices at any time, including at the face-to-face meeting. Victims are invited to contact the VSOT therapist any time they have questions or want to talk about the abuse and feel the VSOT therapist may be helpful—even years after the event. Referring a therapist for the victim may be necessary as well.

The victim's therapist prepares the victim (and parents/guardian) for the closure meeting by reviewing questions and clarifying the family's expectations for the meeting. The therapist reaffirms that the offender is at fault and helps the victim choose how to make the

Stage 1 Therapist Letter
Following is the initial letter sent by the VSOT therapist to Tammy's parents.

Dear Theresa and Tom:

   Thank you again for spending so much time with me on the phone
this week telling me your side of what happened between Michael and
Tammy. I know that talking about the abuse again can be uncomfortable
and even painful. Yet it is just that detailed information of what
you know happened and the effects it had on Tammy and yourselves
that allows me to do a complete assessment and treatment plan. This
ensures that Michael is held fully accountable for his actions and
their consequences.
   Enclosed is a copy of the release-of-information form signed by
Michael's parents. I am glad I could answer questions you had concerning Michael and his therapy. Please call if other questions or concerns come up.
   Also enclosed is a release-of-information form for you. I would
like you to sign and return it in the stamped envelope. This will
confirm the verbal release you gave me this week so I can include
your information and concerns as part of the assessment and therapy
goals. A second release allows me to talk to Tammy's therapist.
   Finally, you will find a brief description of the victim-sensitive
offender therapy stages of treatment [Figure 7.1] that summarizes
the process in which Michael and you can participate, if you so
desire.
   Again, thank you. And do call if I can be of any help. I'll write
again as Michael approaches the last stage of his therapy.

       Respectfully,
       Walter Bera, LP

Stage 3 Therapist Letter
Note that many if not most cases in which the VSOT model is used are hindered by
the lack of an active victim therapist, and each case has unique features. Letters
need to be modified to reflect the actual circumstances of the case. Following is an
example of the letter from the VSOT therapist used in Stage 2.

Dear Theresa and Tom:

   Michael has been making steady progress over the last several
months. He will be completing the primary phase of treatment in the
next few months. I promised to write you at this point to provide
you with some options that you and Tammy might find personally helpful
or therapeutic.
   Part of Michael's tasks near the end of treatment is to write
letters of apology to you and Tammy—personal apologies he owes you

Figure 7.2. Therapist Letters in VSOT

for the sexual abuse he perpetrated. I would like to define some possible options for you that I reviewed with Tammy's therapist for your consideration.

1. You and Tammy can meet with Michael, his parents, and myself. You are in charge of who attends or does not attend. You can ask any questions you want and receive the letters personally. I suggest my own or Tammy's therapist's office as a neutral site, or you may choose any other site that you think might be appropriate.
2. You can receive the letters through the mail. Feel free to call me if you have any questions after receiving them.
3. You can continue the no contact contract.

Take some time to talk it over and call me if you have any questions or when you make your decision. When, where, and how you want to meet or receive the letters is completely your decision. My role is to attempt to provide options for healing or closure and convey or facilitate your wishes to Michael and his family.

I can be reached at 555-1212.

Respectfully,
Walter H. Bera

Figure 7.2. Continued

meeting room feel as safe as possible, including bringing favorite stuffed toys and providing seating arrangements.

The offender is also prepared for the closure choice the victim has made. The VSOT therapist asks the offender any questions raised by the victim and relays the answers. The no-contact contract is continued, the letters are sent, or the meeting is scheduled. The VSOT therapist prepares the offender emotionally for the meeting, if that is the victim's closure choice.

The goal of Stage 3 is to facilitate the most complete therapeutic closure possible, given the specific circumstances and personalities of all involved. The case example that follows is a simplified composite. Baby-sitter offenders may molest children in several families, but to focus on the process, this history concentrates on just one victim family.

Case Example

Michael was a 15-year-old boy living with his mother and 10-year-old brother in a college neighborhood. His parents had divorced 8 years before, and his father moved to another state soon after. The children continued to see their father for extended visits and on holidays. Michael's mother, Mindy, was an instructor in the college's English department and the custodial parent of Michael and his brother.

Michael had always been characterized as very family centered, shy, and sensitive. He also was considered a good baby-sitter and regularly cared for the neighbors' 5-year-old girl, Tammy.

Suspicions were aroused when Tammy told her mother that her "gina" hurt, and her mother observed some irritation around Tammy's vaginal area. In answering questions, Tammy made it clear that Michael had been sexually abusing her under the rules of a "special and secret game."

Shocked, Tammy's mother called Child Protection Services for advice. A social worker interviewed Tammy and there was a follow-up medical exam. The police interviewed Michael who, after considerable questioning, admitted a few instances of fondling. The police told Michael not to contact Tammy. The two families stopped communicating as well.

After Michael's limited offense disclosure, the courts sent Michael and his family to PHASE for assessment. He and his family were accepted for the initial PHASE assessment/education program. In Stage 1, during the first month of treatment, the therapist explained that releases of certain information were needed in order to do a complete assessment and to inform Tammy's parents that Michael and his family were involved in therapy. Michael and his mother signed releases of information for the therapist to receive copies of Michael's statements to the police. They also gave permission for the therapist to contact Tammy's parents to find out how Tammy and her parents were doing and to begin a potential process of healing.

After receiving the signed releases, the VSOT therapist called Tammy's parents, Tom and Theresa, the next day. Theresa answered and the VSOT therapist explained who he was and let her know that Michael was currently in the assessment/education phase of an adolescent sex offender treatment program. He also explained that Michael and his mother had signed releases of information so the therapist could talk to Theresa and Tom about Michael's case. The VSOT therapist followed up with a letter detailing the conversation (see Figure 7.2).

Theresa said she was thankful the therapist had called because there had been no communication between the two families since the investigation 3 months before. The family had been concerned about how Michael was doing and wondered if Mindy was mad at them for reporting the abuse and if there was any new information on what Michael had done to Tammy.

The therapist told Theresa that Michael was slowly opening up and that Mindy was not angry at them, but there was little new information on the abuse itself since Michael was just beginning the program. The therapist assured Theresa that she and Tom would receive new information as it came out in Michael's therapy.

Tom and Theresa shared information about Tammy's reactions to the abuse that had manifested since the initial investigation. Tammy had remembered more abuse incidents involving Michael. She had nightmares, enuresis, and phobias that appeared to be abuse related. Tammy's parents asked for a therapy referral, saying that they were beginning to realize that the abuse had more of an effect on her—and on them—than they first thought. Theresa disclosed that she had been a victim of sexual abuse herself as a child; she worried about whether that had "contributed" to her not seeing or realizing that Tammy was being sexually abused. Tom wanted to know whether the *Playboy* magazines he had in the bedroom might have been used in Michael's abuse of Tammy.

The VSOT therapist assured Tom and Theresa that this new information would be used in Michael's assessment and that their specific questions would be followed-up in the course of Michael's therapy. They were referred to a victim therapist who was comfortable working with an offender therapist. The VSOT therapist asked the family to sign release forms allowing him to get copies of Tammy's statements to the Child Protection Services worker. The victim therapist asked the family to sign releases of information so she could consult with the VSOT therapist. After hearing why it was necessary, Tom and Theresa agreed to sign.

During Stage 2 (Michael had been in treatment just over 3 months), Tammy disclosed more specific details of the abuse to her parents and therapist, who relayed the information to the VSOT therapist. The VSOT therapist confronted Michael with the new information, and he finally admitted a 2-year history of regular sexual contact with

Tammy, including fondling, oral sex, and "humping" Tammy until he ejaculated. Michael wrote an abuse biography detailing his new information on how he abused Tammy. He had, for example, abused Tammy in the bathroom, and this information helped explain Tammy's fear of the bathroom and her enuresis. After the VSOT therapist shared this information with Tammy's therapist and parents, who talked about it with Tammy, Tammy's bathroom phobia and enuresis stopped.

Michael expressed increased remorse as he realized that his abusive actions were having long-term effects on Tammy and her family, as well as on him and his family. In addition, he clarified that while he did use one of Tom's *Playboy* magazines in the course of abusing Tammy, he had discovered them after he had already started his abuse behavior.

Michael was now able to write sincere letters of apology to Tammy and to Tom and Theresa. In family therapy, Michael made a heartfelt apology to his mother for all he had put her through. Mindy said she forgave him and told him she was satisfied with his progress so far. She also said she was glad to know that Tammy, Tom, and Theresa's needs were taken into consideration in the therapy process.

The VSOT therapist contacted Tammy, Tom, and Theresa's therapist to give a progress report on Michael and to let the family know that they could receive his letters of apology at the end of Michael's therapy, if they wished. Tammy's therapist reported that Theresa was dealing with her own childhood sexual abuse in the course of Tammy's victim therapy, but that Theresa's childhood sexual abuse trauma did not add an additional emotional burden to Tammy's experience. In fact, processing Tammy's experience of abuse was helping Theresa work through something she had buried for years.

The VSOT therapist wrote Tom and Theresa, along with Tammy's therapist, to outline their closure options: continuing a no contact contract, receiving Michael's letters of apology through the mail, or having a face-to-face process session with Michael (see Figure 7.2). The VSOT therapist talked to Tammy's therapist before sending the letter and offered to answer any questions Tammy's parents might have about their closure options. Tom and Theresa, after talking with Tammy's therapist and Tammy, decided they wanted a face-to-face meeting in Tammy's therapist's office.

The goals of Stage 2 were completed with the progress assessment of Michael and Tammy. The treatment plan and expectations were revised accordingly.

Michael was assessed as being ready to prepare for closure. He was demonstrating remorse for his actions in the content of his abuse biography and letters, by complying with treatment plan and program contracts, and by expressing worry about Tammy's welfare. His language in therapy had shifted from blaming Tammy and Child Protection Services for his current problems to accepting responsibility for both his abusive actions and their consequences to himself. In fact, Michael went a little overboard, turning "accepting responsibility" into self-blame and self-hate. He became very depressed for a short time until he was reminded that, although he had done something very wrong, he was now in the process of making amends. At this time, he rewrote and reread his abuse biography and letters and they were accepted by his therapist, his mother, and his offender-treatment group (see Figure 7.3). Michael's treatment plan was revised to focus on encouraging him to provide honest, open answers to the questions Tammy and her parents had asked and on preparing for the in-person closure meeting.

Tammy's therapist used play therapy, among other techniques, to create an environment safe enough for Tammy to talk more freely about Michael's abuse. Including Tammy's mother in some sessions was an important step in showing Tammy that, despite what Michael had told her, she had not been "bad" and would not be punished or abandoned for breaking the secret-keeping rules of Michael's "game." It was explained to Tammy that Michael broke the rules in making her play such a mean game with him and making her keep a secret that hurt her. Tammy expressed appropriate anger at Michael (represented by a male doll) for tricking her and making her keep "bad" secrets.

The therapist prepared Tammy for not ever being alone with Michael because he had done a hurtful thing. When Tammy expressed sadness that she would not get to play the "good" games with Michael any more, the therapist explained that Tammy's friends and family could not be positive that Michael would never hurt her again, and they wanted to keep her safe. The therapist asked Tammy if she would like Michael to say he was sorry for tricking her and hurting her, and Tammy said yes. The therapist, Tammy, and her parents worked on

some questions they wanted Michael to answer. The therapist relayed their questions to Michael's therapist.

In Stage 3, after Michael had been in therapy for 8 months, a meeting was arranged at Tammy's therapist's office. The meeting format
was agreed on in consultation between the parents, Tammy's therapist,
and the VSOT therapist. Michael would take the initiative in reviewing his abuse biography and answering any questions asked by Tom,
Theresa, or Tammy. Michael was prepared for the meeting with role
plays in his offender-treatment group. Tammy's therapist prepared
her clients at the same time, working on their questions and what
they could reasonably expect from the closure session.

Tammy and her parents arrived at their therapist's office ½ hour
before the scheduled meeting time so they could feel settled, comfortable, and in control before Michael, Mindy, and the VSOT therapist
arrived. Michael and his support people arrived and were seated facing Tammy's family and therapist. After the VSOT therapist reviewed
the structure of the meeting, Michael began.

With the help of his therapist, Michael summarized his abuse biography. Michael and his therapist answered Tammy's, Tom's, and
Theresa's questions as they arose. As Michael read his letter of apology to Tammy, he started to cry, saying he felt really bad because he sin-
cerely liked Tammy and realized how he had used her affection for
him to hurt her, as well as abusing Tom and Theresa's trust. Tammy appeared unmoved—she could not seem to believe that Michael, who
had been in such a position of power over her, was reduced to tears
and guilt. The VSOT therapist offered Michael's letter of apology to
Tammy, and she accepted it. After she looked at the letter, Tammy
asked her mother to hold it for safekeeping.

Michael read his letter of apology to Tom and Theresa, who gra-
ciously accepted it. Tammy said that the abuse was not her fault but
Michael's, and her statement was confirmed first by Michael and
then by all the participants. Tammy said she was glad he had gotten
the help that he needed, especially because she had been worried he
might do it to other little girls. Tom and Theresa were satisfied with
the process and relieved to get information they needed. They also
said that they forgave Michael. Mindy observed that she and Michael
had grown closer as a result of facing Michael's abusive behavior.

Dear Tammy,

    I don't know what words to use. I'm sorry for sexually abusing you. It wasn't your fault in any way, it was all mine. It will never ever happen again to you or any one else. I hope this letter will help in overcoming the bad experiences I put you through.

          Sincerely,
          Michael

Dear Mr. and Mrs. Smith,

    I'm very sorry for sexually abusing your daughter. You don't have to believe me, and I will not go on and on and try to say I'm sorry the amount of times it would take to heal your wounds. I don't think there are any words that can describe the deep feeling of hate in my heart for the things I did. I really am very sorry, and I hope that in time you won't hate me. But if you do, I can't blame you. I did such a bad thing, I just can't express my feelings of how very sorry I really am.

          Sincerely,
          Michael

Figure 7.3. Michael's Letters of Apology

    The families discussed what level of contact would be appropriate in the future. They clarified that it would take some time to trust Michael fully but that they wished to continue to communicate as neighbors, with the parents freely exchanging phone calls. Both families agreed that Michael could never again be placed in a position of trust with Tammy. This session ended with handshakes, and a few weeks later Michael graduated from PHASE.

TREATMENT RESULTS

    The VSOT program was designed to be victim sensitive throughout the treatment process. At the time of the initial assessment, the safety of the victim is put foremost during offender placement recommendations. Throughout the program, language is encouraged that benefits the victim by confronting all offender misattributions and by teaching offenders to use self-responsible language. During the final closure choices, sensitivity to the victim involves restoring power and control by having the victim decide what type of closure will occur and where and with whom it will take place.

Following is a summary of closure choices made in the VSOT program over a 3-year period, categorized by offense type. The closure method chosen can usually be predicted by the frequency of contact and degree of intimacy between the offender/family and the victim/ family prior to the abuse disclosure.

Sexual Abuse Within the Nuclear Family (Incest)

The vast majority of incest cases are resolved with a face-to-face closure meeting between the offender and his younger siblings. This is typical of the practice now used with family-based incest treatment programs. A handful end with a letter of apology (see Figure 7.4) when the family has other abusive or very disorganized features or the offender (or victim) has been rejected by the family and is in an out-of-home placement.

Sexual Abuse by an Extended Family Member (Incest)

This type of sexual abuse typically occurs in a baby-sitting situation or family gathering, where an uncle or cousin takes advantage of his niece/nephew or other related child. The majority of these cases end with a face-to-face reconciliation meeting. Some end with letters of apology (see Figure 7.4), usually because the victim's family lives some distance from the offender's family and they have only occasional contact.

Sexual Abuse by a Neighbor

A minority of cases in this category resolve in face-to-face meetings. Those that do commonly involve the next-door neighbor, a close family friend, or others who live very near to the family and where there are firm social ties with regular contact. Less intimate

The following letters were written by adolescent sex offenders who participated in PHASE. They are for illustrative purposes only. These letters should be written in language that is clear and sensitive to the age and needs of the recipients. The letters are not complete or exhaustive in themselves, but are a part of the overall VSOT model.

Brother-Sister Incest
These letters were written by a 15-year-old boy to his 5-year-old sister and his parents.

Dear Nancy,

    I am very sorry for sexually abusing you. I took advantage of a trust that should not have been broken. This isn't at all your fault; it's all mine. I will work to make sure it will never happen again, because I love you and am getting help from Walter and the guys in the group.

    Love,
    Your Brother,
    David

Dear Mom and Dad,

    I'm very sorry for sexually abusing Nancy. I know it was hard on you both and still is. I will work to ensure that it will never happen again through the help I am receiving from Walter and the group; but the main reason is because I love you both and I don't want to hurt you or Nancy again.

    Love,
    Your Son,
    David

Extended-Family Sexual Abuse
This letter was written by a 16-year-old uncle to his 6-year-old nephew, who had trusted and loved him and feared he was angry at him for breaking the abuse secret.

Dear Bill,

    I'm sorry. I'm sorry that I sexually abused you. There are a few things I want you to know. First of all, I'm not mad at you for telling others about what I did to you. What happened was not your fault, and in this way, I will be able to get some help straightening myself out. What I did to you was very wrong, and the counseling I'm receiving now is helping me to realize that.

    Sincerely,
    Matt

Figure 7.4. Sample Letters of Apology

Exposer
This letter was written by a 17-year-old male to a 34-year-old woman to whom he had
exposed himself from his car in a parking lot.

Dear Janet,

   I feel that you have the right to an apology from me. I honestly
don't know exactly how to begin apologizing for the terrible episode
I caused you. I have no explanation to offer you for what I did.
You mustn't take it personally, because you did nothing to cause my
actions. You were only an innocent victim. I know I've caused you a
great deal of pain. It must have been very shocking to you. I feel
that I have directly insulted you, and I know you were very offended.
I hope you can accept my apology, and even if you don't, I can understand that.
   It was my personal problem only. The legal system has helped me
very much. I have learned many things through being given information
and getting counseling. I've learned better morals and respect. Right
now I have a better understanding of myself and other things that
can help me control or even completely diminish my problem. I'm going
to try very hard to put this all behind me and get started on the
right track toward a better life.
   I'm very, very sorry.

     Brian

Fetish Burglar
This letter is from a 16-year-old fetish burglar who stole underwear from his mother.
She had been quite frightened by her son's behavior because she discovered her
cut-up underwear under her son's bed. In time he was able to explain that he cut
the underwear's leg holes so that he could get them over his large thighs in order
to cross-dress, not as an angry action against his mother.

Dear Mom,

   I am sorry for what I did, and I am sorry for all the pain and
fear that I caused you. As you know, I am getting help for my problem
of cross-dressing and stealing women's clothes. I feel I am making
progress with this problem as well as with our relationship. I promise
that it will never happen again but I also know that there is nothing
I can say to get rid of the grief. I hope to prove in time that you
can again love and trust me.

     Love,
     Ned

Figure 7.4. Continued

relationships typically end with a letter of apology (see Figure 7.4) because the victim's family wishes for a "less formal" resolution.

A few cases involving baby-sitting by a neighborhood acquaintance (e.g., where the offender was a baby-sitter known to the community or the son of a daycare provider) end in face-to-face meetings. Because the relationship was simply functional, the victim's family usually severs all ties. Most choose to learn the details of the abuse through the VSOT therapist and elect to receive a letter of apology through the mail. A significant minority of the families opt for a continued no contact contract monitored by the VSOT therapist and probation officer.

In a park or playground child-molestation, because there was no prior relationship with the offender, most victims choose to receive the letter of apology in the mail. When they are first contacted by the VSOT therapist, most express thanks for being able to learn the results of their reporting the abuse. Again, a significant number of these families choose a continued no contact contract and say they will keep the therapist's telephone number should any problems arise in the future.

The Nontouch Sex Offender

The category of nontouch offender includes those who steal underwear, expose their genitals, window peep, or make obscene phone calls. If the underwear stealing or exposing is directed toward close family members, the cases necessarily resolve with face-to-face closure meetings. The meetings help the victim understand a behavior that seems bizarre and inexplicable.

Nontouch cases involving neighbors and strangers to the offender usually end with letters of apology (see Figure 7.4) received through the mail. The VSOT therapist answers the victim's questions and offers explanations of the offender's behavior to help put some of the victim's concerns to rest.

The Group-Influenced Offender

The victims of this type of abuse are typically peers of the offenders. The abuse occurs in a group setting, such as a party, school bathroom, playground, or sporting event. Characteristically, the offenders blame the victim. The victim usually feels humiliated and confused. Peer gossip and rumor tend to isolate the victim further. As a result of the situational and attributional processes involved, all of these cases end with an emotionally distant letter of apology, supplemented by a detailed explanation from the VSOT therapist. Many victims in these situations move to new schools and neighborhoods in an attempt to sever all ties and escape the lingering social impact of the abuse.

The Acquaintance Rapist

The victims of date-rape are generally very angry and traumatized by the forced sexual abuse. They usually express relief that the offender is in treatment and anger about the assault, the legal process, and the emotional aftermath. Because the victim's experience is typically very different from the story the offender tells, the therapist can use that information to confront the offender. Some victims accept a letter of apology from the offender on the condition that it is sincere, and all request an assured no contact contract.

SUMMARY AND IMPLICATIONS

The systemic/attributional perspective and the VSOT model offer a fundamentally new approach to the treatment of sexual abuse. Increasing numbers of programs are implementing victim-offender communication components, and guiding protocols are being established (National Adolescent Perpetrator Network, 1993; Yokley, 1990). In a study of 323 juvenile offender treatment programs, 232 (or 72%) use victim apology as a treatment technique, ranking 10th in techniques of greatest use (Knopp, Freeman-Longo, & Stevenson, 1992). This chapter demonstrates that the VSOT process can occur in clear, safe, structured stages from the initial assessment to final closure. The treatment section demonstrates the broad range of offenses that can benefit from such an approach and provides an indication of the type of closure often selected. In fact, closure choice can often be predicted by the frequency of contact and degree of intimacy of the victim-offender dyad and their respective families prior to the abuse disclosure.

This chapter concludes with some examples of VSOT model implications for therapy and the organization of research and treatment of interpersonal violence in general.

It is possible to treat sexual abuse successfully despite an "untreatable" offender. As occurs in some incest cases, the offenders can be so sociopathic that they cannot be treated with conventional therapy. But the VSOT model can help the victim, spouse/parent, and other siblings in the family gain a rational view of the abuse and the offender; the hurt parties can heal by growing beyond the offender's limitations.

Such offenders usually agree to participating in marital and family clarification (not reconciliation) sessions in which their sociopathy quickly becomes obvious. This helps an enmeshed spouse and blaming siblings "let go" of their distorted view of the offender and become more sensitive to how the victim was isolated and used by the offender.

Victim/offender treatment coordination teams should become an integral part of offender therapy. Just as the field now sees the need for multidisciplinary teams for effective and efficient investigation and adjudication of child abuse, so too could the treatment of victims and offenders of sexual abuse and other interpersonal violence benefit from coordination teams. Setting up such teams would involve defining the team (the "professional system" in Figure 6.1), and its task around the victim-offender dyad and their respective needs. Coordination of information and efforts leads to treatment and management that is significantly more informed, safer, and complete, while being shorter in duration and less costly than traditional approaches.

The unit of research in interpersonal violence should be the victim-offender dyad. Sexual abuse studies and interpersonal studies in general focus on either victims or offenders and the data analyzed in their respective groups or subgroups. If the organizing unit of research becomes the victim-offender dyad, the contextual interactional dynamics of sexual abuse could be richly studied. Questions such as the voracity of abuse memories, descriptions, and attributions could be addressed by having members of the victim-offender dyad relate their version of the abuse events. Research on issues of prevention and treatment could also be enriched by analyzing the victim-offender dyad.

The VSOT model offers a structure for possible closure years after the sexual abuse has ended. One case example involves a 30-year-old incest victim. Her father abused her from age 6 through 12. She only revealed the abuse after she moved away and engaged in therapy. For a variety of reasons, she decided not to prosecute. The father, although not denying the abuse, only sought general psychoanalysis.

The victim came to therapy to complete her incest work. The father was contacted via phone, and after discussion about the VSOT model and process as well as reviewing potential legal concerns, he agreed to participate. After some months, correspondence, and phone calls, the daughter received the confirmation of the full truth of her experience and the apology she had always wanted. In addition, the father offered economic restitution, which further helped heal the relationship between these estranged family members.

It is possible for victims to receive information and an apology for abuse that occurred when they were too young or not ready to re- member. A couple came to therapy to create closure in an unusual situation. The father had been a sexual compulsive whose behavior included penis-vaginal rubbing, a form of incest with his two daugh- ters, 6 months and 2½ years at the time of discovery. The behavior had gone on for some months with the older girl and a shorter time with the infant. The father had been sentenced to out-of-home place- ment, workhouse time, and treatment, which he by all accounts successfully completed.

The victims were now entering their early teens and had no recollection of the incest. Therapists had previously recommended against bringing up the abuse, as the memories could be potentially traumatizing to the girls. The present dilemma revolved around the fact that the extended family and relatives were aware of this abuse history, but the victims were not. The parents feared that the victims would learn of their abuse through an awkwardly and potentially traumatic slip at a family gathering. They felt the girls were old enough now and deserved to learn their history in a complete, coherent, and responsible process.

After some preparation, the girls did hear their father's abuse history and later received a heartfelt apology. Rather than being made uncomfortable, they were relieved because both knew "something" had happened in their past but never knew what kind of questions to ask or of whom.

Many questions remain in the application of various victim-offender communication models. Legal, confidentiality, ethical, and therapeutic issues will become clearer and protocols will be established as more programs begin to use these emerging models. The successful negotiation of these details will determine the ultimate limits of this promising new direction.

PART III

A Model for Working With Adolescent Male Prostitutes

DON LeTOURNEAU

8

Adolescent Male Prostitution: A Social Work/Youth Work Perspective

CHAPTER 1 OFFERS a brief historical perspective of childhood and adolescence as well as a discussion of erotophobia, homophobia and sexual identity development as they relate to adolescence. An understanding of these issues is critical to understanding the foundation and context of the social institution of street youth, particularly adolescent male prostitutes. This chapter explores those themes in more specific ways and provides perspective to an area of adolescent male sexuality that has been tragically ignored.

As chapter 1 points out, few adult prerogatives are more firmly protected than sexual behavior. And few adolescent behaviors create the kind of adult discomfort that adolescent male prostitution manages to achieve. Such prostitution represents adolescents engaged in willful sexual behavior, adolescents involved in the illegal activity of prostitution, and most anxiety producing, adolescent males involved in significant amounts of homosexual behavior. It is hard to image any social phenomenon that combines such a powerful mix of social taboos and neuroses.

The available cultural paradigms for viewing and understanding adolescents have a clear gender differentiation. On the one hand, young women are increasingly viewed as the victims of a patriarchal male society that oppresses, sexually exploits, and sexually assaults them.

On the other hand, young men are increasingly viewed as threats to society and in need of control. The rising level of violence, characterized by sexual assaults, gang violence, juvenile crime (predominantly perpetrated by young men), and seemingly random attacks by young men, are seen as evidence to support these perceptions.

Lost in these gender-polarized dichotomies is a way to view adolescent males involved in prostitution. This view contradicts the popular theory that young males who are sexually abused grow up to become sex offenders. It contradicts the image of adolescent males as violent and perpetrators of crimes (many adolescent male prostitutes do engage in criminal behavior other than prostitution but in no greater proportion or level of violence than adolescent female prostitutes). And it contradicts the images of adolescent males as sexually aggressive and exploitative of their sexual partners.

The distorted cultural dichotomies have contributed to the lack of research, inquiry, and attention to adolescent male prostitution, despite the fact that its reported incidence has increased dramatically in recent decades (Boyer, 1989).

The author's efforts to research, serve, advocate, and educate about the issue of adolescent male prostitution have consistently been met with resistance from most areas of human services, research, and professional education. The resistance is seldom overt and hostile and is probably unconscious and not deliberate, but it is resistance nonetheless. It is as though information about male prostitution threatens passionately held "beliefs" about males or there is simply no theoretical framework within which the information can reside.

It is our hope that the information presented here will make its way into the repertoire of mainstream human service professionals and that a framework can begin to be constructed that allows for more diverse and authentic paradigms of adolescents. Current views are one-dimensional and limiting ways of understanding adolescent "victims/survivors" of both genders and obscures their potential for adaptation and survival.

This chapter begins with a review of the historical and recent research literature that is relevant to male prostitution. It then offers a critique of the research, its findings relative to the "causes" and "effects" of adolescent male (and female) prostitution, and the conventional view of adolescent prostitution. The variety of methods and types of intervention and prevention aimed at adolescent prostitution are discussed; chapter 9 presents a model of intervention called detached youth work.

THE HISTORICAL LITERATURE

Male prostitution is described in two bodies of literature. The historical literature includes both the history of prostitution (Amos, 1877; Bailey, 1956; Benjamin & Masters, 1964; James, 1951; Sanger, 1937; Scott, 1968) and the history of homosexuality (Bray, 1982; Burg, 1984; Foucault, 1980, 1986, 1988; Weeks, 1981). The second body of literature is research literature on adolescent male prostitution in the last 40 years (Allen, 1980; Boyer, 1989; Boyer & James, 1983; Butts, 1947; Caukins & Coombs, 1976; Coombs, 1974; Craft, 1966; Deisher, Eisner, & Sulzbacher, 1969; Fisher, Weisberg, & Marotta, 1982; Gandy & Deisher, 1970; Ginsburg, 1967; Hoffman, 1972; Jersild, 1956; MacNamara, 1965; Reiss, 1961; Weisberg, 1985).

The historical literature is only reviewed in the modern research by Boyer and James (1983). However, the historical literature provides a valuable perspective for understanding the present configuration of adolescent male prostitution. Much of the literature on the history of homosexuality has only recently been available, but it is critical in understanding homosexual prostitution. Adolescent male prostitution is certainly not older than homosexual behavior, but it is thousands of years older than homosexuals as an identifiable class of individuals.

Recent research literature tends to view adolescent male prostitution as a post-World War II phenomenon that emerged with the contemporary male homosexual subculture (Fisher et al., 1982) or as a logical construction in the social identity of young males who are homosexual in contemporary society (Boyer, 1989). Although there is little doubt that "hustling" has become an integral part of the modern gay male community and that cultural attitudes toward homosexuality predispose adolescents with this orientation to view themselves as "deviant," the historical literature indicates that the parameters of male prostitution are much broader. Pederasts and women have played major roles in the history of adolescent male prostitution, yet are virtually ignored by researchers. Few writers have attempted to integrate the history of male prostitution prior to the 18th century with current information.

From a historical perspective, three major assumptions can be made about adolescent male prostitution. First, male prostitution is as old as female prostitution. The earliest records of prostitution refer to "religious" or "temple" prostitution (James, 1951). Although the term *prostitution* is not particularly accurate to describe these temple ministrants, who were dedicated to a deity and performed ritual intercourse with supplicants as a part of worshiping their deity, there is evidence that some people offered their sexual services along with temple ministrants for less than ecclesiastical motives (Bailey, 1956).

Benjamin and Masters (1964) state: "Male homosexual prostitution is, so far as we know, about equally as ancient as the female hetero-sexual variety. Homosexual temple prostitutes existed among the Hebrews and in India. Boy harlots plied their trade in the antique civilizations of Egypt, Persia, Greece, Rome, China, and Japan, as else-where" (p. 284)

These male temple prostitutes were the source of the Biblical denouncements of sodomy, sodomites, and catamites and created the linking of homosexual behavior and idolatry in Western cultures (Scott, 1968). The Hebrews, like most other cultures at the time, employed female temple prostitutes under a variety of euphemistic titles, but male temple prostitutes were a part of rival religions, and therefore condemned (Scott, 1968).

This connotation of sodomy and idolatry is further evidenced in the translations of the Greek word *hierodoulos* (temple ministrants). Most Biblical translations render the word as "whore" or "harlot" for females and "sodomite" or "catamite" for males (Bailey, 1956). These translations display a limited understanding of the role and function of these early temple ministrants while obscuring the role of males.

The second major assumption that can be derived from the histori-cal perspective is that male prostitution has always been as prevalent and extensive as female prostitution, even more so at certain times in history. Most texts indicate that the earliest temple prostitution was as prevalent by males as by females. During the classical period of the Greeks and Romans, male prostitution probably exceeded female prostitution (Bailey, 1956; Benjamin & Masters, 1964; James, 1951; Scott, 1968).

Although there is little specific information about male prostitution from the Middle Ages, there is little reason to believe it was less prevalent. The Roman system of licensing and taxing brothels remained the practice in Europe throughout the Middle Ages and accounts survive that indicate that males were as much a part of the brothels as females and provided sexual services to both men and women (Bailey, 1956; Scott, 1968).

Throughout the Renaissance and Victorian period, there are well-documented accounts indicating the prevalence of male prostitution in European cities (Bray, 1982; Burg, 1984). Weeks (1981) notes that Havelock Ellis, Iwan Bloch, Magnus Hirschfeld, Sigmund Freud, and Alfred Kinsey all commented that male prostitution was little less evident than female prostitution.

The final assumption that can be derived from the historical literature is that children and adolescents have always been a significant portion of those involved in male prostitution. Boys as young as 4 years old were bought on the slave markets of Rome and taught passive pederasty for work in the brothels (Lloyd, 1976). Many young boys during the Middle Ages and the Renaissance who could not secure an apprenticeship were recruited or forced to work in brothels or as "kept" servants with overtones of prostitution (Bray, 1982; Burg, 1984). Many of the age-of-sexual-consent laws that were passed at the close of the 19th century were aimed at protecting children from recruitment to prostitution (James, 1951).

These assumptions raise more questions than they answer. If male prostitution is as old and as prevalent as female prostitution and has always involved young boys and adolescents, why does so little literature describe and analyze it? Foucault (1988) points out that what has changed is not the behavior but the way in which the questions are asked and the importance they are given in philosophical and moral debate:

> In the first centuries of our era, compared with the lofty formulations of the classical period, reflection on the love of boys lost some of its intensity, its seriousness, its vitality, if not its topicality.

This does not mean that the practice disappeared or that it became the object of a disqualification. All the texts plainly show it was still common and still regarded as a natural thing. What seems to have changed is not the taste for boys, or the value judgment that was brought to bear on those who had this partiality, but the way in which one questioned oneself about it. An obsolescence not of the thing itself, but of the problem; a decline in the interest one took in it; a fading of the importance it was granted in philosophical and moral debate. (p. 189)

Weeks (1981) observes that "writings on male prostitution began to emerge simultaneously with the notion of homosexuals being an identifiable breed of persons with special needs, passions, and lusts" (p. 113). Bloch suggests that the first use of the term *prostitute* to describe males appears in Duchesne's (1853/1909) *De la prostitution dans la ville d'Alger la conquete.* Yet historical accounts indicate that males have been involved in behavior that can be labeled prostitution (even if it was not called that at the time) since the earliest cultures.

The linking of male prostitution and homosexuality has more to do with cultural categories and perceptions of human sexual behavior than with natural categories of human sexual behavior. Is male prostitution viewed as homosexual prostitution because it involves exclusively homosexual behavior or because of the homosexual identities of the customers? In the historical accounts, the proportions of which customers were male, female, or pederast is debatable and virtually impossible to determine. But evidence suggests that homosexual men were not the only customers of male prostitutes and, as Weeks (1981) points out, "historians and social scientists alike have failed to fit everyone who behaves in a homosexual manner within a definition of 'the homosexual' as a unitary type" (p. 113). As is explored latter in this chapter, current research literature indicates that a significant number of customers are women.

The most recent research suggests that young male prostitutes are more likely to identify as homosexual than previous research indicated (Fisher et al., 1982), yet a common approach of most of the studies of male prostitution is to collapse the homosexual and bisexual categories together as homosexual. Even though this practice has been criticized for implying that homosexuality is a homogeneous category and that sexual orientation is a polarized and immutable state

(De Cecco, 1981), Boyer (1989) defends the practice on the grounds that her study is one of cultural categories rather than natural ones.

The biases of early researchers against homosexuality, the collapsing of bisexual and homosexual identity categories of the more recent research, the inability of historians and social scientists to fit everyone who practices homosexual behavior into a homosexual identity, and the lack of data concerning sexual orientation development in adolescence that is based on natural rather than cultural categories creates skepticism concerning the labeling of male prostitution as homosexual prostitution. This focus on the homosexuality of male prostitution is more the result of the cultural discomfort with the image of males as prostitutes than because of the truly homosexual nature of the phenomenon. The most bisexual period of the male life cycle is usually during adolescence, and attention should be focused on the adolescent aspect of male prostitution rather than its "homosexualness."

THE RESEARCH LITERATURE

There is little research on male prostitution, and much of what has been done is not particularly useful in understanding adolescent male prostitution. In many cases, the research tells us more about the researchers than the subjects being studied. Perhaps the biggest limitation of the literature is that it displays dated attitudes toward homosexuality in general and adolescent homosexuality in particular. Most researchers tend to accept obsolete pathological diefinitions of homosexuality (Butts, 1947; Caukins & Coombs, 1976; Craft, 1966; Coombs, 1974; Jersild, 1956; MacNamara, 1965; Reiss, 1961). Boyer (1989) suggests that "subject and researcher agreed on a mutual denial of homosexuality" leading to research that offers little insight into the phenomenon (p. 155). This illustrates a consistent problem in researching youth in prostitution. These youth become very adept at perceiving adult biases and tell adults what they want to hear (Baizerman, Thompson, & Stafford-White, 1979). To these youth, researchers may be just a different variety of customer.

Other limitations of the research include sampling biases that limit applicability to broader populations. Only two studies have been based exclusively on adolescent populations, and these were done with boys who were incarcerated or from a researcher's psychiatric practice, limiting their value (Craft, 1966; Hoffman, 1972; Reiss, 1961; Wienberg, 1972). Most research has studied only small samples in one or two locales (Caukins & Coombs, 1976; Coombs, 1974; Deisher et al., 1969; Deisher & Gandy, 1970; Ginsberg, 1967). Many studies look at only one type of prostitution and fail to reflect the diversity of male prostitution (Craft, 1966; Deisher et al., 1969; Ginsberg, 1967; Hoffman, 1972; Reiss, 1961; Wienberg, 1972). Finally, most of the research was done during the 1960s and early 1970s before an awareness of the social problems of runaway behavior and physical and sexual abuse of children, and therefore fails to look at the relationship these social problems have to adolescent prostitution.

The most ambitious recent research on adolescent male prostitution is that performed by Urban and Rural Systems Associates (URSA) between 1979 and 1981 as a result of federal hearings on juvenile prostitution and pornography in 1977 (Weisberg, 1985). These hearings resulted in funding for a number of research projects that examined the sexual exploitation of juveniles (males and females) and led to the work by Boyer and James (1983) on adolescent male and female prostitution. URSA (1982) looked at data from several cites around the United States and combined ethnography, service provider surveys, profile analysis (data supplied by service providers on clients involved in male prostitution), and a literature review to generate the first nationally based study on adolescent male prostitution. Seattle-based researchers played an especially important role in this research because of the work of Deisher, James, and Boyer at the University of Washington, and because two agencies in Seattle supplied nearly one-half of the profiles for URSA's profile analysis.

The Findings of the Research Literature

The "typical" adolescent male prostitute can be described as a white, 14- to 18-year-old boy from a broken/neglectful, low- to middle-income family. He has a history of physical and/or sexual abuse, is a high school dropout, and is unemployed, unskilled, and self-identified as gay or bisexual. He is a runaway or throwaway (often the result of his emerging sexual orientation) who regularly uses drugs and alcohol, has a juvenile justice record, and is increasingly reliant on social service systems for food, housing, medical, and employment assistance (Boyer & James, 1983; Deisher, Robinson, & Boyer 1982; Fisher et al., 1982).

With some subtle variations, the research and historical literature describes four basic types of adolescent male prostitution: street hustling, bar hustling, kept boys, and call service or "professional" hustling (Allen, 1980; Caukins & Coombs, 1976; Fisher et al., 1982). These types primarily reflect the locale of the hustling and are fluid when used to identify boys. A boy may engage in one or all of these types during his entrance into, participation in, and exit from prostitution. These four types also reflect the classes of hustling and are reasonably consistent with the historical literature (Bray, 1982; Burg, 1984).

Street Hustling

A 17-year-old hustler recently met a 15-year-old hustler:

"Girl, how long you been hustling the streets?"
"About a year and a half."
"You must not be any good then. If you been out here that long you shoulda done had yourself a book full of names and be sittin' by the phone instead of out here peddlin' your ass on the street corner."

The street hustlers of the literature and experience are boys who are the relatively permanent inhabitants of the "streets," as opposed to those who visit or pass through the streets. The streets are where most boys are introduced to and begin their careers in prostitution, which means this locale is inhabited by boys of all types. Street hustlers are distinguished as the lower class hustlers by their inability to anticipate and conduct their lives with the future in mind (Banfield, 1973). Those who visit or pass through the streets may choose to be present oriented and live moment to moment, but are capable of moving on or out of this milieu.

Street hustling is the most wide open of all the types of hustling. One can encounter all types of people looking for all types of sexual encounters. This is the very reason many hustlers look for more predictable and reliable ways to hustle, yet it is also this adventure and risk that keeps (traps) some and draws others back. In the most general terms, street hustling means standing on a street or corner and establishing contact with a customer in a car through eye contact. Although virtually anything is negotiable, the most common sex sold on the streets is fellatio and it most often involves the customer preforming fellatio on the hustler.

Although seldom defined, the streets as described in the literature is really a metaphor for the meeting ground of a variety of *deviant* subcultures (drugs, prostitution, strip shows, bookstores, gangs, homeless, criminal) that exist in all cities. The term is often loosely used in an attempt to describe a milieu of these overlapping subcultures and the social space common to them. It may refer to a specific physical location (such as Polk Street and the Tenderloin in San Francisco, Times Square in New York, West Hollywood in Los Angeles, Hennepin Avenue in Minneapolis) but is better conceptualized as a metaphor for the confluence of these marginal subcultures. Gang members, prostitutes (male or female), delinquents, or homeless youth have their own as well as shared territory on the streets. Sometimes these territories are relatively stable over time (such as those mentioned above), but more often they are subject to migrations and changes. Police intervention/harassment, public awareness/attention, urban gentrification/development, and the interests of the youth themselves are but a few of the variables that influence the actual physical location of the streets.

Because of the illegal and/or marginal nature of these subcultures that inhabit the streets or public space, it is difficult to obtain "hard" or quantifiable data describing the individuals who live and/or work there. Ethnographies (Fisher et al., 1982) or other qualitative methods are more suited to studying these subcultures. There is an identifiable gay male subculture within which street hustling by boys takes place, but these boys may also participate in the activities of the other subcultures that are a part of the streets.

The boys who street hustle are often the most troubled and delinquent of the boys who engage in prostitution. They are survival oriented and live by hustling whatever they can (e.g., drugs, sex, larceny, panhandling) and are likely to identify as heterosexual or bisexual. They are also likely to have extensive histories of physical and sexual abuse and involvement with the juvenile justice system (Boyer, 1989; Deisher & Gandy, 1970; URSA, 1982).

A useful way to conceptualize these boys is to understand them as having traumatic histories before coming to the streets or early in their street careers, and becoming trapped by the cycle of exploitation they are exposed to on the streets. The resiliency and/or adaptive skills of these boys is minimal and they become the easiest targets for exploitation by street predators. That predation further damages the resiliency of these boys and perpetuates further exploitation.

At times, this group can appear to be either "victims" or "predators," depending on the behavioral sample observed. The high prevalence of sexual abuse histories and prostitution behavior combined with delinquent activities make these boys among the most difficult to work with.

Street hustlers are in the most need of basic social services. Their inability to anticipate the future means they live from crisis to crisis. Needs for food, housing, and medical care are the immediate priority, but street hustlers often need educational services, employment and training services, legal advocacy, mental health services, and case management services. They are often, however, unable or unwilling to maintain participation in these services, and so leave social service providers feeling like a revolving door when these boys drop out of programs only to present themselves again when they are in a crisis. This lack of continuity often leads to a permanent termination from services they have frustrated, leaving these boys to turn increasingly to the streets for their survival needs.

Case Example

Mark first "ran away" from home when he was 13. His mother was an alcoholic who divorced when he was 4. He had a sister who was in foster care because one of his mother's boyfriends had molested her, and Mark had been in foster homes and group homes for his delinquent behavior. He was molested when he was 10 by a friend of the family his mother had recruited to be a "positive male influence" on him, but he had never told anyone.

In school, Mark was in special education classes for his behavior. He got in fights often, was caught stealing in school, and was referred to juvenile court for his truancy. This and shoplifting led to his placement in foster care. His "bad attitude" and "oppositional behavior" landed him in a group home. He barely graduated from the group home and was returned home at 12.

Mark would not listen to his mother and her rules, and one night when he came home late and found his mother drunk, they got in a huge fight and she kicked him out. By now Mark knew plenty of kids on the streets; he started hanging out with them and sleeping where he could. When he became desperate for money, a friend told him about a guy who would pay him to give him a blow job and Mark decided to try it. The guy had lots of drugs and alcohol and offered Mark a place to stay for a while.

Mark met other guys who would let him stay for a while and he sold small amounts of drugs for some of them. He also got pretty good at stealing cars and breaking into the houses of guys he used to stay with. By the time Mark was 17, he had spent time in a couple of juvenile correctional facilities for his delinquent behavior, but none of the counselors or therapists had ever suspected his prostitution behavior and he never told anyone. Everyone, including Mark, was more comfortable talking about his delinquency.

On the streets, Mark would hustle and deal while staying with one of his friends or until he got enough money for an apartment. He was always running out of money and getting evicted. He also got ripped off and in fights a lot. Somebody he had crossed or the cops were always looking for him. Mark always had grand plans for getting a "straight" job and going to college after he got his GED, but not long after he got a job he would lose it because he was up late partying the night before and could not get up for work.

Bar Hustling

Bray (1992) describes the brothels of male prostitution in London during the Renaissance as "likely to have been taverns where prostitutes could entertain their clients. Such taverns, together with young male prostitutes walking the streets and alleys of Elizabethan London, probably offer the principal way we should envisage homosexual prostitution in the London of the time" (p. 89). Bray also describes the "molly houses" (places where homosexual men would meet) of the time as being taverns or private homes where drink was sold and one could have sexual encounters.

Weeks (1981) observes that "the most basic purpose of the homosexual subculture in the nineteenth and early twentieth centuries . . . was to provide ways to meet sexual partners," and "As early as the 1720s, these meeting places had been known as 'markets,' corresponding to the contemporaneous use of the term 'marriage market' " (p. 121).

Bar hustling differs from street hustling primarily in that it is more focused and more gay oriented. The distinctions can be fairly subtle and the overlap between the two is often considerable. Bar hustling occurs around the edges of the "markets" where gay men meet to find sexual partners. In many cities this is the gay bars, but it can also be gay neighborhoods, parks, bookstores, or, in the past, bath houses. The territory is more exclusively gay than where street hustling occurs, which can be territory shared with other subcultures.

The boys who hustle in these areas are more likely to be gay identified and to have run away or been kicked out because of their emerging homosexuality, are as likely as street hustlers to have been sexually abused, and are drawn to the gay markets as a part of making meaning out of their emerging sexuality (Boyer, 1989; Boyer & James, 1983; Fisher et al., 1982). URSA found that, in comparison to street hustlers, bar hustlers are from slightly less dysfunctional families, have completed slightly more school, were older when they ran away, and were older when they first had sex and when they first started hustling; neither type was likely to have been involved with social services and juvenile justice agencies (Fisher et al., 1982).

Bar hustlers are generally more competent and more able to anticipate the future in their lives than street hustlers. Bar hustlers often look for "sugar daddies" and can look like kept boys in this respect. They are very mobile and can act as travel companions for men who take them on trips or who are from out of town and offer them rides to new places, particularly in winter. This is especially true of the west coast between Seattle and Los Angeles and the east coast between Miami and Boston, where there are corridors of cities boys can move between with relative ease.

These boys enjoy the attention and power they derive from older gay men, but, as some researchers have noted, there can be a hostile dependency between these boys and their customers/sugar daddies (Allen, 1980; Boyer & James, 1983; Caulkins & Coombs, 1976). Some of these boys hustle to stabilize their lives and identities as gay men, whereas others become trapped by the cycle, resenting the exploitation by adult gay men while lacking the skills or abilities to escape it, in part because of how lucrative it can be.

Bar hustling also includes what URSA and other researchers have described as situational or part-time hustlers (Allen, 1980; Fisher et al., 1982). These are usually older adolescents and can include college students, who hustle in the bars when they need extra money or for the excitement. (URSA's typologies describe situational hustlers participating in street hustling as well as bar hustling.) There are stories of young men who have put themselves through college and graduate school this way (URSA, 1982).

Bar hustling is the area of male prostitution that has grown the most rapidly during the last two decades, and no doubt reflecting the growth and visibility of the gay male community in most larger cities (Boyer, 1989; Fisher et al., 1982). The boys who hustle in and around the gay bars are increasingly gay identified with a probable history of sexual abuse. Although somewhat less acute, their social service needs are similar to those of street hustlers, but bar hustlers are less likely to receive those services in an atmosphere that understands or accepts their homosexuality. The homophobia (or, at the very least, heterosexism) of most youth-serving agencies leads many of these boys to be wary of such programs. The most effective service provision is usually the result of programs by or in conjunction with local gay and lesbian social service organizations.

Case Example

Greg began running away from home when he was 14. He was well known to the juvenile police officer in his suburb for his habitual running. There was never any indication of delinquent behavior other than running. Greg lived with his older sister and mother, who had never married. His mother was eccentric and controlling, but there was no indication of abuse or serious problems at home.

Greg knew he was gay when he was 13; he began running to hang out downtown and at a local gay park. He soon met other gay-identified boys and plenty of gay men who let him stay with them. It did not take long for Greg to figure out how to make money, since most of the boys he knew hustled and most of the men he stayed with would spend money on him. Greg soon had a regular clientele and only spent time on the streets to party and hang out with the other boys.

In a somewhat neurotic way, Greg's mother would regularly call and harass the local juvenile officer and chastise him for not finding her son and getting him away from those "perverts" who were "poisoning" her son with ideas about homosexuality. A few times the officer was successful at tracking Greg down and bringing him home, but Greg never stayed for long due to his mother's incessant lectures about perverts and homosexuals. Eventually the officer was successful at having Greg arrested while he was turning a trick, and Greg was sent to a group home.

Greg continued to hustle occasionally while in the group home (without their knowledge) for extra spending money and clothes, but this behavior eventually dissipated. He would still hang out in the same places, but more for the peer relationships than for sex or money. While on the streets, Greg had stayed high most of the time, primarily on marijuana but frequently on cocaine. The group home tried to get him to go to outpatient treatment or at least AA groups, but Greg was not interested. He continued to smoke marijuana while in the group home (without their knowledge), but, like the hustling, this behavior dissipated over time and eventually Greg no longer got high.

Over his mother's vociferous objections, Greg was eventually placed in a gay foster home, graduated from high school, and went to college.

Call/Professional Hustling

Hetaera and male courtesans are at least as old as the Greeks; Bailey (1956) notes a revival of hetarism and courtesans in the 12th and 13th centuries. Today, call boys/men service upper-class men and women who require discretion and can at least imitate an acceptable level of social status.

As described in the literature, these boys usually work the upper-class bars and hotels and occasionally work for call services or upper-class houses of prostitution (Allen, 1980; Caukins & Coombs, 1976; Fisher et al., 1982). Those that provide their services to men are mostly gay identified and see themselves as professionals (Fisher et al., 1982). They may engage in prostitution on a part-time or full-time basis, or, as URSA describes it, on a vocational or avocational basis (Fisher et al., 1982). Those who provide their services to women most often identify as heterosexual and often work the strip shows for women and/or for private dance circuits.

In most of the research, professional hustlers are a small percentage of those studied, but it is not clear whether this is the result of this group making up a small portion of males involved in prostitution or the result of their skill at concealment. Whatever their numbers, they exist and are the most competent and least troubled of the young men who are involved in prostitution. They represent the "upper-class" of male prostitution in that they are able to anticipate a future in their lives and conduct their lives accordingly.

Call boys are the least likely of all types of male prostitutes to request services from social service agencies and are not likely to see themselves as needing such services. On occasion they may involve themselves in individual psychotherapy, but often this is not related to their involvement in prostitution, and they may not even reveal that information to their therapist.

Case Example

Tony was kicked out of the house when he was 16. He was a straight-A student from a middle-class family in the suburbs with three kids and mom and dad. Tony had never been in trouble, but, as the oldest child and male, his father had high expectations for him. However, Tony did not want to play sports, and it was getting harder and harder for him to hide his homosexuality from himself and his father. When Tony finally told his father, his dad kicked him out.

Tony quit school and stayed with a friend's family until he got a job and his own place. Free to pursue his sexuality, Tony managed to get into the gay bars and started experimenting with sex. One of the bars that had regular strip shows had an amateur night, and some of Tony's friends talked him in to trying out. He liked it, and was recruited to do it on a regular basis. The money was the most appealing part for Tony, since he made only a little above minimum wage at his job. Through the other guys that danced, Tony also learned how to make even more money with men who booked him for private parties and for sex. With his looks and intelligence, Tony soon had a regular clientele and quit dancing. He became so popular that he raised his prices and became more selective.

Tony finished his GED and financed his college education through hustling.

Case Example

Ed's mom divorced when he was 2 and never remarried. His mother had gone back to college and law school, and was a workaholic. Ed and his mother got along, but he always had the feeling that he reminded his mother of the mistake she made in marrying his father, whom he never knew. Ed's first sexual experience was with his best friend's mother when he was 13. She was wealthy and divorced and no one seemed to question that he spent a lot of time at his best friend's place, even if his friend was not there.

Ed had learned to be very charming with older women and began to notice how they looked at him and acted toward him when he was downtown or at the mall. When Ed was 16, a woman in her 30s picked him up at a shopping mall, and he wound up staying with her for several days. She took him to bars and out for dinner and told him that he acted older than his age that he seemed to know what a woman wanted. After this happened a few more times, and Ed was not coming home much or going to school, his mother and he began to fight; Ed finally quit coming home. One of the women he stayed with took him to a bar that did a male strip show for women, and talked him into trying out. He did and pretty soon he had enough money to get his own place. Through some of the guys he danced with Ed learned about a service that booked guys for private parties, and pretty soon he had developed a clientele that paid him to do more than dance.

This form of prostitution often presents the dilemma of whether prostitution can be a "healthy" career choice for an individual or whether it is inherently exploitative and/or abusive to the prostitute. Free from most of the debilitating effects of the streets and lower-class forms of prostitution, professional hustling's effects are more limited to the impact of fee-for-service sex. The arguments for and against these perceptions are most often constructed around passionately held beliefs about human sexuality and the theology of sex and seldom on the basis of research.

Kept Boys

Emperor Hadrian of Rome was so captivated by his "kept boy," Antinous, that statues of the boy were set up all over the Roman Empire (Lloyd, 1976). (Although earlier writers on this subject display fairly homophobic attitudes, more recent accounts suggest the relationship between a kept boy and his "master" to be quite complex; see Yourcenar, 1954.) Bray (1982) describes boys of Renaissance England who lived in households with the status of servants but whose relationship with the masters of the household had strong overtones of prostitution. Boys who were conscripted to the expanding navies of the 17th and 18th centuries often ended up being known as the "carpenters, cooks, or fiddler's boy" (Burg, 1984, p. 38). Today one can read the newspapers to find stories of local and national public figures who are embarrassed to be caught employing young men in dubious roles that have strong overtones of prostitution.

Kept boys are a type of male prostitution because of the obvious financial arrangements that are a part of a primarily sexual relationship. Other than acknowledging their existence, the research literature offers little insight into the lives of kept boys. The overlap between kept boys and bar hustlers in older adolescent boys even leads many to combine the types as one (Allen, 1980; URSA, 1982). However, there are actually two very distinct groups of boys who can be considered kept.

The first group is the kept boys of the literature, who are older adolescent boys and might hustle the bars or work the call services when they do not have a sugar daddy. The fluidity in the types of hustling they participate in indicates that they are a part of the upper class of hustling. Kept boys in this group are almost exclusively gay identified and often form complex relationships with the men who keep them. Their relationships can have a difficult mixture of "trick," lover, mentor, friend, and parent. There is a mutually manipulative quality to these relationships that can create hostile dependencies for both parties, adding to the complex nature of the relationship.

Although homophobic attitudes can lead some to oversimplify these relationships, there are obvious parallels to these relationships that are not interpreted so simplistically in the heterosexual world. The practice and tradition of kept girls and mistresses offer the most insight into the world of these kept boys.

Case Example

Damion grew up in a rural area as the son of a local sheriff's deputy. He had some minor troubles with the law (shoplifting and theft) and began drinking a lot when he was about 15. His father kicked him out of the house when Damion started identifying as gay at 15, and Damion made his way to the city in search of other "queers." He found the local "cruising" area and began hanging out and sleeping where he could. Soon he was hustling, and before long he "fell in love" with one of his tricks.

Damion moved in with his lover (he never called him a sugar daddy even though Damion was 17 and his lover was 43), but he still hustled on occasion. His lover would try to get him to get a job, quit hustling, and finish school, but Damion only wanted to get high, party, and shop. They would have fights and Damion would leave for a while until his lover would beg him to come back.

After that relationship ended, Damion found others, which would last several months until the hostile dependency of both parties would blow it up. Sometimes Damion's lovers would get violent and beat him up, but this would only give Damion more ammunition to make them feel guilty and a chance to extract a large favor (such as shopping) to make up.

Damion even learned to hook up with men who would take him to Los Angeles, Miami, or the Caribbean on trips. As he got older (20s) and his appeal diminished, Damion began staying with men longer and would even help some find younger boys on the streets.

The second group of boys who can be considered kept are those who are kept by pederasts. Pederasts, as the word is used here, represent a subculture of men whose primary sexual interest is pre- through postpubescent boys. Clinically, these men can be considered pedophiles and/or hebophiles, but these diagnostic categories,

although accurate, fail to capture the community these men participate in, the historical traditions they share, and the patterns they
develop. Although recent research illustrates that the data about
pedophiles has broadened considerably in recent years, little clinical
or research data are available about men who molest adolescents.

The pederasts referred to here are best typified by the membership
of the North American Man Boy Love Association and the types of
individuals involved in boy-sex rings that are reported by journalists
occasionally. One of the most infamous examples of such a report is
documented in *The Boys From Boise,* a ring that involved over 100
boys and numerous public officials (Gerassi, 1966). These pederasts
should not necessarily be considered gay men, though they can present themselves as such. Pederasts move through the gay male subculture and the streets and are alternately parasites and predators in
those worlds.

The boys who are kept by pederasts are much younger (8 to 15)
than other kept boys and are most often recruited to the relationship
while they are still living at home or early in their runaway/throw-
away career. They may be ambivalent or confused about their sexual
orientation and are likely to have been involved in pornography. This
pornography is seldom the commercial pornography that attracts
public attention but the private pornography that is more characteristic of the pederast community. Local and national networks of
pederasts facilitate the exchange of private pictures and home videos
with other interested pederasts.

These boys most often come from abusive, neglectful, or dysfunctional families and are initially the most isolated of the boys in prostitution. Gradually, these boys may be exposed to the world of the
streets and/or prostitution through their association with the pederast,
and eventually either the youth or the pederast severs the relationship and the boy moves on to street hustling as a means of survival.

Boys kept by pederasts are difficult to research because of their
inaccessibility, but there is some description of this phenomenon in
the literature on investigation of sexual abuse and missing children
by law enforcement agencies (Burgess, 1984). This literature is more
relevant to the prosecution of pedophiles than to the boys who are
kept by pederasts and seldom acknowledges the relationship of this
phenomenon to male prostitution.

Case Example

Joey was the middle of five children in a two-parent household in the suburbs. Both of his parents worked and Joey was on his own a lot by the time he was 10. Joey and some of his friends in the neighborhood would hang out at the home of a man named Dave. Dave worked nights and was around a lot during the day and let the neighborhood boys play his stereo, smoke, and even drink once in awhile. None of the boys told their parents about what went on at Dave's for fear of ruining a good thing, and, since Dave helped coach a little league team in the community, none of the parents worried too much.

After Joey got in some trouble in school and for shoplifting, Dave suggested to Joey's parents that Joey come along on a camping trip. Everyone thought it might be good for Joey. While on the trip, Dave molested Joey, and when they came back Joey's behavior continued to deteriorate. Even though Joey was uncomfortable with what was going on, Dave made it sound like it was a natural thing.

Joey was eventually placed in a group home because of the trouble he was getting into, but he ran away and went to Dave, who promised not to turn him in. Joey stayed with Dave for several months. Dave had lots of camera equipment and talked Joey into posing for him, saying he could be a model. He even got him to pose nude by showing him some art books on nudes.

Joey eventually got arrested while trying to shoplift and was sent to a residential treatment program, which he also ran from. He stayed with Dave a few days but started hanging out downtown and learned fairly quickly that there were other men like Dave who would let him stay with them. He also quickly learned about hustling.

This graduation of sorts is often the path to the more obvious forms of prostitution for many boys. Many researchers note the early sexual abuse histories of the boys who become involved in prostitution and theorize a correlation between these histories and the boys' subsequent involvement in prostitution (Boyer, 1989; Coombs, 1974; Deisher et al., 1969; Fisher et al., 1982; Jersild, 1956). A weakness of the literature is that little or no distinction is made regarding the types of abuse boys experience prior to their involvement in prostitution. There is no information about the duration, frequency, or specific sexual acts involved and often little or no data about the relationship between the abuser and the boy.

The author's experience suggests that a significant amount of the abuse documented by the research could be accounted for by the prolific careers of pederasts. There are many pathways into prostitution for boys; it is impossible, based on the literature, to determine how many find their way through pederasts, but the topic certainly deserves more attention than it has received.

There is a possible parallel between the young pimps who do the recruiting and early socialization of young women prostitutes and the similar role that pederasts play in recruiting and socializing young men. The parallels lie primarily in the skills that pimps and pederasts have at identifying youth who are most vulnerable and in the elaborate seductions they are able to employ. Pimps and pederasts are much more able than social service agencies to supply vulnerable youth with housing, food, clothing, and affection.

An important difference between pimps and pederasts, and possibly the reason for the lack of inquiry into pederasty, is the difference between what drives male and female prostitution. Female prostitution is more profit or economically driven, whereas male prostitution is more sexually driven. The subculture of female prostitution (pimps and prostitutes) is generally organized around business principles and what is profitable. The subculture of male prostitution and the role of the pederast are organized around sexual tastes and/or obsessions, and often subjugate profits to those interests. In this sense, adopting the mind of the pederast is not as easy as adopting the mind of the pimp. Most people understand the profit motive and capitalism, but few are comfortable with the world of the pederast. A more thorough understanding of how this pederast subculture operates would shed light on adolescent male prostitution.

WHAT IS MISSING FROM THE RESEARCH LITERATURE

Following are examples of areas the research has ignored or contributed little to but that offer much potential for increased knowledge and understanding of not only male prostitution but adolescent male sexuality.

Drag Queens

Roman boys who were castrated and dressed as girls were in great demand in the brothels of Rome. Benjamin and Masters (1964) report that in the 19th century Dr. Jacobus Sutor found boys of 11 and 12 in the brothels of Beijing who had been partially castrated and taught to cross dress and assume a feminine gender role when he visited China. Cross-dressing male prostitutes are a common and prominent feature of male prostitution in the Middle and Far East.

Drag queens or cross-dressers have been and are a common feature of male prostitution throughout the world, yet there is virtually no research on this unique aspect of prostitution. The adolescent boys who cross-dress and prostitute on the streets of American cities today raise important questions about ethnicity, homosexuality, and gender role expectations in our culture. They are disproportionately boys of color, primarily African American, Hispanic, and American Indian. This situation leads to pointed questions about gender role rigidity for males within different ethnic and cultural milieus.

Drag queens are not transvestites, as they are often called, because of the primarily public nature of their cross-dressing and because their cross-dressing is not primarily related to sexual arousal. Rather, it is primarily related to gender role presentation. They are also not transsexuals, as they sometimes are diagnosed, or at least few of them meet the criteria necessary for surgical consideration. Drag queens often talk of feeling more feminine than masculine, which can mislead clinicians into thinking they are transsexuals, but seldom do they actually want to be a woman. This is often a metaphorical way for them to talk about the qualities of being feminine. Most striking is that the same behavior in women is seldom, if ever, considered a sign of pathology or even deviant.

Case Example

Allen/Alexis was 16-year-old African American male who had been doing "drag" since he was 13. He said a customer had first gotten him to try it, and he felt safer dressing as a woman than as a man. In his predominantly African American community he reported less harassment for dressing as a woman than as a male who identified as gay. He and the group of "queens" he socialized with would confuse

and confound uninitiated youth workers with their mixing of pro-
nouns. A favorite phrase of Allen's/Alexis's was "I'm more woman
than you could ever handle and more man than you could ever hope
to be." He also once commented that a therapist was more "woman"
than he was, which was interpreted as a reference to the therapist's
nurturing qualities.

Allen/Alexis would prostitute with a variety of customers. Some
were "closeted" gay men who wanted to pretend they were having
sex with a woman but knew he was male. Some were openly gay
men who were extremely "butch" and wanted a "feme" counterpart.
Often he would prostitute in areas where he could pass as a woman
with men who did not know he was male. On those occasions he
would restrict the transaction to preforming fellatio on customers to
prevent them discovering his genitals.

Allen/Alexis had briefly taken black market hormones to stimulate
breast development but had no desire to have a sex change. He also
had several different wardrobes corresponding to different styles
such as "slut," "businesswoman," and "entertainer."

Heterosexual Male Prostitution

Badgley (1984) found that 50% of the 229 adolescents (145 females, 84 males) interviewed reported that they had been approached for sex by women. This is one of the few studies to ask the
question, what would we learn if we asked more?

Informal interviews with clients and street outreach workers from
around the country reveal that virtually all have anecdotal accounts
of boys who trick occasionally to exclusively with women. The accounts vary greatly as to the type and style of prostitution with women,
but the one consistent theme is that women seldom to never want
brief and orgasm-focused sex from the boys. It is virtually always a
kept-boy style of prostitution. The boys always spend at least the
night and often days with the woman and the sex is qualitatively
different than that which occurs with male customers.

There is little doubt that the phenomenon exists, likely in numbers
that would surprise most practitioners, but there are virtually no data
on which to speculate. Perhaps the more pertinent question is why
have these questions not been asked more?

The Effects of Prostitution

Boyer (1986) is the only researcher who has conducted longitudinal studies to analyze the exit process from street life and the impact of social services directed at street youth. The bulk of the research on prostitution consists primarily of field interviews and case studies that describe the phenomenon, its causes and motivation, and the needs of the youth involved.

Because of the wide diversity of the types of prostitution boys may engage in and the similar diversity of the boys themselves, it is impossible to say much in a general way about the effects of prostitution on young men. It is important to distinguish the effects of the streets from the effects of prostitution. The lower-class forms of prostitution such as street hustling can have much more debilitating effects than the higher-class forms such as the call services, but this is more likely the result of the higher levels of predation and deprivation that are characteristic of lower-class prostitution as the result of actual fee-for-service sex. The violence, drugs, and frequent arrests that are more common in the lower classes of prostitution create effects that can be independent of the effects of sex for money.

There are at least three important variables to consider in assessing what impact prostitution may have on individuals who are involved. The first is the life experiences of the boy prior to his involvement in prostitution. This is important in evaluating the resiliency and/or adaptation skills the boy possesses. Boys who have extensive histories of deprivation, poverty, physical/sexual abuse, neglect, or institutionalization become much easier targets of predation by everyone from customers to the police. It is as though prostitution has an exponential effect on the history a boy brings to prostitution. The more troubled he is before he becomes involved in prostitution, the more troubled he will become by his involvement. This does not mean that those who manage prostitution with more competency have not experienced significant trauma. Resiliency in children allows some to adapt more effectively than others and to show less effect from trauma, but it is unlikely that those who are getting the most "beat up" by their involvement in prostitution were not the most "beat up" before they got involved in prostitution. As is explored later, however, one must not automatically assume that all boys in prostitution have significant histories of abuse and neglect.

The second variable in assessing the impact of prostitution is the extent and duration of the boy's involvement in prostitution. Boys who make brief forays into prostitution and move on suffer fewer effects than those who remain involved for a long time. Those who prostitute on a part-time basis with regular customers suffer fewer effects than those who prostitute many times a week with customers off the street. Those who begin their prostitution careers in early adolescence and are still involved in late adolescence, regardless of the class of prostitution, are likely to have lasting and significant effects. The most immediate and obvious of these effects is in the domain of living skills such as housing, education, employment, money management, and relationship skills, all of which may be minimal and crisis oriented. The less obvious effects are in the domain of mental health and self-esteem. Many boys are adept at masking the latter effects even if they are significant.

The third variable in assessing the impact of prostitution has to do with the sexual orientation of the boy. Weeks (1981) observes that "homosexual roles and identities are historically constructed" and that "the social definitions and subjective meaning given to the orientation can vary enormously. . . . If this is the case for the clients of male prostitutes, how much more true is it for the prostitute himself who must confront two stigmatized identities—that of the homosexual and that of the prostitute" (p. 115). The fact that homosexual behavior, especially in the context of child abuse or prostitution, does not necessarily give rise to a homosexual identity makes sorting out this issue extremely difficult. Hence the obsession of the research literature with "Are they gay or are they not?"

Although Boyer's (1989) research has contributed greatly to the understanding of homosexual identity formation in young male prostitutes, there is little or no corresponding research on young men who identify as heterosexual or bisexual. It is important to note that over one-third of the boys in Boyer's prostitute sample identified as bisexual or between a 2 (mainly heterosexual/substantial degree of homosexual) and a 4 (mainly homosexual/substantial degree of heterosexual) on Kinsey's 7-point scale.

If it is difficult for researchers and clinicians to make sense of the sexual orientation of young males in prostitution, it is even more difficult for the young men themselves. The only conclusive thing that can be said about the sexual orientation and identity development of young males in prostitution is that it is likely to be problematic and confusing for both the young man and those who work with him.

Case Example

By the time Johnny was 17, he had been arrested over a dozen times for offenses ranging from soliciting to shoplifting. He had been beaten up by cops, customers, and other street kids and was a permanent fixture of the "gay ghetto" street hustling scene. Johnny had been severely physically and sexually abused from 4 to 8 and had grown up in 12 foster homes, 3 residential treatment centers, and 1 correctional facility.

Case Example

Greg started running away when he was 13 to explore his emerging homosexuality. His suburban middle-class family was reasonably functional but homophobic. After hustling with regular customers for about a year, Greg was arrested and spent time in a group home and a gay foster home. Greg had more difficulty dealing with the homophobia of his mother and the juvenile justice system than with his prostitution experiences.

Case Example

Bob ran away from his foster home at 14 and learned to hustle after being approached many times in the bookstores he liked to hang out in. When he was 16, he identified as homosexual and moved in with an older lover who turned out to be abusive. After leaving that relationship, Bob started having sex with women and became confused about his sexuality. After identifying as bisexual for a period of time, Bob settled on a heterosexual identity.

Case Example

Jeff had been hustling since he was 13 but adamantly stated he was not homosexual. He was involved in a lot of delinquent behavior

and spent some time in correctional facilities. Jeff had been violently
sexually abused by a man when he was 10. Jeff finally realized he
was in love with his best male friend when he was 16; after the reali-
zation, both quit hustling. They eventually both identified as homosexual but continued to have sex with women on occasion.

The Conventional View

Much of the current research and literature concerning adolescent
male prostitution focuses on how entrance into prostitution is a
problem manifesting "deviance" and/or "pathology" that is caused
or influenced by a number of possible variables such as early sexual
experience, sexual abuse, homosexuality, dysfunctional families,
low self-esteem, and drug/alcohol abuse (Mathews, 1989).

In the conventional view, the variables mentioned are thought to
work singly or in combination to induce an adolescent to enter
prostitution. There is an implicit assumption that the sexual activity
of prostitution violates the norms of acceptable sexual behavior, and
therefore involvement in it is considered "sick" and/or deviant. This
is even more true of male than female prostitution because the sexual
behavior often involves homosexuality. Although there is little doubt
that these variables contribute to the vulnerability of some youth to
become involved in prostitution, the generalizabilty to all youth in
prostitution is suspect and these variables provide little insight into
the more fundamental processes that place adolescents at risk of
involvement, contribute to their continued involvement, and present
barriers to exiting street life and prostitution.

Before reviewing the variables, it is important to note two methodological issues in the research on adolescent prostitution that
affect the results. The first is the problem of sampling or who is
studied; the second issue is how data are collected once the subjects
are identified. The most accessible subjects for research are those
who are arrested, incarcerated, in treatment, requesting help/services,
or most visible on the streets. If one assumes that a significant proportion of young people involved in prostitution is not accessible
through these means, then it is difficult to generalize the research

findings to all youth who are involved in prostitution. These types of methodological problems have parallels in the research on homosexuality (Gonsiorek, 1982, 1991) and sexual abuse (Finkelhor & Browne, 1986) yet are seldom acknowledged in the literature on adolescent prostitution.

The reliance on primarily quantitative methods of data collection is inherently problematic in regard to adolescent prostitution. It usually means the young person must fit his or her reality into a predetermined set of questions and/or categories that convey to the youth a lot about what the researcher already thinks and wants to hear about, rather than what the youth sees as important and relevant. For example, a young hustler was having a conversation with a social worker. The young man began to relate his family history, and was asked why he was sharing that information, to which the response was, "Isn't that what social workers want to know?" At 16, this young man was already adept at perceiving the professional biases of social services professionals and responding to those biases in the manner the professional were most comfortable with.

These qualitative methods also rely on the relative honesty of the subjects and the interpretations of the interviewer. These are somewhat unreliable given the legal and moral judgments of the behavior being studied and the extremely short-term nature of the relationship between the youth and the researcher.

Finally, these methods assume that the answers that youth give do not change over time. In reality, the answers to such simple questions as who are you, where are you going, and where did you come from change significantly over time.

Early Sexual Experience/Sexual Abuse

The research literature clearly indicates that a significant number, if not the majority, of young males in prostitution were sexually or physically abused and/or psychologically maltreated while they were growing up (Boyer, 1989; Deisher et al., 1969; Fisher et al., 1982). Yet many young men are abused and maltreated and do not become involved in prostitution and many young people involved in prostitution were not abused. Clearly there is a need to consider other variables that, in combination with abuse, lead to a young person's involvement in prostitution. It is also misleading to overemphasize one variable to the exclusion of others, such as the disenfranchisement of youth, the mixed and double messages about sexuality that are targeted at youth, the inability of social services to provide assistance to street youth, the disintegration of families and communities, and the climates of futility that many young people grow up in.

Homosexuality

The percentage of young men involved in prostitution who identify as homosexual has increased significantly over the last 2 decades; prostitution can be understood as a logical construction in the social identity of young males who are homosexual (Boyer, 1989). However, many young men are involved in prostitution who do not identify as homosexual, some male prostitution does not involve homosexual behavior, and considerable prostitution is bisexual. Researchers commonly ignore the diversity in the sexuality of males in prostitution by dichotomizing the samples into groups of homosexual and heterosexuals and suggesting that bisexuality is the same as homosexuality. Boyer (1989) defends this practice by suggesting "that the study is not one of natural categories but of cultural ones" and arguing that "individuals draw upon the existing cultural categories in their attempts to gain self-understanding" (p. 179). This dichotomization has also been criticized because it implies that homosexuality is a homogeneous category and that sexual orientation is a polarized and immutable state (DeCecco, 1981). The relationship between homosexuality as a socially/culturally constructed identity and male prostitution is poorly understood. Because adolescence is perhaps the most bisexual period in the human development life cycle, more research is required to uncover the depth and meaning of sexual orientation as a variable influencing an adolescent's involvement in prostitution.

Dysfunctional Families

Every year over 1 million young people run away from their families to escape problems or seek adventure on the streets (Children's Defense Fund, 1990). If the young person is unable or unwilling to return home, survival becomes a serious issue. As needs for basic food and shelter become more acute, prostitution becomes a realistic and viable alternative to meet these needs. A difficult family or living situation may bring an adolescent to the streets, but the decision to engage in prostitution depends on other factors such as the length of time a person has been on the streets, the intensity of survival needs, and the influence of friends and street peers.

Low Self-Esteem

A common perception is that a poor self-image leads adolescents to become involved in prostitution. In a study of personality characteristics of 30 young women who had been involved in prostitution for over a year, Thompson (1988) found that most had a positive self-image, and the young women who had the worst self-images had all spent time in residential treatment programs because of their prostitution activity. When asked why they used some of the negative labels they employed for themselves, the women commonly responded, "that's what they told me in treatment." Mathews's (1989) study of adolescent prostitution in Toronto found that the low self-esteem reported by adolescents after they began their involvement in prostitution resulted not from the work itself but from the harassment, judgment, and persecution from police, social workers, and others.

Drug/Alcohol Abuse

The myth persists that drug or alcohol addiction drives some people to prostitution to support an ever-increasing habit and harder drugs. Although many young people involved in prostitution use drugs and alcohol, it is not known how this usage is in any way different from the drug- and alcohol-using population in general. The relatively recent development of crack addicts prostituting to get more crack is as yet poorly understood. The more common scenario is a development of or increase in drug or alcohol abuse as a means of coping with the loneliness and stress of street life.

The Problem With the Conventional View

The tendency of traditional social research and social work practice to view involvement in prostitution as a symptom of personal
pathology or as deviance implies a preunderstanding that is normative. A view that if a young person is a prostitute, it can be assumed
that certain things must be true about his or her background, personality, and motivation gives rise to uniform intervention approaches
and labeling that is one-dimensional. Personal pathology/deviance
explanations isolate the phenomenon of adolescent prostitution in
the individual. This view is limited in that it deflects awareness of
the broader social and economic forces that place many youth at
risk for involvement in prostitution (or gangs, homelessness, delinquency, or drug abuse) and it fails to illuminate the social interactions that affect a youth's life once he or she enters prostitution. Not
surprisingly, social policy and social service interventions based on
the conventional view have failed to reduce or contain the number
of adolescents involved in prostitution (or gangs, homelessness, delinquency, or drug abuse).

Viewing prostitution as the symptom of personal pathology/devi-
ance also fails to address the consumers of adolescent prostitution.
There are definite and identifiable markets for the sexual services of
adolescents. The question should not be what is wrong with adolescents that they prostitute, but why do so many adults want to have
sex with adolescents? If there are such clear markets for the sexual
services of adolescents, how come more young people do not become involved? The customers are usually adult males, but a study
in Toronto found that half of the adolescents interviewed had been
approached for sex by women (Badgley, 1984). The lack of research
and attention directed at the consumers of adolescent prostitution is
difficult to defend and raises questions about the focus on the adolescents involved.

The conventional view also minimizes or ignores the economics
of adolescent prostitution. For young people with acute survival
needs who posses few employment skills and have no permanent
address and possibly no identification, prostitution presents a viable
option for quick money. Working for minimum wage at a fast-food
restaurant can appear as exploitative to some adolescents as prosti-

tution. The economics of street survival has been expressed as, "Once I was on the streets, I knew I could steal, sell drugs, or sell sex. There was less chance of getting busted if I sold sex, and I figured I didn't hurt anybody else." For many young people on the streets, prostitution is not a moral or a mental health issue but one of economics. These young people decide that, at some level, prostitution is acceptable, though indeed this decision is made in desperation and with a very limited range of options.

Individual pathology/deviance explanations fail to recognize that prostitution is not a monolithic form of behavior. There are many different types of prostitution and many different types of prostitutes, each with his or her own reasons and explanations for why he or she got involved in prostitution and why he or she stays or leaves. If one listens long enough, those reasons and explanations are likely to change over time as the young person's awareness of himself or herself and the world he or she lives in changes. As Mathews (1989) states, "The conventional view fails to consider the lived, felt reality of adolescents on the street, and as a result social work programs based on this theoretical orientation are meaningless and irrelevant to these young people" (p. 8).

A Contextual View

Mathews (1989) is one of the few researchers to address the social context in which prostitution occurs. His social effects model "rejects the individual pathology concept and attempts to ground adolescent prostitution in a wider social context" and "views entrance into prostitution not as a problem for the adolescent but as a solution" (p. 8).

Mathews identifies two types of "social effects." The first are "factors which originate in society and social relationships and which inform and/or influence an adolescent's process of entrance into, and maintenance in, prostitution as an income producing activity" (p. 8). These factors include elements such as the convoluted media images about sexuality targeted at adolescents, tacit social acceptance of prostitution, and the "contradictory messages that come from a government that finances itself, in part, through drinking, smoking, and gambling (lotteries), yet advocates restraint and morality when it comes to sex" (p. 8).

The second factors "consist of more negative elements and are best understood as being consequences suffered by the adolescent prostitutes as a result of society's judgment against what they do" (p. 8). These include the loss of traditional support structures (family, friends, school, church), the narrowing of life choices available, the acquisition of a "criminal" role, and the entrenchment in street lifestyle and values that makes transition back to the straight world more difficult.

Mathews's model details how needs, skills, values, models, and subculture interact and lead to an adolescent's decision to enter prostitution, to become entrenched in prostitution, and to exit from prostitution. This model views prostitution as a satisfier of basic needs (work—for money to buy food and shelter) and as a consequential choice for young people with few resources (skills, contacts, and emotional support).

Mathews suggests that the most important factor in a young person's decision to exit prostitution is a highly supportive significant other or model (this could include youth workers, social workers, exprostitutes, family members, boyfriends, girlfriends, or street workers) outside of the prostitution community. As a young person leaves prostitution, he or she frequently loses income, status in the street community, and stability and control over his or her life. The establishment of a significant relationship provides more incentive for a young person to change than anything else.

Mathews's research falls within the tradition and is consistent with a re-emerging body of literature and new research that confirms the importance of significant adult relationships in fostering resilience, protective factors, and healthy development in adolescents, especially high-risk adolescents. This growing body of recent research and scholarship complements older literature on the role of youth workers and mentors as powerful agents in helping adolescents overcome significant obstacles to their development. (This research is discussed in more detail in chapter 9.)

Young people exiting prostitution also have a variety of street friends and other models exerting influence in the opposite direction, and can vacillate between the streets and the straight life for considerable periods of time. They experience great ambivalence as they contemplate choosing between competing cultural patterns of work, remuneration, and lifestyle that make the prospects frightening and imposing. This ambivalence leads many professionals to question the "true" motivation of the young person who vacillates between hanging out with old friends and trying to stay out of prostitution while developing the resources to maintain a nonstreet life.

This can be a particularly dangerous period of time for some young people both emotionally and physically. Emotionally because significant others outside of the subculture of the streets can question the motives and genuineness of the youth's desire to leave prostitution and withdraw their emotional support at a time when the youth needs it most. Physically because the cultural rules, values, and norms of behavior are different in the street subculture than in the straight world. In the straight world, police and social workers are the "good guys" and friends can be trusted not to hurt you if you disagree with them. On the streets, police and social workers are the "bad guys" and no one can be trusted not to use physical force or intimidation if they do not like what you are doing.

For example, frequently a youth leaving prostitution has considerable knowledge and information about a host of criminal activities (drug dealings, theft and burglary rings, sex rings, political corruption) that police and others are interested in to use to prosecute the "bad guys." The new values the young person is learning (trust the "good guys") often leads him or her to want to cooperate with the police in investigating and prosecuting the individuals the youth has knowledge about. This makes the young person a threat and a target for those same individuals. In the 15-year history of the Street Program at the Lutheran Social Services of Minnesota, eight young people were murdered and many others were harassed and intimidated during this stage of exiting prostitution. The irony is that many young people who cooperate with authorities in these types of investigations because they want to help and want to do the right thing end up feeling as betrayed by the "system" as they did by individuals on the street. In both situations they are used and manipulated for goals that have nothing to do with their own well-being.

This points to the young person's need for the emotional support of a significant other as he or she attempts to make the transition between cultures. The young person's ultimate decision to leave appears to be strongly affected by a need for genuine emotional relationships. Once a young person begins to experience the genuineness and stability of a relationship with a positive model, the young person can begin to sort out his or her other needs, values, and skills (resources) in order to establish priorities and determine a plan for leaving the streets.

Through a relationship with a significant other, a young person can find access to his or her needs for work, housing, support, and assistance. This greatly enhances the likelihood of leaving prostitution. This also opens up the possibility of getting the young person involved in specialized training programs to develop the skills that will enhance his or her prospects of maintaining traditional types of employment. Although the street values the young person acquired are likely never forgotten, the person can reevaluate them in light of new emotional relationships and the stability of a new living situation.

9

Prevention of and Intervention
With Male Prostitution

THROUGHOUT HISTORY, "interventions" with prostitution have ranged from licensed regulation to suppression and control through law enforcement. Licensed regulation has most commonly been utilized. Suppression and control through law enforcement are primarily a development of the late 18th and 19th centuries.

Because the most visible adolescent prostitution is on the streets, and most adolescents are introduced to prostitution through the streets (even if they move on to higher-class forms of prostitution), interventions or attempts at prevention tend to focus on the social phenomenon of street youth. Although adolescent male and female prostitution have a range of similarities and differences, the approaches to working with male and female prostitutes have been relatively similar. This chapter discusses some of the approaches to interventions and presents a detached youth work model. Unless otherwise noted, the discussion and model apply equally to both males and females. A thorough knowledge of the uniqueness of each form of adolescent prostitution is necessary for effective service provision, but it would be a mistake to build separate programs or interventions for males and females.

Baizerman (1989) suggests a public health model and vocabulary to organize and analyze the discussion of intervention and prevention attempts. It is important to distinguish the different levels of

261

prevention and, although all interventions may be preventive, it is possible and useful to specify precisely, if abstractly, what one hopes to prevent.

In public health, distinction is made between and among three levels of prevention: primary, secondary, and tertiary. Primary prevention means keeping a phenomenon from occurring, secondary prevention means keeping a phenomenon once present from occurring again and/or becoming debilitating, and tertiary prevention means rehabilitation.

Public health also distinguishes between a social group of actual people and a population/group as a logical or empirical category of people. There is also distinction among the levels of intervention called clinical (e.g., Joe), population/group (e.g., 14-year-olds; runaways; left-handed, blue-eyed boys) and social institutional (e.g., street youth).

Prevention of adolescent prostitution may mean controlling its magnitude and configuration by eliminating or preventing the recruitment of certain populations/groups (e.g., younger youth) and/or by changing how the street subculture is connected to a variety of other social institutions (e.g., police, child protection, youth-serving agencies), social structures (e.g., the job market), and social phenomena (e.g., exposure to HIV). This does not represent a moral acceptance of street youth or prostitution, rather an acceptance of the phenomenon as being real and beyond the current willingness and/or ability to make it go away. Adolescent prostitution is morally unacceptable, but it exists and persists. Its consequences can be diminished on youth who are on the streets for whatever reasons or causes.

This raises the question of whether the prevention of a phenomenon is possible without an understanding of what caused it. The short answer is yes; controlling a phenomenon also prevents it from becoming more serious, lasting longer, and entailing more debilitating consequences. Of more significance when thinking about cause is the distinctions among individuals, population/group, and social institutional. The causes for each are themselves different phenomena, with increasing complexity and abstractness as one moves from the specific, concrete individual to a theoretical entity such as the social institution of street youth.

Even more important may be the choice to pay more attention to continuance than to cause. The key analytical and action questions may be what and how adolescent male prostitution and street youth are sustained. Adolescent male prostitution as a part of the larger subculture of street youth (e.g., prostitutes, homeless, gangs, delinquents) is embedded in a reticulum of social structures and processes. Adolescent prostitution is sustained by its interconnections to functionally and geographically related social systems.

Table 9.1 organizes these concepts and grounds them to an understanding of services to youth involved in prostitution.

These levels of prevention (primary, secondary, and tertiary) and levels of intervention (clinical, population/group, and social institutional) are used to organize the following review of intervention models for youth in prostitution.

THE SOCIAL INSTITUTIONAL LEVEL

Prevention and intervention at the social institutional level are complex and difficult due to the multiple variables involved and the difficulty in mobilizing support in social, economic, and public policy within which the social institution of street youth is embedded. This section does not analyze in detail the social, political, economic, and religious contexts that contribute to the cause and continuance of street youth and prostitution, but provides a brief overview of some of the major trends and issues related to the social phenomenon of street youth. Having no more youth on the streets, making it possible for all youth to get off the streets, making street life different (i.e., more bearable or less damaging), making it possible for youth to have a nonstreet life, and creating a healing environment (i.e., making services and opportunities for nonstreet life available) are indeed difficult if not impossible tasks to accomplish fully, but there is ample room for improvement.

At this time in American history it is not possible to escape the conclusion that we face an imminent crisis regarding our nation's children and youth. It is not necessary to recite the litany of reports and research that document the multitude of ways that youth are in crisis. One of the most recent documents reports that fully one half

TABLE 9.1 Public Health Prevention

	Clinical Level	*Population Group*	*Social Institutional*
Primary Prevention	Keeping Joe (a youth) off the streets	Keeping X type of youth off the streets	No more youth on the streets
Secondary Prevention	Helping Joe get off the streets	Helping X type of youth get off the streets	Making it possible for all youth to get off the streets
	Preventing Joe from being further damaged by his street life	Keeping street life from becoming more damaging to X type of youth	Making street life different (e.g., bearable or less damaging)
Tertiary Prevention	Helping Joe have a nonstreet life	Helping X type of youth have a nonstreet life	Making it possible for youth to have a nonstreet life
	Reversing the damages caused by Joe's street life	Reversing the damages caused by X type of youth's street life	Creating a healing environment (i.e., make available services and opportunities for nonstreet life)

of America's youth are at serious to moderate risk of not reaching productive adulthood (Carnegie Corporation, 1992).

There is growing consensus in the reports that chronicle the troubles of youth that the most important influences on young people today have arisen as a consequence of social and economic upheaval and injustice. This consensus argues that the various ways of getting into trouble—not just trouble with the law—can be seen as statistically probable reactions to these influences. In other words, troublesome adolescent behavior says more about the situation than about the young person. In the Carnegie Corporation (1992) report, James Comer, a cochair of the Carnegie Task Force, describes the changes that have influenced youth:

> Two massive sets of social and economic changes have occurred along parallel tracks, and they intersect most acutely at the point when young people attempt to make the transition from adolescence to adulthood, from dependence to independence—or, better yet, interdependence, for that is what productive adulthood in our country really means. I see these two tracks as the following: a significant increase in the number

of skills needed for successful adulthood and a significant decrease in
the ongoing support and guidance offered to young people during their
growing up years. These two trends have created a serious problem in
our country—indeed, I believe, a crisis. (p. 18)

Comer describes the nation's postindustrial shift from a manufac-
turing and industrial base that was able to absorb almost all workers
to an economy rooted in an information and service base. With this
shift came new and greatly accelerated educational requirements
that necessitated higher levels of individual development and adequate family and community functioning to promote that level of
development.

What has actually occurred has been a decrease in the support
young people feel from their families and communities as they struggle
to move through their development and meet the more accelerated
educational and skill requirements for successful transition to adulthood. Some of this decline in support is the result of poor or nonexistent public policy related to youth development, but the decline
also reflects the greater demands for work placed on many parents
and the disintegration of neighborhoods and communities as safe and
nurturing environments for children and youth.

The results of this lack of support for children and youth can be
seen in the rising levels of adolescent violence, delinquency, and self-
destructive behavior. As young people grow up without the support
and guidance they need, in conditions of great stress and adversity,
such as poverty, neglect, abuse, parental inattention, depression,
alcoholism, criminality and unsafe neighborhoods, the probability
of engaging in high-risk behavior increases. A sad reality of American
life is that when families, schools, and communities fail to provide
for the needs of children and youth, some people attempt to exploit
those unmet needs with little or no regard for the welfare of youth.
The current rise in gang behavior among adolescents is perhaps the
most striking example of this reality. Young people's needs for safety,
protection, support, discipline, structure, and meaningful interaction
with adults is exploited by organized adults who use the youth for
their own political and financial gain. Pimps and pederasts have long
used these same tactics with youth at risk.

As young people grow through adolescence without the support they need and with ever higher levels of development necessary for a successful transition to adulthood, many are left in a social and economic backwater. This enforced marginalization gives rise to feelings of anger, rage, alienation, and hopelessness, which can be seen in their behavior.

It is this aspect of risk that defines the popular term *high-risk youth*. More youth today are at risk not because they have some personal qualities or pathologies that identify them, but because the conflict between social and economic policy has affected greater numbers of youth, increasing the statistical chances that greater overall numbers of youth will "crack" under the strain. Some groups of youth are more at risk than others owing to factors such as class, ethnicity, gender, and locale, but a significant number remain marginal in every meaningful social and economic sense until they reach their mid-20s and possibly longer. It is no surprise that there is increased crime, mental illness, drug abuse, homelessness, and prostitution due to this enforced marginalization.

The trouble in which young people find themselves reveals far less about them than it does about the environment in which they grow up. The terms *at risk* and *in trouble,* common concepts in working with young people today, are often misunderstood. The implication is often that to describe a young person in either of these ways is to point to some enduring characteristics that can be attributed to the individual concerned. Developmental theory is often employed to describe how a young person is implicated in his or her own "trouble" or risk. We suggest that at risk and in trouble are not adjectives that describe individuals, but they are prepositional phrases that refer to the situations in which people find themselves. Risk and trouble, in other words, denote circumstances; they do not define people.

This position does not exclude the possibility that there are some young people for whom risk is in some sense a personal characteristic, or whose troubles are deep-seated. But it does imply that this situation is not easy to demonstrate, that it is unlikely to be true for more than a small minority, and that a "situational" perspective should always be the one to which first consideration is given.

Much attention has been paid in the last decade to the educational and family situations of young people, but the "third leg," so to speak, of the human development triangle has received far less attention. If family and school constitute two of the primary sources of development and support for young people, the third leg represents those experiences that young people have in their neighborhoods and the larger community. An ancient African proverb admonishes that "it takes an entire tribe to raise a child."

With the exception of infancy, no time of life compresses more physical, intellectual, social, emotional, and moral development into so brief a span as the period called adolescence. The importance of community environments and institutions in contributing to that development is well supported by both research and practice. The opportunity to make those contributions arises largely during non-school hours, yet few American communities work consciously to seize that opportunity.

The Carnegie (1992) report states:

> The passage through early adolescence—guided by family, encouraged by school, and supported by community—should result in healthy outcomes. That is the case for many American youth but not for many others. Instead of safety in their neighborhoods, they face physical danger; instead of economic security they face uncertainty; instead of intellectual stimulation they face boredom; in place of respect, they are neglected; lacking clear and consistent adult expectations for them, they feel alienated from mainstream American society. (p. 9)

Historically, the social and behavioral sciences have followed a problem-focused approach to studying human and social development. This "pathology" model of research traditionally examines problems, disease, illness, maladaptation, incompetence, and deviance. The emphasis is placed on identifying the risk factors of various disorders such as alcoholism, mental illness, criminality, and delinquency. The identification of risks does not necessarily provide a clear picture of what strategies are needed to reduce the risks.

More recently, there has been a growing amount of literature and research on "protective factors," "resiliency," and "youth development" (Benard, 1991; Garmezy, 1991; Gibbs & Bennett, 1990; Search Institute, 1993; Watt, 1984; Werner & Smith, 1982). This research, which is well reviewed by Benard (1991), examines the high-risk children who become healthy, competent young adults and have found "remarkable evidence of strength, courage, and health in the midst of disaster and adversity" (Watt, 1984, p. 22).

This research, along with the increasing theoretical acceptance in the child development field of the transactional-ecological model of human development, in which the human personality is viewed as a self-righting organism that is engaged in active, ongoing adaptation to its environment (see Bronfenbrenner, 1974), has resulted in a growing interest beyond the identification of risk factors for the development of a problem behavior to an examination of the protective factors: those "traits, conditions, situations, and episodes that appear to alter—or even reverse—predictions of [negative outcome] and enable individuals to circumvent life stressors" (Garmezy, 1991, p. 421).

The importance of this research to the prevention and intervention fields is obvious: If the personal and environmental sources of social competence and wellness can be determined, better preventive interventions can be planned and focused on enhancing the personal and environmental attributes that serve as the keys to healthy development. This is especially true for the social institution of street youth, who live, work, and play in among the most high-risk environments. Too often, prevention and intervention strategies with these youth underestimate their resiliency and overemphasize their risk for disorders such as alcoholism, mental illness, criminality, or delinquency. Such strategies also unduly individualize the problems of street youth and ignore the social and environmental factors that contribute to the phenomena of street youth and adolescent prostitution.

Although this discussion is general with regard to adolescents, young males have been particularly hard hit by the social, economic, and political changes of the last few decades and the extension and marginalization of adolescence. Unlike the biological rite of passage of menses for young women, the rites of passage for young men have always been culturally defined and determined. Modern societies have been unable to maintain coherent rituals for males to identify their passage out of childhood and into adulthood. Chronically high unemployment rates and a 25% drop in earning power over the last 2 decades for young males (a 60% drop for young African American males) have left these young men more dependent for longer periods of time and further undermines their transition to adulthood (The Forgotten Half, 1988). During this extended dependence and marginalization, young men are murdered, assaulted, incarcerated, and complete suicides more than any other age or gender group in America, and far more than in any other industrialized nation ("More Young Men Killed in U.S.," 1990; Search Institute, 1993). This book also suggests that young males are sexually abused in greater numbers than is reported or generally believed. Young men are not just the perpetrators of increased levels of interpersonal and sexual violence, they are also the victims of it.

A question that needs to be asked of current public policy is the extent to which it assumes (or does not) that individual problems have environmental roots. Policies and resource allocation seem to reflect the view that young people and their parents are largely responsible for their own problems. Unemployment, bad housing, run-down schools, racial and sexual violence, and questionable police behavior not only do not excuse individual or collective acts of rage or despair, but they often do not even explain them.

A particular gender differentiation in this last policy shift is disturbing. It is reflected in the fact that the majority of the adolescents in juvenile correctional programs are male, and the majority of the adolescents in community and institutional mental health programs are female. The common stereotypes are that young men are "delinquents" or "criminals" and that young women are "troubled" or "victims." Although both labels (delinquent/criminal and troubled/victim) create responses that young people do not necessarily want or need (i.e., control), the rationale for the one is to protect the community and the rationale for the other is to protect the individual. The situation and/or environment are likely to be used to explain, even if they do not excuse, the behavior of young women.

The statistical categories or situations in which young people are at risk or disadvantaged (e.g., abused children, ethnic minorities, school dropouts, inner city youth, youth from broken homes) can be facilely described. Membership in any of these categories makes it much more likely, in a purely statistical sense, that trouble of some kind will occur. Young people in one or more of these categories are at risk because some feature of their social environment puts them at a disadvantage. It is worth noting that the term *disadvantaged,* a less fashionable term these days, implies a fundamental issue that *at risk* does not, namely social justice.

These trends and policies refute the popular notion that youth make up a privileged group, and suggest that today is an especially difficult time for the young, particularly if they are in any way disadvantaged. Young people are in the front lines of the economic and political battles that rage around them and in which they are not allowed to actively participate. They attract the stereotypes and images that portray themselves as the ultimate causes not only of their own troubles but of other people's problems as well. And youth are on the receiving end of regressive social policies that seem to overpower attempts to liberalize and enrich the experience of growing up.

THE POPULATION/GROUP LEVEL

Population/group interventions target logical or empirical categories of youth who are at risk or involved in prostitution for prevention efforts (primary, secondary, or tertiary). Examples of these kinds of interventions are shelter and services for runaway and homeless youth, HIV-risk reduction for youth in prostitution, drug abuse prevention for homeless pregnant girls, and employment and training services for homeless youth.

In the last 20 years, most models of intervention at this level have grown out of adolescent health programs and runaway shelters for youth. Adolescent health programs have their roots in adolescent medicine, which represents the collaboration of the schools of medicine, public health, and social work in universities during the 1960s. These programs were a response to the unique medical, developmental, psychosocial, and health-care needs of adolescents. Deisher, who conducted research on male prostitution in the 1960s and has been instrumental in developing programs for youth in prostitution in Seattle, was among the early pioneers of adolescent medicine. Los Angeles Children's Hospital, which has long been involved in providing health care and coordinating services to youth in prostitution, is an example of an adolescent health-care program that grew into a comprehensive service system for these youth.

Runaway shelters developed out of a response to the youth who dropped out in the 1960s; these shelters expanded greatly during the rise in runaways in the 1970s. The expansion of these programs was in part a result of the federal Runaway Youth Act of 1974 and the funding made available through the Youth Development Bureau of the Department of Health and Human Services. Some of these programs continue to evolve and now attempt to serve homeless youth through funding from the legislative renewal of the Runaway Youth Act and the National Network of Runaway and Youth Services. Like adolescent health programs, these shelters and programs have experienced the increasing population of runaway and throwaway children in the last 20 years and have attempted to adapt to the changing service needs of the population of youth most likely to become involved in prostitution.

With the emergence of homeless youth and the threat of HIV infection in the 1980s, adolescent health-care programs and runaway shelters joined forces in many locations and developed the concept of multiservice centers and service provider collaborations in an attempt to consolidate resources and provide a more comprehensive range of services for street youth. The alliance arose because the shelters had access to the youth, and adolescent health programs had expertise in health care issues. The services these collaborations provide include street outreach, drop-in centers, shelter, health care, employment and training services, educational programs, transitional living skills programs, advocacy, and case management services.

A key development in the inclusion of services in such programs of adolescent males involved in prostitution was the emergence and growth of lesbian and gay social service organizations in the 1970s. These organizations gave gay-identified boys a reason to trust that their sexual orientation would be respected and that gay-identified, gay-sensitive staff would be available to them. The emerging expertise of lesbian and gay social service organizations added new insights to the problems facing gay youth and contributed to the development of services specifically designed for these youth, including prevention efforts such as support and coming-out groups.

Unfortunately, these organizations, which were at their high point in the 1970s and early 1980s, are often consumed by the need for AIDS services or have not survived or retained their effectiveness in more politically and fiscally conservative times.

Each of the last 3 decades has seen dramatic increases in the growth of disenfranchised and alienated youth due to social trends and policy shifts and the corresponding socially constructed definitions of the problems they face (Weisberg, 1985). The "hippies" became the "runaways" who became the "prostitutes" who became the "homeless" who have now become the "gangs." As the social alienation of these youth has increased, they have become less willing to participate in programs designed to meet their ever-expanding needs, and service providers have become increasingly reliant on outreach as the most effective means of involving youth in program participation.

These alienated youth are the easiest, although not the only, pool on which predators, such as pimps and pederasts, look to recruit youth to prostitution. These youth do not all become involved in prostitution but a significant number do, and those that do not are likely to become involved in one of the many other deviant or criminal subcultures of the streets, such as drugs or theft, thus increasing their alienation.

The theory behind intervention programs that target this population is that youth have a basic right to services that will allow them to grow and develop, and, if given access to services that respect their right to choose, most youth will choose alternatives to street life and prostitution. It is the simple idea of offering a carrot instead of a stick; or, from a behavioral perspective, offering reinforcement instead of punishment-based alternatives. These interventions allow youth to build, in their own way, on their competencies and adaptive abilities rather than focusing on their disabilities. These interventions allow youth to choose the time and place in which they will face their victimization and make their own meaning of it. If all they want is to get a job and housing so they can go back to school, that is what they are offered. The boundaries about who is allowed to get close and how soon are left to the youth to control. Adults earn the right to restore the trust that was betrayed; they cannot assume that because they mean well, youth should trust them.

Access to services and the changing needs of youth present problems for service providers. These two issues of access and needs are the points around which many programs or collaborations of programs struggle and/or fail in their efforts to serve youth involved in prostitution and street youth in general. A more basic concern is the integrity of the model itself, which is alien and suspect to many law enforcement, mental health, social service, and public welfare agencies. Maintaining a noncoercive approach to the direct and indirect challenges of such systems is a continuous struggle.

Access can be thought of as the entry point back into the broader society for youth involved in prostitution or street life. That gateway for youth is embodied in the outreach worker. The relationships outreach workers are able to form with youth are the basis for the access the youth has to the possibilities the youth worker has to offer. The youth worker represents an agency or program to the youth on the street. The youth do not trust programs, for which they have little concept (e.g., program philosophies, protocols, service flow charts, and bureaucratic structures), but may trust an outreach worker who works for an agency to work with them toward other possibilities.

Outreach workers are also gateways for the programs that employ them. It is through these workers that agencies have access to the youth they intend to serve. Outreach workers must keep the agency responsive to the needs of youth and can be the source of information and experience on the changing needs of alienated youth. This is reflected in the evolution of the programs that developed out of serving runaway youth in the 1970s.

Despite the critical role the outreach worker plays in the success or failure of programs designed to serve disenfranchised youth, outreach work is often assigned to entry-level staff with little or no training or support. They are overworked, underpaid, and seldom taken seriously. They work to establish credibility with youth on the street and similarly have to work to establish credibility at their agency. The management of this tension by both the worker and the agency is the key to whether a program can provide the access and maintain the growth necessary to achieve its goals of helping the youth it intends to serve.

Case Example

Establishing rapport with street youth often requires that an outreach worker be accessible by spending long hours hanging out with and listening to youth. This work often occurs in the evening or late at night on street corners, in coffee shops, or at other street youth hangouts. These youth are often not willing to show up for appointments during the day at an agency office until they have established a trusting relationship with the worker, which could take weeks or months.

This willingness to cultivate relationships with youth on the street runs counter to the ethic in many youth work agencies of "if the kid doesn't show up for the appointment he or she must not want help very badly." Other youth workers may suspect outreach workers of being manipulated by youth because they are willing to go out and find kids rather than wait until the kids come to them. They are also often suspicious of anyone who is willing to work the unusual hours that outreach workers are and of people who are seldom around the office.

THE CLINICAL LEVEL

Clinical intervention models target individuals who are at risk or involved in prostitution for prevention efforts (primary, secondary, and tertiary). Clinical intervention models most often view prostitution as a symptom of pathology or deviance, and tend to isolate the problem in the individual while paying less attention to the environmental factors. These models profess a desire to help youth but can end up punishing the "victim" because they are willing to use coercion to provide interventions. There are primarily two types of clinical intervention models: the criminal/legal and the mental health.

Criminal/Legal Intervention Model

The assumption that adolescent prostitution is child abuse is a common feature of most juvenile justice systems. There is typically a belief that prostitution is harmful to an adolescent and that his or her continued involvement is likely to lead to other criminal acts. This belief suggests that it is in the child's "best interests" to prevent continued or further involvement in prostitution, even if incarceration is necessary. If a youth is unwilling to accept whatever assistance or programs are offered, police, probation, child welfare, and child protective agencies often use the extensive powers of the juvenile court to coerce the youth into accepting services.

These actions are usually initiated by the police, who are aware of youth on the streets involved in prostitution. Patrol or vice officers (seldom juvenile officers) will bring some charge against a youth to initiate a court action and allow for the detention of the youth to prevent running away from a shelter. This varies with each local jurisdiction and is usually a result of agreement among the police, juvenile justices, and city/county attorneys as to what charges the prosecuting attorneys will uphold and the justices will not throw out of court. Because legislation often changes and civil rights abuses are sometimes challenged, there is an evolving nature to these charges. Generally, they comprise whatever will accomplish the goal of obtaining legal leverage over the adolescent. Once in the juvenile justice system, the youth is either given such unattractive "options" that he or she is coerced into "choosing" what the court intends, or the youth is ordered into criminal justice programs that are designed for a variety of criminal offenses. With the increase in juvenile sex offender treatment programs, it is not uncommon for juvenile justices to order youth involved in prostitution (particularly males) into these programs. The rationales for this are specious at best, and are often the result of the system's exasperation over not knowing what else to do with youth who refuse to be "helped."

Numerous problems are inherent in these coercive approaches. Weisberg (1985) offers an analysis of the difficulties in using law enforcement and the juvenile justice system as an intervention approach to adolescent prostitution. Most of the problems stem from inadequate investigation and prosecution of the real offenders in adolescent prostitution—the customers. Law enforcement agencies lack the training, resources, or willingness to perform the investigations necessary to prosecute these cases adequately. They therefore prosecute the victims of prostitution in attempt to force help on those unwilling to accept it, further alienating youth who have often suffered much already.

However, if law enforcement agencies were willing, trained, and equipped to investigate adolescent prostitution and prosecute the customers who demand the services and youth were processed through child protective agencies as victims of sexual abuse, different outcomes might ensue and different questions might be raised. Law enforcement agencies do not typically coerce other child sexual abuse victims into treatment. Such behavior might appropriately be construed as further victimization. Yet this is precisely what happens in adolescent prostitution.

The system unfortunately often violates youth in a way not unlike that of the perpetrator. At its core, child sexual abuse is a gross violation of personal boundaries and choice. A child's right to say no and personal and physical boundaries are violated. Whether the violations are the result of seduction, tricks, manipulation, or physical force, the child on some level knows a violation even when unable to put words or meaning to the events. Child protective and law enforcement agencies often perpetuate similar violations on adolescents involved in prostitution.

Instead of identifying and building on the resiliency of the child, the system often saps the youth's strength. Youth involved in prostitution, and street youth in general, exemplify this issue most dramatically. These youth, who most often have extensive histories of abuse, develop adaptive coping strategies that often are functional in that environment, though often not desirable or adaptive outside of it. They run away from abusive homes or situations. They become suspicious and distrustful of adults. They fight to regain and maintain control over their lives, and develop elaborate survival strategies beyond the abilities of many adults to cope with situations.

Instead of building on their resiliency, protective factors and adaptive skills and seeing them as resourceful within a dangerous environment, these youth are often returned to the homes they find abusive, reinforcing that they have little or no control over their lives. Their judgment is impugned for not trusting service providers to have their best interest at heart, and the resources that would allow them to avoid resorting to prostitution or crime for survival are withheld. It is paradoxical that juvenile justices often order a youth to a treatment or correctional program for extended periods of time at exorbitant rates, whereas less expensive programs that provide outreach, shelter, and employment training for the same youth are barely able to secure minimal funding, if they are funded at all.

Case Example

In Minnesota, Juvenile Court Judges refer young people involved in prostitution to inpatient or residential treatment programs that range from exclusive treatment centers that charge up to $900.00 per diem to county correctional facilities that cost $250.00 per day. By comparison, two transitional housing programs in the Minneapolis/ St. Paul area that provide housing subsidies and case managed health care, counseling, independent living skills training, employment training, educational opportunities, and legal advocacy do so for well under $50.00 per youth per day.

Mental Health

Mental health approaches generally assume the conventional view of prostitution as a symptom of personal pathology resulting from such factors as prior sexual abuse, family dysfunction, and/or chemical abuse by the youth or youth's family (Mathews, 1989). Interventions by mental health approaches can be psychoanalytic, cognitive/ behavioral, or behavioral, and settings can include correctional, inpatient hospital, residential, group homes, and outpatient.

Utilizing individual, group, and family therapy, mental health approaches seek to address the individual pathology or disorder of the adolescent and/or his or her family as a means of intervening in the youth's prostitution behavior. These approaches often include social services such as education, employment training, and independent living skills as part of their treatment plans but as secondary rather than primary issues. Because they generally assume that prostitution is a manifestation of personal deviancy and/or pathology, mental health approaches seldom are exclusively designed to treat prostitution behavior, and are more often general mental health programs designed to treat disorders in adolescence. Mental health approaches have significantly different configurations depending on their source of referral and intake. Those whose primary source of referral (and payment) are public agencies, such as juvenile court, child protection, and child welfare, most often are part of models that rely on law enforcement and coercion for interventions. Those that rely on referrals from individuals and other private social service agencies are usually parts of models that rely on participation by the client for interventions.

Because adolescents have far fewer patient rights than and are often considered the property of parents, "commitment" or coercion into mental health programs and institutions is far easier to accomplish with adolescents. Depending on state laws, parents and public agencies (child welfare and protection) often have few clear standards for such commitments. Independent review or appeal processes for the adolescent are rare.

A unique problem institutional and residential mental health programs face in working with boys in prostitution is responding to gay-identified boys who are sexually active in a residential living setting. Homophobic staff and residents often harass these youth, who are offered little or no institutional protection. Most residential programs are unprepared for sexual activity among same-sex residents. This discomfort and inexperience in dealing with homosexual behavior in adolescence is a reason why many programs minimize or ignore a boy's involvement in prostitution and focus instead on antisocial or delinquent behavior. The prevalent attitudes in residential and institutional mental health care for adolescents regarding adolescent homosexuality are that the boys are too young to know, it is a phase they will grow out of, or the same-sex orientation is the result of individual pathology. Seldom are these institutions able to embrace and affirm an adolescent's homosexual identity. This failing seriously impairs whatever treatment these programs offer.

Mental heath rationales for coercion are based on the belief that an adolescent's prostitution behavior is a danger to himself or herself and possibly to others; as such, it must be controlled for the youth's own best interests. In the service of corrections, mental health is primarily concerned with protecting the community. In the service of child protection and child welfare, mental health is concerned primarily with protecting the adolescent from himself or herself and from further exploitation.

Correctional mental health programs are either general and designed to facilitate change in the delinquent behavior of adolescents, or they are sex offender programs that also address delinquent behavior, but in more specific ways and with a major emphasis on sexuality that the general approaches often lack. Another distinction between general corrections and sex offender programs is the more frequent use by the sex offender programs of a broader variety of treatment strategies and techniques, whereas the general corrections programs are primarily dependent on behavioral techniques and strategies.

Although it is not unusual for adolescents involved in prostitution to be court ordered into sex offender programs, this is inappropriate. The rationales that prostitution is technically a sex "crime" and/or that sex offender programs work on victimization issues (which youth in prostitution often have) are dubious, and any possible gains from these approaches are contradicted by the overwhelming messages of blaming the victim and holding children more accountable for sexual behavior than adults.

Inpatient hospital and residential programs (such as residential treatment and group homes) are often used by corrections to treat adolescents in prostitution but are primarily used by child protection and child welfare agencies (or by parents who employ these agencies or their insurance to pay for and place their children). The treatment philosophies can range from psychoanalytic to behavioral, and the way these programs address issues can be general (e.g., "ranches" or "homes" for boys) or quite specific (e.g., inpatient chemical dependency treatment programs). Inpatient hospital and residential programs incorporate the treatment of prostitution into their strategies of treatment for the disorders of adolescence or the specific problems they are set up to treat. If a youth is in a residential treat- ment program for adolescent boys, such as a boys' ranch, the treatment plan may include some special attention to the boy's prostitution involvement, but this attention usually will be in the context of a more general treatment plan that addresses perceived "core" issues, such as prior sexual abuse or family dysfunction. If a youth is in a more specific program, such as a chemical dependency treatment program, prostitution may be addressed, but again as a manifestation of a perceived central issue such as drug or alcohol addiction.

Case Example

John would run away for months at a time and then come home. He had done it so many times his parents had quit calling the police when he left. When he was 16 and came home from one of his "trips" his parents talked him into checking into a chemical dependency treatment program. They knew he used drugs and convinced him he had a drug problem.

During treatment, John talked about his prostitution behavior, but the focus was always on his chemical use and "what he would do to get high." During family counseling, they talked about how physically abusive his father had been and how his family had a hard time accepting his homosexuality.

When used as parts of noncoercive models, mental health programs are based on the belief that adolescent prostitution is child abuse and that, as victims/survivors, these youth need access to mental health services as part of their recovery from that exploitation and the likely sexual abuse they have experienced. These primarily outpatient programs are usually a part of the continuum of services that are accessible through the outreach programs described earlier, although therapists in private practice or community mental health clinics often see youth and young adults who are self-referred.

Outpatient mental health programs can utilize individual, group, and family therapy and employ a full range of treatment strategies and philosophies when treating adolescent prostitution, but often programs that are designed to treat prostitution specifically emphasize group work and occasionally individual and family work in conjunction with that. This therapy commonly uses cognitive/behavioral or self-help approaches and focuses on prostitution and "the life" or lifestyle issues of prostitution. When these programs are part of the service continuums of outreach programs, these mental health services are often case managed with other social services.

Family counseling is often difficult for youth who are referred to mental health services through street outreach programs. Some have no family. Others have family who refuse to participate due to rejection of the youth (e.g., because of the youth's homosexuality or conflict with a stepparent who forces a choice on the biological parent) or because they are exhausted/disillusioned from past attempts at family counseling (e.g., they had bad experiences or have seen little or no results from their efforts), or because of denial of the family's dysfunction (e.g., alcoholism, incest, physical abuse). The work in outpatient mental health programs around issues of family dysfunction and family therapy often would be helpful to the adolescent; however, unlike adolescents, families cannot be coerced into treatment.

Another difficulty of family therapy with adolescents who have been on the streets is the result of managing a normal developmental process gone awry. It is quite normal for older adolescents (15 to 17) to begin individuating from the family and asserting independence. Adolescents who have experienced the freedom and autonomy of the streets and attempt to move home or reestablish ties with their family often find it very difficult to tolerate the control or guidance that parents quite rightly exert. For youth who have managed the horrors of the streets, being a "normal" child again is difficult. It is as though they skipped a step and are expected to come back and do it over, which can be difficult—if not impossible—to do, even if they want to.

A critical aspect of the configuration of mental health services for youth in prostitution is the issue of funding or fees. There is clearly more money in providing services through coercive models and institutional programs. These programs charge fees to either the county who refers or places the youth or the insurance company of the parents who place the youth. Youth in prostitution have very little money to pay for mental health services themselves, and as a result, mental health providers who wish to serve them through noncoercive models must recruit funding through grants. When available, this type of funding is limited and results in minimal outpatient programs.

The newest models of service to homeless youth are decentralized residential treatment programs. They provide shelter, transitional housing, a range of social services, mental health services, and case management, all accessible to the youth through self-referral. The funding for such programs is, however, difficult to construct (usually from a variety of funders) and falls far short of the per diem per person fees that traditional institutional mental health programs receive from insurance or counties.

These new service models have received the support of the Adolescent Services Division of the National Institute of Mental Health, which sponsored a conference in 1991 that invited runaway and homeless youth service providers to become a more integral part of the mental health service systems for "seriously emotionally disturbed adolescents." These runaway and homeless youth programs have demonstrated effective models for working with children's mental health systems despite their chronic underfunding, particularly in comparison with traditional mental health services.

Case Example

Greg found out about the prostitution group at a mental health clinic through a flyer at the drop-in center for street youth. He liked the support and understanding he got from other guys in the group about how hard it was leaving street life and how tempted he was to go and party with his old friends at times. Those had been his only friends for a long time. After a few months, the group therapist talked to Greg about trying to get his family in for counseling, but only his mother would come. It helped though: Greg was starting to get along with his mother and she was talking about how she was finally getting comfortable with his lover.

DETACHED YOUTH WORK: A MODEL

For a complete review of the history and practice of detached youth work, the reader is directed to the research of Thompson (1990). Much of what follows borrows heavily from her work and from the author's long professional association with her.

To understand the type of youth work involved in working with street youth, youth in gangs, and youth involved in prostitution, it is helpful to look at the history of detached youth work in the United States. Literature dealing with detached youth work can be found in law, sociology, psychology, social work, and criminal justice disciplines and in the popular press. For the sake of brevity, only information from the United States is included here; considerable foreign and international literature on the subject lends credibility to it being a cross-cultural model.

The History of Detached Youth Work

From the mid-1960s until the present, virtually no literature has been published in the United States on detached youth workers or

detached youth work programs. Possible explanations for this include the following. First, by the mid-1960s, detached youth work
was no longer a new and exciting approach to working with gangs;
it had been around for 20 years and it was effective, according to
those in the field (New York City Youth Board, 1952). Yet no one
had developed a solid theory of detached youth work. No established
discipline claimed it as its own, and there was no consensus regarding the roles and functions of detached youth work.

Second, the nature of gang behavior shifted. What consisted mostly
of public fighting and terrorizing neighbors in the 1960s began to
evolve into a more private (even secretive) behavior that involved
more drug and organized criminal activity. In 1965, the New York
City Youth Board noted this shift as it was beginning: "New demands
of narcotic addiction, school and employment are replacing fights as
the focal point of the gang's concern" (p. 58). The public began to
see gangs as less troublesome. This continued until recent years with
the attention given to drive-by shootings and increased levels of
public violence.

A third explanation arises from the preceding one. The behavior
of adolescent gang members was seen by many until the late 1960s
as within the range of "normal adolescent" behavior, and the problem was defined as a societal problem ("social issue") of finding more
appropriate channels and activities for young people. This view gave
way to a more "medical" view of gang behavior as resulting from
"troubled" or psychologically "disturbed" young people ("personal
problem"). During this same time, social concern was shifting from
the lower-class adolescent to the middle-class adolescent (i.e., the
rise in the public attention given to the Flower Child Movement, the
protests of the Vietnam War, and the Civil Rights Movement were
driven mostly by middle- and upper-class young people).

The fourth reason for the lack of literature on detached youth work
has to do with the biases of youth workers toward scholarly work,
including research about their own practice. Youth workers did not
develop their own literature, almost as a reaction against the academic
and scholarly disciplines that declined to claim detached youth work
as part of their discipline. Konopka (1972) describes the reluctance
of social workers to adopt the methods of social group work on which
detached youth work is based. For Konopka, social group work (i.e.,

detached youth work) is distinguished by its emergence from self-help groups and movements of democratic group action such as youth services, recreation, the labor movement, settlement houses, and community centers, whereas casework, which is the oldest method of social work, has its origins in philanthropy movements, such as the Charity Organization Society, which distinguishes sharply between the giver and the receiver of social services.

The early programs of detached youth work are important because they set the tone for later programs. And the detached youth workers themselves are important because they represent the essence of youth work itself.

Theory and History of Juvenile Gangs and Delinquency

To understand the emergence of detached youth work, it is important to examine the context of juvenile gangs and juvenile delinquency from which detached youth work is developed.

The wealth of writing and scholarship about juvenile delinquency from the late 1950s to the mid-1960s is an indication that juvenile delinquency was a "growth industry" for academics at that time. Among the research, the work of Shaw and Jacobs (1940) and the "Chicago School" had a significant impact on detached youth work. Shaw found that delinquency and crime tends to be confined to delimited areas and that delinquent behavior persists despite demographic changes in these areas. He speaks of "criminal traditions" and the "cultural transmission" of criminal values. In this tradition, "delinquency, for the most part was seen as a result of a reversible accident of the person's social experience" (Kobrin, 1959, p. 22).

Cloward and Ohlin (1960) expand the notion of cultural transmission and argue that delinquency arises because opportunities are blocked to lower-class youth who want the same things as other youth but cannot find socially legitimate ways to achieve "success." Cloward and Ohlin suggest that these lower-class youth move into criminal activity, prove their manhood through fighting, or retreat into chemical use as ways of responding to their lack of opportunities.

A third theory, the cultural approach (Kvaraceus & Miller, 1959) looks at lower-class neighborhoods as having developed a relatively stable subculture in which forms of criminal and delinquent values and behavior are accepted and normative. Lerner (1957) proposes a fourth theory that views delinquency as a manifestation of the general breakdown in community standards (i.e., social disorganization). A fifth approach is psychogenic: An adolescent's family and early childhood experiences are seen as predictive of later troubles (Aichorn, 1935; Redl, 1945). Another perspective is that delinquent behavior is related to "rites of passage" (Bloch & Niederhoffer, 1958). In this view, delinquency is seen as a normal process that some adolescents pass through on their way to adulthood, but that they "age out" of eventually.

A seventh approach views delinquency from a situational perspective where a youth is seen as acting out as a way of reducing personal tensions. This approach shows an obvious psychological-psychiatric theory base.

Bernstein (1964) subscribes to a multiple causation model. He suggests that "delinquency is not a unitary diagnostic category. It is behavior which is in conflict with the law within a designated age range. Its origins are diverse not only from one youth to another, but also within any one youngster" (p. 25).

The early views of gangs implicitly, and often explicitly, saw them as normal manifestations of adolescent developmental tasks and needs. A basic tenet of these views was the conception of delinquency as within the normal range of adolescent behavior and not pathological. The behavior was certainly not "typical" and was socially "deviant," but not "crazy." For example, Thrasher (1927) says:

> Gangs represent the spontaneous effort of boys to create a society for themselves where none adequate to their needs exist . . . the failure of normally directing and controlling customs and institutions to function efficiently in the boy's experience is indicated by the disintegration of life, inefficiency of schools, formalism and externality of religion, corruption and indifference in local politics, low wages and the monotony of occupational activities, unemployment, and lack of opportunity for wholesome recreation. (p. 37)

Freeman (1956) states that the "phenomena of the corner crowd is a natural function of the situation" (p. 15) and Lerman (1958) asserts that to understand gang behavior, one must consider factors other than personality dynamics, for example:

> The internal relationships of the group and the evolved roles, status, structure, norms, and persistency of interaction of the individual's immediate peer group; the pressures toward conformity and the potentiating effects of group participation, predominant values of the significant people and institutions within the neighborhood life space affecting the individual and his primary reference group; the mode and style of personal controls of behavior prescribed, permitted, and proscribed by outside sources, and the reality aspects of the specific problem situation with which the individual is confronted. (pp. 71-72)

Gang Work

Campbell (1984) comments on the decline in the number of articles and literature on gangs and gang behavior in the mid-1960s in a book on girls and gangs:

> In the sixties, for example, it was widely believed that gangs had finally disappeared. Absorbed into youth politics, some argued. Fighting in Vietnam, said others, or turned into self-destructive junkies. It seems likely that their disappearance was a media slight of hand. New York stopped reporting gang stories and the rest of the country followed suit. Gangs die out and are reincarnated regularly by the media whenever news is slow. As a phenomenon, gangs have never been put to rest. Though they may be inactive for a few months or a few years, they are quietly living in the tradition and culture that has sustained them for over a hundred years in the United States. (pp. 5-6)

In the last few years, the popular press has again picked up on gangs, resulting in a proliferation of attention on gangs and gang behavior. Public concern about crime is fueled by stories in the popular press about primarily minority youth involvement in gangs and criminal or delinquent behavior. The public dialogue, heavily influenced by a law enforcement perspective (i.e., the "war" on drugs), seems to ignore the long history of gangs in America and the lessons learned in understanding gangs and delinquency.

Much like the conventional view of adolescent prostitution mentioned in chapter 8, the popular public opinion of gangs seems to unduly locate the problem as within an individual youth and/or his or her family. Despite decaying and increasingly violent neighborhoods, poor schools, and chronic poverty, young people are expected to "just say no" to drugs and gangs. Even more, they are often seen as morally weak or corrupt if they succumb to these powerful influences in their lives.

The predominant early view of juvenile delinquency held that such behavior arose out of societal conditions and that gangs were a natural consequence of such conditions. That view also assumed that, although troublesome to society, gang behavior displayed "normative" adolescent developmental responses to conditions. Thus early social service agencies, churches, and leisure time organizations attempted to involve gang members in their programs. Thrasher (1927) describes this early work:

> In the early 1920's businesses, the YMCA, the Boy Scouts, the settlements, the parks and the playgrounds, and the Boys Clubs attempted to take over the gangs and turn them into social or athletic clubs. The politicians and the saloon keepers have also learned the trick of taking over these gangs and making clubs out of them, but their motives have usually been rather more for their own aggrandizement than for the good of the boys. (pp. 509-510)

These early programs and attempts to co-opt gangs were not very successful. These programs were unable to draw boys, or when they did, the boys were disruptive and seen as a threat to others. The failure to incorporate the boys into ongoing programs probably prompted the settlement houses and early leisure-time agencies to send some workers into the community to work with these boys. This was not done systematically, however, and was not called detached youth work. It probably involved the use of indigenous young men and was focused on involving male adolescents in athletic activities (Thrasher, 1927). Some of the neighborhood associations affiliated with the Chicago Area Project in the early 1930s used detached youth workers, but again did not label them as such. In a 25-year assessment of the Chicago Area Project, Kobrin (1959) states, "In all probability, the Area Project was the first organized program in the

United States to use workers to establish direct and personal contact with the 'unreached' boys" (p. 27).

Explicit Detached Youth Work Programs

More attention was not given to gangs until World War II, when there was an increase in adolescent delinquent gangs. One response to the reemergence of gangs was to create detached worker programs. These appeared almost simultaneously in many large cities, as social service agencies and governmental units came to recognize that traditional building-centered programs were ineffective in controlling and preventing gang disruption (Kobrin, 1959; New York City Youth Board, 1965). One study in 1947 reported that fewer than 10% of problem youth were attending in-building programs (Dumpson, 1949).

The words "detached youth worker," "gang worker," "area worker," "social group worker," "streetworker," "corner worker," "corner group worker," "extension worker," and "street gang worker" are descriptions of where the worker does his or her work and with whom he or she works.

Lerman (1958) provides a definition that fits most detached youth work programs reviewed here: "A non-membership, community located professional service provided through a single worker who works in an environmental situation over which s/he has limited control and who extends service to a group without prior request from them for service" (p. 45). A more comprehensive definition comes from the Boston Special Youth Project.

> Detached work involves intensive contact with a corner-group where the worker meets the teen age group in their natural environment. By close association with them and getting to know their needs as a group and as individuals, the worker forms a positive relationship and helps them to engage in socially acceptable activities which they come to choose. The basic goal is helping them to change undesirable attitudes and patterns of behavior. (Freeman, 1956, p. 21)

The first explicit use of the phrase "detached youth worker" appears in 1947 in a New York City Youth Board plan for the Central Harlem Street Club Project (Thompson, 1990). This plan suggested that such workers were part of the Youth Street Club Program. The detached youth worker programs in New York City, Los Angeles, Boston, and Chicago have received the most attention in the literature, although there are references to programs in San Francisco (Bernstein, 1964), Philadelphia (Bernstein, 1964; Philadelphia Department of Welfare, 1964), Detroit (Bernstein, 1964), and Cleveland (Bernstein, 1964; Welfare Association of Cleveland, 1959).

The Efficacy of Detached Youth Work

Until the literature on detached youth work began to dissipate in the late 1960s, it was replete with testimonials and claims as to youth work's effectiveness (Ackely & Fliegel, 1960; Bernstein, 1964; Caplan, Deshaies, Suttles, & Mattick, 1964; Dumpson, 1949; Freeman, 1956; Kobrin, 1959; Juvenile Delinquency Evaluation Project, 1960; New York City Youth Board, 1952, 1962, 1965). These studies of detached youth work document the efficacy of the approach and identified some of the major themes related to the work.

In terms of outcomes, these studies indicate that the most dramatic changes that occur from detached youth work are in the arena of public group behavior. Public delinquency (e.g., theft, vandalism, and fighting) is reduced the most. The second most dramatic changes occur in the area of individual public behavior, and the least dramatic in individual private behavior (e.g., drinking, gambling, sex). Bernstein (1964) believes that changes in private behavior are almost always linked to other changes such as school, jobs, and relationships with youth workers and adults. Among the other desirable outcomes from detached youth work are:

- More youth staying in or returning to school
- More youth involvement in organized activities of other agencies
- More successful referrals to other professionals
- More youth obtaining and maintaining employment
- More youth taking individual responsibility for their own actions
- Improved relationships between the target youth and the community
- Improved health care of the youth involved
- Improved attitudes on the part of youth toward his or her future and his or her ability to affect it

More dramatic and personal examples of the effectiveness of detached youth work can be found in Bernstein's (1964) study. He discovered several situations where groups of youth who were not being served by detached youth workers acted out in dramatic ways in order to obtain the attention and services of a detached youth worker.

The Evolution of Detached Youth Work

Even though the literature and research about detached youth work faded and disappeared, the practice of it did not. Youth work's origin, evolution, and practice parallel the work for which it was designed. It shares much with gangs, which move in and out of the spotlight of public and academic attention but do not cease to exist in the absence of that attention. It is possible to trace the evolution of detached youth work through the moral panics and youth crises that have ebbed and flowed over the years. Adolescent prostitution emerged as a dominant issue of the mid-1970s with news stories, congressional hearings, and ensuing research. Homelessness became the issue of the 1980s, and the conceptualization of homeless youth emerged out of the runaway programs of the 1970s designed, in part, to address and prevent adolescent prostitution. In the 1990s, the crisis is again gangs. There are youth workers (not many) whose careers have spanned the last 2 or 3 decades who find amusement in the changing language, symbols, and "problems" while they continue to do essentially the same work with the same client groups (sometimes even with the children of former clients).

That amusement does not belittle the evolving complexity of the problems that youth face or the increasing danger or severity of those problems. But it does serve to illustrate part of the essence of detached youth work. Thompson (1990) describes that essence as:

> a stance which is actualized as a praxis depending upon the unique moment, the unique youth, in a unique context. Detached youthwork then is contingent: it depends. Hence there is no single method, skill or approach. . . . If what a detached youthworker does "depends," how can (s)he be expected to tell you what (s)he does. Each youth, each moment is unique. Yes, there are commonalities and patterns, but they are abstractions. The concrete, specific is what matters. Here too, and

unknowingly, the detached youthworker speaks like an Existentialist: it depends on the meaning, the moment, the choice, and the action. (pp. 86-95)

Detached youth work, which seems intrinsically tied to work with the most marginal and alienated of youth, is not related to the work through the problems these youth display (e.g., gangs, prostitution, homelessness), but through the ability to create authentic helping relationships with these marginal and alienated youth and to effect more positive outcomes than would likely occur. The knowledge base of detached youth workers has been expanded to include a more diverse population of youth, and the language systems used to describe and define those youth has changed and gotten more complex, but the art of creating, sustaining, and "manipulating" relationships has remained the essence. Relationships are the skill of detached youth work:

> Given who these workers choose as youth clients, i.e., "street kids," their willingness and ability to create "real relationships" is impressive. It is the major rationale for this kind of youth work, as well as being at times a challenge to other human service professionals. These workers "connect" with the unconnected and (thought to be) unconnectable. (Thompson, 1990, p. 97)

Thompson's research documents that current detached youth work is the same as that which has been practiced historically, with three major differences. The first is that current detached youth workers do not work exclusively with gangs of youth but with individual alienated youth on the streets or with logical empirical categories of youth (e.g., youth in prostitution, youth at risk for AIDS, homeless youth). As in the past, the longer a youth worker remains in the work, the more he or she becomes involved in a variety of problems both on the individual and community level.

Another difference is that agencies that employ detached youth workers today do not have an explicit belief in the intrinsic value of detached youth work but rather see it as a recruiting method for agency programs. These agencies often call their workers outreach workers and define the function of these workers as marketers and public relations workers between the population of youth identified for service and the building-centered employer. One of the most extreme examples of this is the federal funding made available in 1991 for teen health clinics to employ outreach workers to promote prenatal care and clinic use in homeless, drug abusing, pregnant, adolescent females.

The third difference is that women are now commonly found among detached youth workers, as well as among clients. Historically, work with gangs was done by men with adolescent males.

THE THEORY OF ADOLESCENCE UNDERLYING DETACHED YOUTH WORK

The detached youth workers of the 1950s often challenged the more dominant psychiatric perspective of young men involved in gangs as troubled individuals; social group workers (i.e., detached youth workers) often challenged the distinctions social work's case-work method made between the giver and the receiver of social services. Today's detached youth worker often challenges conceptualizations of adolescents and adolescence (i.e., youth the person versus youth the stage of human development).

Kurth-Schai (1988) describes a conceptual continuum for mapping contemporary thought concerning the nature of adolescence. On one end of the continuum, youth are seen as victims of adult society, with the assumption that youth are vulnerable and in need of adult protection. She traces this image from the early years of the industrial revolution to the current images of youth as victims of physical, sexual, and emotional abuse. In addition to this overt victimization, Kurth-Schai includes as victims objects of adult sentimentality characterized by the view that youth are "economically worthless but emotionally priceless."

On the other end of the Kurth-Schai continuum is the view that youth are threats to adult society, with the assumption that youth are dangerous and in need of adult control. She also traces this image from the early days of the industrial revolution to the current images of gangs and juvenile crime, and attributes the perpetuation of this view to lack of contact and caring for other people's children.

In the middle of the continuum is the view that youth are learners of adult society, with the assumption that youth are incomplete, incompetent, and in need of adult guidance. Kurth-Schai traces this image to 20th-century academic models of child and adolescent development represented by the socialization and enculturation theories of sociologists and anthropologists and the universal stage theories of developmental psychologists. She further notes that:

> As guidance may include elements of protection and control, assumptions derived on the basis of this conceptualization may be used in support of either of the first two images. . . . [Y]outh therefore are perceived in terms of their incapacities and inabilities, and it is assumed that adult intervention is essential for their proper development. (p. 115)

Lacking from these conceptualizations of adolescence is the potential of young people to contribute to the social order. Kurth-Shai summarizes:

> By conceptualizing children as objects of sentimentalization we trivialize their thoughts and actions. By seeing youth as objects of socialization we obscure their "social insight and environment-shaping competence." By regarding youth as victims we obscure their potential for adaptation and survival. By perceiving youth as threats to society we ignore their potential as catalysts for positive social change. (1988, p. 117)

The consequence of failing to acknowledge the social potential of youth is serious:

> The secret message communicated to most young people today by the society around them is that they are not needed, that society will run itself quite nicely until they—at some distant point in the future—will take over the reins. Yet the fact is that society is not running itself nicely . . . because the rest of us need all the energy, brains, imagination and talent that young people can bring to bear on our difficulties. For society to attempt to solve its desperate problems without the full participation of even very young people is imbecile. (Toffler, 1974, p. 15)

Detached youth work challenges the definitions of adolescence as simply the transition period from dependent childhood to self-sufficient adulthood or as a "marginal situation" in which new adjustments must be made, namely those that distinguish child be-havior from adult behavior in a given society (Muuss, 1962). These definitions of adolescence are guilty of what Goodman (1970) refers to as the "underestimation fallacy." Konopka and the Center for Youth Development and Research of the University of Minnesota (1973) offer a more comprehensive definition of adolescence:

> We do not see adolescence exclusively as a stage that human beings pass through, but rather as a segment of continuing human development. We reject the common conception that adolescence is solely prepara-tion for adulthood, except that everything in life can be considered to be preparation for what follows. We believe adolescents are persons with specific qualities and characteristics who have a participatory and responsible role to play, tasks to perform, skills to develop at that particular time of life. The degree or extent to which an adolescent experiences such responsible participation will determine and maxi-mize his/her development. (Konopka, 1973, p. 2)

The key for Konopka and much of the recent research and litera-ture on resiliency and youth development is responsible participa-tion. Benard's (1991) review of the resiliency and protective factors research points out that high expectations from families, schools, and communities and meaningful participation and involvement of youth are key factors in fostering healthy development and resiliency in adolescents. Detached youth work has and does share this concep-tualization of adolescence.

Rather than viewing adolescence as inherently problematic, diffi-cult, and full of risks for health-compromising or disordered behav-ior, detached youth work views adolescence as full of opportunities, possibilities, and potential, even with "troubled" youth. This is another way in which detached youth work challenges the views and con-ceptualizations of adolescents. The population that detached youth work selects as clients is generally viewed as troubled and the agencies employing youth workers most often apply a pathology or disease approach to working with youth. Yet, detached youth work shares more conceptually and philosophically with the youth development field (e.g., 4-H Extension programs, YMCA/YWCA, Boy/Girl Scouts), which fosters healthy development and provides youth with opportunities to master developmental tasks rather than focusing on the elimination of problem behaviors.

Because of this development approach, an essential component of the knowledge base of detached youth work is child and adolescent developmental theory; an essential component of the practice of detached youth work is the critical analysis and evaluation of the applicability of developmental theory to the everyday lives of youth.

The work of Gilligan and others in recent years challenges and expands traditional developmental theories of adolescence. Gilligan, Ward, and Taylor (1988) note that, because Piaget's view of knowing and thinking is based on mathematical and scientific knowing and thinking, the revival of Piaget's work in the 1960s signaled a move toward stronger math and science education and the decline of curriculum that teaches history, languages, writing, art, and music. Implicit in Piaget's theories of cognition is the belief that young people have little insight and "knowing" that is valuable to adults (Gilligan et al., 1988). Erikson (1963) gave us the concept of adolescence as seeking identity, and emphasized separation, individuation, and autonomy, which seems at odds with the human condition of interdependence and has likely contributed to the egocentric and narcissistic behavior that is so common to adolescence today (Gilligan et al., 1988; Konopka, 1973). Erikson's moratorium as a condition of adolescent development is an explicit denial of the adolescent's ability to participate, contribute, and experience accountability in society. Kohlberg's general inattention to the moral development of young women has been challenged by Gilligan et al., who have created a whole new set of questions to ask about the meaning of self, development, and relationships. The deep sense of outrage, despair, and disconnection that Gilligan et al., Konopka, and Miller have tapped in young women has contributed to theories of adolescent development of both boys and girls (Gilligan et al., 1988).

Konopka (1973) suggests the concept of adolescence as an "age of commitment" in which the youth struggles between dependency and independence as he or she moves into the true interdependence of humanity. Konopka describes this age of commitment as including the search for self, but also points toward the "emotional, intellectual and sometimes physical reach for other people, ideas, ideologies, causes and work choices" (p. 11).

The key concepts of adolescence for Konopka (1973) are:

1. The experience of physical and sexual maturity
2. The experience of withdrawal of and from adult benevolent protection
3. The consciousness of self in interaction
4. The re-evaluation of values
5. Experimentation

Woven into these concepts are the qualities or characteristics of adolescents. Experimentation is coupled with a mixture of "audacity" and "insecurity," reflecting adolescents' unique willingness to try out new ideas and relationships as well as the uncertainty that comes with the withdrawal of protection. "Loneliness" and "psychological vulnerability" are qualities of adolescents that reflect the lack of a bank of positive experiences to draw on when experimentation results in defeat or the outcome is negative. "Mood swings" are the result of a series of tensions created by the move from dependence to interdependence. Omnipotence tangos with feelings of helplessness and inadequacy, "it won't happen to me" plays hide and seek with the fear that it will, confusion results from being expected to act like an adult one minute and being treated like a child the next. A strong "peer group need" creates a willingness to subjugate personal needs to cooperation and group acceptance. Finally, adolescents need to be "argumentative" and "emotional" because they are in the process of trying out their own changing values and relationships with the outer world.

Based on this concept of adolescence, Konopka (1973) believes that programs and systems for serving youth should be judged by the opportunities they afford youth and the credibility they enjoy. They should provide the opportunity for youth to experience making choices and commitments while experimenting with a variety of roles to try out those choices and commitments. They should enjoy credibility from the validity of the program in the eyes of those served.

One is hard-pressed today to find programs serving youth that meet these criteria. Such programs exist but are more the exception than the rule. Unless real options are available, "making choiccs" becomes an empty phrase for young people. Pseudo decision making does not promote developing commitment. Therefore, intervention should be focused on the removal of limiting factors, and law and policy should be used to support healthy development rather than to control and contain socially disapproved behavior.

KEY ELEMENTS OF SUCCESSFUL DETACHED YOUTH WORK PROGRAMS

The discussion of detached youth work so far has been abstract and theoretical, more about a "stance" than about practice. To an extent this is part of the nature of the work, but some things can be said about the characteristics of successful detached youth workers.

In addition to Thompson's research (1990), two research projects have focused on what works with youth: a joint research project by Search Institute of Minneapolis and the Minnesota Extension Service, University of Minnesota (Search Institute, 1992, 1993) was designed to identify the keys to successful youth work; and an ongoing project of the Community Fellows Program at the Massachusetts Institute of Technology (Starr, 1993) is conducting research on what techniques are effective in working with youth.

Virtually all the research points to the chief skill of youth workers as their ability to create authentic relationships with youth that demonstrate their genuine caring (Search Institute, 1992; Starr, 1993; Thompson, 1990). The deeper question is how that caring is demonstrated and how those relationships are created. Following is a summary of some of the chief characteristics of successful youth work

Respect

An essential characteristic of successful youth workers and youth work programs is a deep value and respect for young people. Good youth workers respect and strive to understand young people and their families (including their values and traditions) and to accept, learn from, build on, and celebrate their clientele's strengths.

Commitment

A part of caring and respecting youth is having a commitment to them—being accessible and available to youth as well as being consistent over time. Relationships are not like "cases" that can be transferred, and alienated youth cannot be dealt with en masse. Alienated youth need to see that youth workers as individuals are willing to commit to long-term relationships and are willing to be available to the youth when they need them.

High Expectations

Youth workers who respect and care about youth see them as intelligent, capable, and deserving. They want and expect youth to succeed and work to give youth opportunities that enable that success. These high expectations do not mean discounting a youth's pain or difficulty; youth workers focus on empowering youth to overcome obstacles by believing in their ability to succeed. Youth workers do not patronize or "coddle" youth by seeing them as "damaged" or unable to achieve much because of the trauma and difficulty in their lives. This can be extremely difficult with youth who have suffered much, and becomes a delicate balancing act between affirming and nurturing while challenging and holding youth accountable. These high expectations are usually applied to youth programs as well, and can lead to youth workers being critical of services that do not provide the best for youth. Although expecting much from young people, youth workers are simultaneously working for structural change that removes barriers for youth to succeed.

Indigenous Workers

There is considerable debate in the field as to the need for youth workers to have the same background (e.g., same race, same economic condition, same personal struggles) as the youth they are attempting to serve. Historically, indigenous workers have been preferred for detached youth workers, and it is fair to say that if youth workers have not come from the same background as the youth they work with, they start at a disadvantage. One youth worker in the MIT study put it this way: "All the degrees don't mean nothing to me. If you are intelligent enough about the streets, to me that's better than any degree that you can ever get, cause you know what's happening. . . . You can better understand and deal with these people" (Starr, 1993, p. 7).

Caring is put forth by some as an alternative to this experiential knowledge. If someone is sincere in his or her caring, the argument goes, youth appreciate that, even if the person is not from the streets. This is an area that needs further study, but it is safe to say that a youth worker who does not share the same background as his or her clients will need to work much harder to demonstrate caring and willingness to learn and understand the background and environment that the clients experience.

Self-Knowledge

Youth workers, particularly those working with street youth, need to know and understand themselves prior to facilitating someone else's growth. This involves assessing one's personal biases and prejudices, understanding one's motives for helping others, having a good sense of personal worth so that unhealthy needs are not being met through one's work in unhealthy ways, and establishing boundaries and limits to prevent becoming enmeshed or overinvolved with clients.

Professionalization

There is a long-standing debate as to the professional status of youth work, especially detached youth work, that most likely has its origins in the early debates about social group work as a legitimate method of social work. Youth work and detached youth work, with roots in social group work, emerged from self-help movements, settlement houses, and community organizations, whereas clinical social work and family therapy, with roots in social casework, emerged from philanthropy movements that distinguished sharply between the giver and the receiver of social services.

This long-standing debate aside, it is worth noting four dimensions of professionalization that detached youth work often challenges and that contribute to the ambivalence of its professional status: the enclosure of professional space, the specialist division of labor, the cult of theoretical training, and the fetishism of technique.

Enclosure. Enclosed professional space—offices, desks, interview rooms—is at once a defense against the outside world and a structure of perception, the gestalt in terms of which a young person's life is viewed. The defense function is particularly illustrated for those working with street youth in the language that workers use, with its talk of the "front lines," working in the "trenches," and client "bombardment." With the images of a hostile environment this language evokes, it is hardly surprising that professionals attempt to create a territory within which they can more easily control the environment.

Yet the sterility that these professional spaces create sets limits on what can be known about a youth and renders this knowledge one-dimensional; how young people function in interviews, classrooms, examinations, and assessments is unlikely to be much of a guide to the rest of their lives. The less willing professionals are to experience young people in a range of settings and the less prepared they are to work with them in a space that is genuinely shared, the more partial and selective their knowledge of young people and the greater their failure to understand what is really important to them will be.

Specialists. The rise in specialties and the fragmenting of young people based on the symptoms they display contribute to the mutual suspicions and stereotypes that infect one separately trained profession's view of another. This is constantly confirmed by the surprise of youth workers, social workers, health-care providers, chemical dependency counselors, teachers, psychologists, and employment/training counselors on those few occasions when they work together long enough to appreciate one another's standpoint. The fact that shared experiences can have such a liberating effect should create caution about the attempts to guarantee interagency cooperation through procedures and "channels of communication." The error is a pervasive one, it being regularly assumed that if only the "machinery" is set up right, an improved service will follow. The whole person cannot be discovered in a filing cabinet of assessments based on behavior observed in unnatural and unfamiliar settings. Young people can only be discovered by those brave enough to venture out into the unprotected and exposed environments where they live.

Theoretical Training. Professional aspirations tend to encourage two parallel developments: an overvaluing of abstract learning, detached from its moorings in experience, and a belief in the effectiveness of short-term interventions at the expense of the more traditional commitment to long-term relationships. Drawing on a range of theoretical disciplines does not mean overriding concrete situations and empirical experiences with distant academic concerns. It does not mean squeezing young people and circumstances into ready-made categories, ignoring the obvious dissonance. And it does not mean prizing erudition above material skills and a basic rapport.

Technique. The fetish of technique is to the professional what the fetish of procedure is to the organization. It is sustained by the vision of an expert reaching deeply into a distressed young person, pulling a few crucial levers, and letting nature or society do the rest. Such an uncompromisingly instrumental perspective, apart from fostering a cynical understanding of what people mean to each other, takes no account of the long-term nature of human processes. Nor does it explain why persistent evidence suggests that the most substantial social work achievements are based on relationships in which a great deal of time, patience, and empathy have been invested.

For detached youth work then, the whole person theme is crucial in an analysis of professionalization and the organizational structure of services for street youth. The four dimensions reflect various ways in which young people are fragmented and their integrity is translated into a series of incomplete and selective images, though it is imagined that unity can be restored by recombining them. The hierarchical nature of organizations and the ways in which they preclassify according to established systems and procedures makes them resistant to innovation and oblivious to subtle changes in the environment, whereas the one-dimensional nature of the professional gestalt converts risky social situations into clients and individual clients into clusters of separate needs.

THE WORK OF DETACHED YOUTH WORK

What follows is an attempt to ground detached youth work in the everyday activities of a detached youth worker. This list is not exclusive, and is particular to detached youth work with street youth. It is meant to give the reader a sample, a feel, a taste of what it means to "do" detached youth work.

Dealing With the
Everyday Life of Street Youth

Hanging out on street corners, shopping malls or all night restaurants until 4 a.m. watching, talking, and listening to street youth. Getting paged at 2 a.m. to help a young person who has been raped, beaten up, or stranded by a "trick" and does not trust the police or the service system to help and has no one else to turn to. Giving young people rides to free dinners offered by churches, the grocery store, the doctor or health clinic appointments, job interviews, counseling appointments, school, their families, or work. Mediating disputes between street youth, between lovers, between prostitutes and pimps, between hustlers and sugar daddies, between youth and parents, and between street youth and police.

Helping Street Youth
Deal With the System

Attending court appearances, institutional staffing, agency meetings, and even family counseling sessions with street youth in the role of advocate and encouraging rapprochement and conciliation. Visiting street youth in detention facilities, residential treatment programs, group homes, and hospitals. "Networking" and case managing individual youth and groups of youth with social workers, probation officers, therapists, counselors, and parents. Using personal and professional relationships to help street youth gain access to services (shelter, housing, health care, education, employment and training, counseling, legal, recreational, spiritual, and cultural) and working to keep those services accountable to the young people.

Collaborating and Community Organizing

Educating and collaborating with service providers (shelter, housing, health care, education, employment and training, counseling, legal, recreational, spiritual, and cultural) to make their services more accessible to street youth and to develop new or expanded programming. Organizing and participating in community groups and coalitions around such issues as runaway and homeless youth, prostitution, gay and lesbian youth, children's mental health, HIV/AIDS prevention, gangs, missing children, and child sexual abuse. Working with public officials, legislators, and policy makers to advocate, testify, educate, and develop new programming for service gaps. Working with researchers to document and identify street youth and their needs better. Attending and presenting at local, regional, and national conferences and think tanks on runaway and homeless youth, prostitution, gay and lesbian youth, children's mental health, HIV/AIDS prevention, gangs, missing children, and child sexual abuse.

Thompson (1990), in describing the major skill of detached youth workers at developing relationships, states:

> Yet, when talking about their work (themselves working; themselves at work), youthwork means skill. Relationship is something they do well, something they know how to do. In their metaphor, they "build" relationships. This is their skill and how, when, and with whom it is used show how, where, and with whom detached youthwork is practiced (i.e., actualized). Given who these workers choose as youth-clients, i.e., "street kids," their willingness and ability to create "real relationships" is impressive. (p. 96)

Detached Youth Work and Supervision

The supervision and employment of detached youth workers can best be understood as a series of tensions that are cultural, structural, and often personal. To borrow a concept from the psychoanalytic

Supervisor = parents,
school,
"the system,"
society

Worker = youth

Figure 9.1. Supervision

literature, there is a "parallel process" (Kahn, 1979; Sachs & Shapiro, 1976) on a systemic as well as a personal level in which the relationship between the detached youth worker and the supervisor closely resembles the relationship between the youth and his or her troubles with the adult world. This relationship is illustrated in Figure 9.1.

The tensions between detached youth workers and supervisors can be seen in a variety of arenas, but they most often are metaphors for the struggle between the youth and society. The detached youth worker defines the work in terms of the youth (i.e., youth teach the worker how to be helpful and the "program" emerges from those needs), and the agency/supervisor defines the work in terms of programmatic and funding goals (i.e., which funders will fund and/ or what hierarchies dictate which preclassified and established systems and procedures of "programs" that squeeze young people and circumstances into ready-made categories of "service delivery"). This tension or strain between the detached youth worker and supervisor is best managed when it is understood, in the psychoanalytic parallel process language, as transference and countertransference or as the unconscious acting out of emotions displaced from one relationship/situation to another relationship/situation.

Many detached youth workers perceive supervision as control, and many agency administrators perceive supervision of detached youth workers as difficult (e.g., they are hard to control, accountability is difficult). Thompson (1990) describes this tension:

"Out of sight out of mind," as the saying goes. This is true for the youthworker while the agency personnel expected to supervise the youthworkers act on the adage "visibility is accountability." The more time the youthworkers spend with youth and the less time with agency staff, the more likely they were "to identify" with the youth. The long hours of listening, observing, and being with youth create, in the youthworker, the belief that (s)he is one of the few adults who can "really" understand the youth. They begin to look at the agency as if they were an outsider, questioning policies, procedures, and even the beliefs of the other agency staff. While the supervisor worries, "frets" and imagines what is happening and why, the anger and the frustration of the worker only increases the concern of the supervisor and a vicious cycle is created. (p. 95)

Baizerman (1988) describes another type of tension between detached youth workers and their agencies:

The detached youthworker wants the authority to be an agent of the agency in the name of the youth. Herein lies another source of tension between worker and employer. Employing agencies tend to be ambivalent about detached youthwork because the gains in status and funds which accrue due to their presence is offset by the tensions and problems attendant to their being employed. Since detached youthworkers work with youth at relatively high-risk to complicated personal and familial troubles, detached youthwork seems to get entangled in a wide array of never ending legal, moral and psychological "problems," as seen by the agency. Nothing is ever simple, neat or "cut and dried," i.e., routine. (p. 3)

This is illustrated by the work with gay-identified adolescents involved in male prostitution. Agency executive directors and boards may feel ambivalent about a detached youth worker's advocation for these obviously underserved youth because such advocacy makes the agency vulnerable to attacks by right-wing Christian and profamily organizations that could jeopardize agency funding or credibility.

Another area of tension is what detached youth work often calls "ethics" and agencies often call "boundaries." Detached youth work is always extending the concept of boundaries by challenging the ethics of the helping professions. The work itself is seen by some as "codependent" or guilty of "overidentifying" with the client. In addition, by the very nature of the work (being out on the streets), detached youth workers are witness to much that is illegal, "immoral," violent, and unjust. Helping and forming relationships with youth in this context means that "doing the right thing" is never an easy judgment. Professional detachment collides with a deep sense of moral outrage. Because detached youth workers are not usually members of an established profession, they often do not have professional socialization into the codified ethical codes of such groups and they often challenge the standards of practice of those professional groups. These challenges are well taken but without a process for reflecting on and understanding them, the worker can become frustrated and lose effectiveness.

Commenting on this, Thompson (1990) observes:

> Detached youthworkers may have psychological insight about themselves and/or their clients. If such insight is present, they still lack a theoretical base or language in which to talk about these insights. Hence, supervision, which is often about what in the worker may be influencing what the worker is doing, can be threatening. The supervisor represents the employing agency, and the detached youthworker tends to be in tension with his/her employer. Thus it is seen how the very ethos of detached youthwork, the lack of formal preparation and personal limitations of the worker join in an anti-supervision dance. (p. 96)

Thompson (1990) summarizes the needs of supervision as:

> Youthworkers appear to be open and willing to supervision if it is reflective, supportive and provides a means to remove barriers and obstacles to services to client youth. Youthworkers want someone to talk to about what they are experiencing, someone who will listen, challenge, confront, and accept. They need, in my opinion, supervision which provides for practical mastery, supervision that helps them put their experiences into personal and work contexts and supervision that can move from the levels of "real and concrete" to the theoretical, and back again. . . . Agencies need to understand the detached youthwork stance. It is important that agency personnel recognize and acknowledge the value of detached youthwork as understood from the perspective of the worker. Administrators must come to understand the inherent structural sources of job strain. The anti-technocratic ideology, the lack of an identified code of ethics, the lack of professional identification and status, the relative isolation, the long hours, and the constant struggle to do the right thing in the right way. With such understanding, administrators would help to prevent "burn out," would help to define "role boundaries." They would provide outside consultants for detached youthworkers and strongly encourage ongoing meetings with youthworkers employed at other agencies. (pp. 106-107)

SYNOPSIS OF THE
DETACHED YOUTH WORK MODEL

The model of detached youth work is presented as a method of working with street youth and youth involved in prostitution. It is a method with a history in the social group work method of social work that has evolved and survived but is usually practiced without formal training and education. This lack of formality reflects the long-standing debate about the professional status of the social group work method and the ongoing challenges that detached youth work presents to the professionalization and bureaucratization of youth services.

Detached youth work embraces the youth development theories of adolescence such as those of Konopka (1972, 1973) and Gilligan et al. (1982), rejects the notion of adolescents as incomplete and incompetent, and explicitly rejects attempts to pathologize and medicalize the problems of street youth. The practice, skills, and objectives of detached youth work are the art of relationships and the displacement of technique by principle.

Finally, although supervision of detached youth workers may be difficult, it is not impossible and can be made much easier by agencies valuing and understanding detached youth work and addressing the sources of structural, cultural, and personal strains of detached youth work.

SUMMARY

Science is said to proceed on two legs, one of theory (or, loosely, of deduction) and the other of observation and experiment (or induction). Its progress, however, is less often a commanding stride than a halting stagger—more like the path of a wandering minstrel than the straight ruled trajectory of a military marching band. The development of science is influenced by intellectual fashions, is frequently dependent on technology, and, in any case, seldom can be planned far in advance, since its destination is usually unknown. (Ferris, 1988, p. 144)

Observations always involve theory. (Hubble, 1985, p. 12)

Our hope is that the information presented in this section will make its way into the repertoire of mainstream human service professionals and that a framework can be constructed that allows for more authentic and diverse paradigms of adolescents, particularly males. For this to occur, the prevailing theories or paradigms of adolescent males must be broadened to include the observations that history and research present; these observations must be accountable for the theories that shape them.

The historical literature illustrates that young men and boys have been the sexual objects of pleasure for men, women, and individuals both eclectic in their desires and exclusively pederast throughout human history, and that prostitution has always involved young men and boys. As Foucault (1988) points out, what has changed is not the "taste for boys," but the way in which the questions are asked and a fading of the importance they are granted in philosophical and moral debate.

In modern times, questions about male prostitution have been largely confined to whether the young men involved are homosexual or heterosexual and how that sexual orientation affects or influences their involvement in prostitution. Although these are intriguing questions, they are difficult to understand or investigate without being grounded in the larger questions of the nature of the "taste for boys" and why it is not granted more importance in philosophical, scientific, and moral debates.

Male prostitution is, in a sense, the visible tip of an iceberg. Above the surface is the activity of prostitution; below the surface are the disquieting issues of young males as "victims" or the objects of sexual exploitation, a range of sexual behavior and motivation that does not conveniently fit the culturally defined categories of homosexual or heterosexual, and gender role behavior that challenges conventional notions of maleness.

Attempts to define male prostitution as homosexual prostitution are but one way to obfuscate and distort the unique maleness of prostitution to fit cultural categories and definitions rather than to describe the reality of those involved. This completely ignores the roles of women and exclusive pederasts as customers, as well as making the erroneous assumption that male customers and the prostitutes themselves fit within a definition of homosexual.

Male prostitution is the most visible form of the sexual abuse and exploitation of young males. Below the surface is the issue of the high prevalence of sexual abuse prior to prostitution in the young men involved. This is but one indication that the documentation of sexual abuse of boys is underreported, and speaks to why it is so hard for boys and young men to voice their experiences and for those experiences to be heard. In a culture where men are defined, by both men and women, as sexual predators, it is difficult for them to tell of their experiences as prey.

In terms of social sex roles, the term *male prostitute* is itself an oxymoron. The term *prostitute* carries a host of negative images more associated with the social role of women than men, making the term *male prostitute* difficult to assimilate into everyday conceptualizations of males.

The framework must be renovated if more authentic paradigms of males are to emerge. More research with better methodology that includes the areas of male prostitution that have been traditionally ignored (e.g,. drag queens, pederasts, women customers) is necessary to better understand these enigmatic phenomena, but the information that research supplies must have somewhere to reside. The available cultural paradigms for males, especially adolescent males, do not easily allow for the incorporation of that information.

The other operative word in adolescent male prostitution is "adolescent." The parameters around the discussion of adolescent involvement in prostitution need to be expanded, the phenomenon needs to be contextualized in a wider social setting, factors in society (values, beliefs, and attitudes) and social relations that have a bearing on the process of entrance into and maintenance in prostitution deserve attention, and the dimensions fundamental to a deeper understanding of the phenomenon need to be delineated.

It is not our intention to condemn as worthless conventional research views and perspectives or to present as entirely oppressive all social service practice. Clearly some young people benefit from the existence of these services. It is also not our intention to appear supportive of adolescent involvement in prostitution, for we believe it to be sexual abuse. But the current simplistic "victim/perpetrator" paradigm does not capture the full nature of the abuse: the economic, social, and political exploitation; the impoverishment of constricted sex roles; and the considerable limitations of current theory and institutions.

Because street prostitution is the most visible form of prostitution (and the most accessible to the young person starting out), it receives the most public attention and tends to become the stereotype of what the life is all about. The truth is, prostitution is a diverse enterprise conducted in private homes, in hotels and nightclubs, and through escort services and pagers, as well as on the streets.

Perhaps the most difficult aspect for people outside the life to understand about street life is the shift in thinking that occurs once a young person has been living "out there" for a while. This thinking can best be described as a "survival mentality" characterized by desperation, hypervigilance, and a need for instant gratification. Most of these youth live a moment-to-moment existence and capitalize on any opportunity, illegal or otherwise, to meet their urgent survival needs.

There is a general tendency on the part of the public and some professionals to want to reduce adolescent prostitution, a complex social phenomenon, to a simple "problem" requiring a simple solution. In essence, the problem is seen as in and with the adolescent. Adolescent prostitution is both a mirror and a microcosm of many of the prevailing values, attitudes, and beliefs of modern society.

Prostitution is not simply the activity of prostitutes but is a phenomenon inextricably interwoven with the social fabric of our society. Consideration must be given to the many components that often get overlooked. A major one is the "markets" that exist for the sexual services of adolescents and the adult male and female customers who use these services.

Adolescent prostitution as an income-producing activity appears to be, for the most part, a short-term career, even when it is pursued on a full-time basis (Mathews, 1989). For many adolescents, it is simply a bridge between impoverished states in a directionless career path; for others it is an acknowledged stopgap en route to other areas of work. In any event, most young people do not appear to remain in prostitution much beyond 3 years, and intrusive interventions can be a factor not only in their entrance into the life but also in their staying in it longer. Criminal records, labeling, forced and irrelevant social service programs, and esteem-lowering persecution and harassment are not only ineffective but encourage the behavior they are trying to stop.

The moral repugnance of adolescent prostitution is difficult to reconcile with the acceptance that it is beyond the current willingness and/or ability to eliminate. This difficulty often leads to simplistic and quick solutions to try and make adolescent prostitution go away or a fatalistic resignation that nothing can be done about it. The intermediary, and more difficult position, is that it is morally unacceptable, but it is here and unlikely to go away. However, its consequences on the youth on the streets can be diminished, and interventions can control its magnitude and configuration by eliminating or preventing the recruitment of certain population/groups (e.g., younger youth) and by changing how the street subculture is connected to a variety of other social institutions (e.g., police, child protection, youth-serving agencies), social structures (e.g., the job market), and other crucial phenomena (e.g., exposure to HIV).

The problem of adolescent prostitution can be addressed on many levels; the most effective approaches are those that are able to develop multilevel and multiservice strategies. Because the social institution of street youth is embedded in a reticulum of social structures and processes and is sustained by its interconnections to functionally and geographically related social systems, approaches that flourish in one location cannot necessarily be transplanted to another location and produce the same results. If models of intervention have value, it is not because they can be replicated, component by component, somewhere else. Indeed, a mechanical metaphor is not appropriate here—an organic one is far more useful. No doubt it is possible to "take new cuttings" and "breed new strains," but this is quite different from the idea that one can engineer identical structures indiscriminately. Rather it is the way of thinking about these phenomena and the underlying principles that can be replicated and transplanted to new environments.

Any model of intervention with street youth needs to be built on at least four principles. The first is to identify situations, not categories, of young people. This means, on the one hand, that efforts should be made to study the wider context in which street youth occur, and, on the other, that those who find themselves in that situation must not be overly pathologized and labeled.

The second principle is that street youth are not aliens. This is a truism but nonetheless a necessary reminder. Economic, institutional, and cultural wedges have been driven between the worlds of street youth and adult society. The distorted images of street youth as prostitutes, gang members, drug addicts, and delinquents call for adults to bear the responsibility for rapprochement between the generations and build long-term relationships and support. Implicit in this principle is the respect for young people as persons.

The third principle is to relate services to needs, not needs to services. Among the layers of organization and bureaucracy, it has become increasingly difficult to see that a "need" is independent of the vast and complicated machinery of youth services. Needs today are most often defined in terms of whatever services are deemed viable. This principle argues for a more empirical approach to identifying and understanding needs. This means professionals must be prepared to gather as much relevant data as possible (about individuals, groups, and communities), be ready to experiment with new ways of asking questions, and be willing to listen carefully to the answers. It means professionals must have the tenacity to sift for clues and search for patterns without assuming that either they or the street youth already know the ultimate outcome. It means professionals must consistently think of themselves as researchers, analyzing data, hoping to be surprised, and trying not to take anything for granted.

The fourth principle is that when organizations and agencies consider the concepts of evaluation and accountability, they should look outward to street youth and the community rather than upward toward managers and administrators. Accountability should ultimately be to the client, not the organization. Tests of an agency or professional's ability have become tied to such criteria as recorded change in client behavior and the capacity to describe one's activities in language so convoluted that anyone outside the profession (and many inside) have difficulty understanding it. Reversing this would mean that a worker's skills would be tested by the client, rather than protected by records and the ability to convert accounts of activities into theoretical codes and organizational ciphers. Implicit in this principle is the belief that joint accountability and mutual evaluation are desirable where workers and clients have developed a relationship of cooperation based on mutual respect and a balance of power.

The detached youth work model presented here is an organic model whose emphasis is on a set of principles rather than a set of techniques or structures. As Thompson (1990) suggests, detached youth work is "a stance which is actualized as a praxis depending on the unique moment, the unique youth, in a unique context" (p. 86). It starts with a problem (street youth), not a program, and its primary tool is the relationships the worker is able to form with youth. Strategies and services emerge from these relationships and the nature of the problems the worker encounters.

At its simplest and most sweeping, the message of detached youth work is this: Youth-service agencies tend not to be able to cope with fluidity, uncertainty, change, and continuity—any form of "becoming" that transcends boundaries in time, space, or role. For both organizational and professional reasons, these agencies are more comfortable with fragments and factors, components and compartments, timetables and targets and everything else that can be defined, discriminated, determined or differentiated. To the degree that this is true, these agencies also fall short of the principles espoused here, and fail in their mission to serve youth.

10

Epilogue

A young man who had a bitter disappointment in life went to a re-
mote monastery and said to the abbot: "I am disillusioned with life and
wish to attain enlightenment to be freed from these sufferings. But I
have no capacity for sticking long at anything. I could never do long
years of meditation and study and austerity; I should relapse and be
drawn back to the world again, painful though I know it to be. Is there
any short way for people like me?" "There is," said the abbot, "if you
are really determined. Tell me, what have you studied, what have
you concentrated on most in your life?" "Why, nothing really. We
were rich, and I did not have to work. I suppose the thing I was really interested in was chess. I spent most of my time at that."

The abbot thought for a moment, and then said to his attendant:
"Call such-and-such a monk, and tell him to bring a chessboard and
men." The monk came with the board and the abbot set up the men.
He sent for a sword and showed it to the men. "O monk," he said,
"you have vowed obedience to me as your abbot, and now I require
it of you. You will play a game of chess with this youth, and if you
lose I shall cut off your head with this sword. But I promise that you
will be reborn in paradise. If you win, I shall cut off the head of this
man; chess is the only thing he has ever tried hard at, and if he loses
he deserves to lose his head also." They looked at the abbot's face
and saw that he meant it: he would cut off the head of the loser.

They began to play. With the opening moves the youth felt the sweat
trickling down to his heels as he played for his life. The chessboard

became the whole world; he was entirely concentrated on it. At first he had somewhat the worst of it, but then the other made an inferior move and he seized his chance to launch a strong attack. As his opponent's position crumbled, he looked covertly at him. He saw a face of intelligence and sincerity, worn with years of austerity and effort. He thought of his own worthless life, and a wave of compassion came over him. He deliberately made a blunder and then another blunder, ruining his position and leaving himself defenseless.

The abbot suddenly leaned forward and upset the board. The two contestants sat stupefied. "There is no winner and no loser," said the abbot slowly, "there is no head to fall here. Only two things are required," and he turned to the young man, "complete concentration, and compassion. You have today learned them both. You were completely concentrated on the game, but then in that concentration you could feel compassion and sacrifice your life for it. Now stay here a few months and pursue our training in this spirit and your enlightenment is sure." He did so and got it. (Sohl & Carr, pp. 43-44)

Our initial attempts to create a more "unified" volume on males as victims and perpetrators of sexual abuse seemed premature, at least for us and perhaps for the field. We found ourselves most comfortable with an increasingly diverging set of perspectives that reflected what each of us believed in, felt we were good at, and respected but did not necessarily share in terms of perspective or skills in the others.

Despite the variety of our perspectives, from individual therapy in which the effects and meaning of the abuse interacts with the development of the self, to family therapy in the context of large and complicated systems, to gritty on-the-streets social work, we share important commonalities.

The first is a deeply felt need to place understandings of sexual abuse in a larger and richer context. This context includes the social forces that disenfranchise youth and drive them into the streets; the complex and changing function that prostitution has played in our civilization; the family systems of both victim and offender as well as the larger "institutional family" (perhaps the most dysfunctional of all) of social service, mental health, criminal justice, and related systems; and the ways in which the experience of sexual abuse resonates throughout the individual psyche. The phenomena of sexual abuse cannot be understood in a fragmented or atomized way. There is no real "field" of sexual abuse, nor should there be.

Rather, there are different ways of understanding the complexity of sexual abuse through the simultaneously limiting and enriching perspectives of particular disciplines. Treating sexual abuse as a specialty area apart from the individual psyches carrying the experience; the families and other systems affected; and the larger culture that is simultaneously horrified, condoning, shaming, and denying regarding sexual abuse merely repeats the alienation, fragmentation, and disenfranchisement that are the hallmarks of the experience. We are integrationist about sexual abuse and promiscuous about the levels on which it needs integration.

There is another commonality in our perspectives: A belief that a helping or therapeutic intervention cannot occur unless there is a pervasive respect for the client. Whether that client is victim or perpetrator, adult or minor, psychologically minded or lacking in insight, well defended or emotionally integrated, cooperative or obstreperous, normatively middle class or living on the edge, the patient or client deserves the good will, complete skills, respect, and understanding of the therapist or helper—concentration and compassion.

This is a truism in any kind of clinical work. However, certain kinds of clinical work, like working with victims and perpetrators of sexual abuse, more readily elicit violations of these norms. The helper who cannot feel warmth or empathy toward a client or class of clients and who cannot simultaneously risk challenging that client or clients should not be working with such individuals. Neglecting this basic stance is the danger of any overly politicized perspective. We suggest that any goal that interferes with or diminishes the overriding principle of operating in the best interests of the individual client is inappropriate and runs the risk of shading into seriously unethical behavior.

That is not to say that such goals are unworthy but rather that their place is not in clinical work. Desires to seek justice for victims, to make the world a less oppressive place for any class of people, to prevent further abuse, and the like, are only reasonable in clinical work if they do not deflect from the individual client's best interests. Interventions rendered in the interest of victims in general, to make examples of certain people or situations, or to create social change, invariably shortchange some individual clients.

The core feature of abuse, sexual or otherwise, is that the rights and interests of an individual are ignored and/or violated to serve the purposes of another. Intervention efforts that zealously attempt to remedy other abuses by deflecting from the centrality of the best interests of the individual client can easily end up as a more exquisitely rationalized form of abuse.

We share an attitude of wringing every drop of utility out of a theoretical perspective or clinical technique. We believe that there is little sacred and a great deal foolish about the theory and practice of clinical work. Such endeavors are only as worthwhile as they are respectful and useful. Clinical theories and techniques are not understandings of human nature, philosophical systems, spirituality, or important in their own right. Rather, they are tools to be used in ways intended, and perhaps in ways not initially intended (but cautiously), to reduce suffering in a way that serves the client's best interests.

We suspect Kohut would not have been pleased to see his ideas about early childhood processes applied to later childhood and adolescent developmental events. Many family system theorists might find tight adherence to specific goals intermingled with potentially high risk interactions with multiple systems at once, in victim sensitive offender therapy, too untidy. Many social workers might perceive the central allegiance to the youth served in the detached youth work model as unnerving indeed.

Our common goal is to utilize clinical theory and technique to accomplish the task of respectful and effective reduction of suffering and to facilitate change in the best interests of the clients. Slavish adherence to theoretical niceties and oppositional delight in trouncing on such niceties ignore the centrality of the needs of the client.

Finally, we share a curiosity about the meaning of our work. Regularly questioning the nature of what one does may not reliably produce wisdom, but we are confident it helps contain clinical arrogance.

We are disquieted by the peculiar convergence of recent cultural trends in the United States regarding children. The 1980s, which witnessed recognition of and "concern" for sexual abuse of children, also saw a massive erosion of social supports, health care, and economic services for children to a level that has not been seen for the better part of a century. Are we as a society concerned about the welfare of children, or are we using children to indulge yet another round of our cultural love-hate obsession with sexuality, our see-saw between excess and repression? Do we focus concern predominantly on childhood sexual abuse so we do not have to address unnerving questions about the failure of our familial, social, political, economic, and healthcare institutions to address the needs of children?

To allow so many children to be without adequate prenatal care, early childhood nutrition, health care, and a viable education or job skills within a violent environment with little prospect of meaningful adult employment; and then to be concerned about these children's vulnerability to sexual abuse seems a sham. If our concern for children is true and deep, we as a society must find ways to address all the ways children are abused.

In this "field" of sexual abuse, where the needs and the demands of clients are high, the database is thin, dogmatism seems to run rampant, and the internal contradictions and avoidance of substantive issues on a societal level make the mind reel, we heartily recommend concentration and compassion.

John C. Gonsiorek

References

Abel, G., Barlow, D., Blanchard, E., & Guild, D. (1977). The components of rapists' sexual arousal. *Archives of General Psychiatry, 34*, 895-903.

Abel, G., Rouleau, J., & Cunningham-Rathner, J. (1986). Sexually aggressive behavior. In W. Curran, A. L. McGarry, & S. A. Shah (Eds.), *Modern legal psychiatry and psychology* (pp. 14-37). Philadelphia: F. A. Davis.

Ackely, E. G., & Fliegal, B. (1960). A social work approach to street-corner girls. *Social Work, 5*(4), 27-36.

Aichhorn, A. (1935). *Wayward youth*. New York: Viking.

Allen, C. M. (1990). Women as perpetrators of sexual abuse: Recognition barriers. In A. L. Horton, B. L. Johnson, L. M. Roundy, & D. Williams (Eds.), *The incest perpetrator* (pp. 108-125). Newbury Park, CA: Sage.

Allen, C. M. (1991). *Women and men who sexually abuse children: A comparative analysis*. Orwell, VT: Safer Society Press.

Allen, D. M. (1980). Young male prostitutes: A psychosocial study. *Archives of Sexual Behavior, 9*, 399-426.

Allport, G. W. (1954). *The nature of prejudice*. Reading, MA: Addison-Wesley.

American Humane Association. (1981). *National study on child neglect and abuse reporting*. Denver, CO: Author.

American Psychological Association. (1985). *Standards for educational and psychological testing*. Washington, DC: Author.

American Psychological Association. (1986). *Guidelines for computer-based tests and interpretations*. Washington, DC: Author.

American Psychiatric Association. (1994). *Diagnostic and statistical manual of mental disorders* (4th ed.). Washington, DC: American Psychiatric Association.

American Psychological Association. (1992). Ethical principles of psychologists and code of conduct. *American Psychologist, 42*, 1597-1611.

Amos, S. (1877). *Laws for the regulation of vice*. London: Stevens and Richardson.

Arendt, H. (1968). *Men in dark times*. Orlando, FL: Harcourt Brace and Company.

Aries, P. (1962). *Centuries of childhood: A social history of family life*. New York: Random House.

Atcheson, J. D., & Williams, D. C. (1954). A study of juvenile sex offenders. *American Journal of Psychiatry, 111*, 366-370.

Awad, G. A., Saunders, E., & Levene, J. (1984). Sexual abuse: Current issues and strategies. *International Journal of Offender Therapy and Comparative Criminology, 14*(1), 105-116.

Badgley, D. (1984). *The committee report on sexual offenses against children: Vols. 1 & 2.* Ottawa, Canada: Ministry of Supply and Services.

Baer, M. (1976). *Ode to Billy Joe* [Film]. Warner Bros.

Bailey, D. S. (Ed.). (1956). *Sexual offenders and social punishment.* London: Hazel Watson and Viney.

Baizerman, M. (1988, November). Do we need detached youthworkers to work with street kids? *Street Children Update: Briefing.*

Baizerman, M. (1989). *Street kids: Where should we focus.* Unpublished manuscript.

Baizerman, M., Thompson, J., & Stafford-White, K. (1979). Adolescent prostitution. *Children Today, 2*(3), 20-24.

Baker, A. W., & Duncan, S. P. (1985). Child sexual abuse: A study of prevalence in Great Britain. *Child Abuse & Neglect, 9*, 457-467.

Banfield, E. (1973). *The heavenly city revisited.* Boston: Little, Brown.

Barbaree, H. E., Marshall, W. L., & Hudson, S. M. (Eds.). (1993). *The juvenile sex offender.* New York: Guilford.

Barnard, G. W., Fuller, A. K., Robins, L., & Shaw, T. (1989). *The child molester: An integrated approach to evaluation and treatment.* New York: Brunner/Mazel.

Bateson, G. (1972). *Steps to an ecology of mind.* Toronto, Canada: Chandler Publishing Company.

Beck, A. T. (1976). *Cognitive therapy and the emotional disorders.* New York: Internation Universities Press.

Becker, J. V., & Kaplan, M. S. (1988). The assessment of adolescent sexual offenders. In R. J. Prinz (Ed.), *Advances in behavioral assessment of children and families: Vol. 4* (pp. 94-118). Newbury Park, CA: Sage.

Becker, J. V., Kaplan, M. S., Cunningham-Rathner, J., & Kavoussi, R. (1986). Characteristics of adolescent incest sexual perpetrators: Preliminary findings. *Journal of Family Violence, 1*, 85-97.

Becker, J. V., Kaplan, M. S., & Temke, C. E. (1992). The relationship of abuse history, denial and erectile response of adolescent perpetrators. *Behavior Therapy, 23*, 87-97.

Benard, B. (1991). *Fostering resiliency in kids: Protective factors in the family, school, and community.* Washington, DC: Northwest Regional Educational Laboratory and the U.S. Department of Education.

Bender, L., & Blau, A. (1937). The reaction of children to sexual relations with adults. *American Journal of Orthopsychiatry, 7*, 500-518.

Benjamin, H., & Masters, R. E. L. (1964). *Prostitution and morality.* New York: Julian Press.

Bera, W. (1980). *Self-defense/assertiveness training in the treatment of sexual assault trauma.* Unpublished manuscript.

Bera, W. (1985). *A preliminary investigation of a typology of adolescent sex offenders and their family systems.* Unpublished master's thesis, University of Minnesota.

Bera, W. (1990). The systemic-attributional model: Victim-sensitive offender therapy. In J. M. Yokley (Ed.), *The use of victim-offender communication in the treatment of sexual abuse: Three intervention models* (pp. 45-76). Orwell, VT: Safer Society Press.

Berger, L. (1974). *From instinct to identity: The development of personality.* Englewood Cliffs: Prentice Hall.

Berman, M. (1982). *All that is solid melts into air: The experience of modernity.* New York: Simon & Schuster.

Bernstein, S. (1964). *Youth on the streets: Work with alienated youth groups.* New York: Association Press.

Bloch, H., & Niederhoffer, A. (1958). *The gang.* New York: Philosophical Library.

Block, J. H. (1983). Differential premises arising from differential socialization of the sexes: Some conjectures. *Child Development, 54,* 1335-1354.

Bolton, F. G., Jr., Morris, L. A., & MacEachron, A. E. (1989). *Males at risk: The other side of child sexual abuse.* Newbury Park, CA: Sage.

Boorman, J. (Director). (1972). *Deliverance* [Film]. Warner Bros.

Boyer, D. (1986). *Street exit project* (Final Report to U.S. Department of Health and Human Services, Grant No. 90-CY-0360). Washington, DC: Office of Human Development Services.

Boyer, D. (1989). Male prostitution and homosexual identity. *Journal of Homosexuality, 17,* 151-184.

Boyer, D., & James, J. (1983). Prostitutes as victims: Sex and the social order. In D. E. J. MacNamara & A. Karman (Eds.), *Deviants: Victims or victmizers* (pp. 109-146). Beverly Hills, CA: Sage.

Bradford, J. M. (1993). The pharmacological treatment of the adolescent sex offender. In H. E. Barbaree, V. L. Marshall, & S. M. Hudson (Eds.), *The juvenile sex offender* (pp. 278-288). New York: Guilford.

Brannon, R. A., Larson, A. W., & Doggett, K. V. (1989). Sexual victimization among juvenile sex offenders. *Violence and Victims, 5*(3), 213-224.

Bray, A. (1982). *Homosexuality in renaissance England.* London: Gay Mens Press.

Bremmer, J. F. (1992). Serious juvenile sex offenders: Treatment and long-term follow-up. *Psychiatric Annals, 22*(6), 113-130.

Briere, J. (1984, April). *The effects of childhood sexual abuse on later psychological functioning: Defining a post-sexual abuse syndrome.* Paper presented at the Third National Conference on Sexual Victimization of Children, Children's Hospital National Medical Center, Washington, DC.

Briere, J. (1990). Accuracy of adults' reports of abuse in childhood: Dr. Briere replies [invited letter]. *American Journal of Psychiatry, 147,* 1389-1390.

Briere, J. (1992a). *Child abuse trauma: Theory and treatment of the lasting effects.* Newbury Park, CA: Sage.

Briere, J. (1992b). Methodological issues in the study of sexual abuse effects. *Journal of Consulting & Clinical Psychology, 60,* 196-203.

Bronfenbrenner, U. (1974). *The ecology of human development.* Cambridge: Harvard University Press.

Brown, M. E., Hull, L. A., & Panesis, S. K. (1984). *Women who rape.* Boston: Massachusetts Trial Court.

Browne, A., & Finkelhor, D. (1986). The impact of child sexual abuse: Review of the research. *Psychological Bulletin, 99,* 66-77.

Burg, B. R. (1984). *Sodomy and the pirate tradition: English sea rovers in the seventeenth century Caribbean.* New York: New York University Press.

Burgess, A. W. (1984). *Child pornography and sex rings*. Lexington, MA: Lexington Books.

Burgess, A. W., & Holmstrom, L. L. (1975). Sexual trauma of children and adolescents: Sex, pressure and secrecy. *Nursing Clinics of North America, 10*, 551-563.

Butcher, J. N., Dahlstrom, W. G., Graham, J. R., Tellegen, A., & Kaemmer, B. (1989). *Minnesota Multiphasic Personality Inventory-2 (MMPI-2)*. Minneapolis: University of Minnesota Press.

Butcher, J. N., Williams, C. L., Graham, J. R., Archer, R. P., Tellegen, A., Ben-Porath, U. S., & Kaemmer, B. (1992). *Minnesota Multiphasic Personality Inventory-Adolescent (MMPI-A)*. Minneapolis: University of Minnesota Press.

Butts, W. M. (1947). Boy prostitutes of the metropolis. *Journal of Clinical Psychopathology, 8*, 673-681.

Calvert, K. (1991). *Children in the house*. Boston: Northeastern University Press.

Campbell, A. (1984). *The girls in the gang*. New York: Basil Blackwell.

Caplan, N. S., Deshaies, D. J., Suttles, G. D., & Mattick, H. W. (1964). Factors affecting the process and outcome of street club work. *Sociology and Social Research, 48*, 207-219.

Carnegie Corporation. (1992). *A matter of time: Risk and opportunity in the nonschool hours*. Woodlawn, MD: Author.

Caukins, S. E., & Coombs, N. R. (1976). The psychodynamics of male prostitution. *American Journal of Psychotherapy, 30*, 441-451.

Children's Defense Fund. (1990). *Children 1990: A report card, a briefing book, and action primer*. Washington, DC: Author.

Cloward, R. A., & Ohlin, L. E. (1960). *Delinquency and opportunity*. Glencoe, IL: The Free Press of Glencoe.

Conte, J., Berliner, L., & Schuerman, J. (1986). *The impact of sexual abuse on children* (Final Report No. MH37133). Rockville, MD: National Institute of Mental Health.

Conte, J., & Schuerman, J. (1987). The effects of sexual abuse of children: A multidimensional view. *Journal of Interpersonal Violence, 2*, 380-390.

Coombs, N. R. (1974). Male prostitution: A psychosocial view of behavior. *American Journal of Orthopsychiatry, 44*, 782-789.

Craft, M. (1966). Boy prostitutes and their fate. *British Journal of Psychiatry, 112*, 1111-1114.

Dahlstrom, W. G. (1993). Tests: Small samples, large consequences. *American Psychologist, 48*, 393-399.

D'Augelli, A. R., & Patterson, C. J. (Eds.). (1994). *Lesbian, gay and bisexual identities across the lifespan*. New York: Oxford University Press.

Davis, G. E., & Leitenberg, H. (1987). Adolescent sex offenders. *Psychological Bulletin, 101*(3), 417-427.

DeCecco, J. P. (1981). Definition and meaning of sexual orientation. *Journal of Homosexuality, 6*(4), 51-67.

DeFrances, V. (1969). *Protecting the child victim of sex crimes committed by adults*. Denver, CO: American Human Association, Children's Division.

Deisher, R. W., Eisner, V., & Sulzbacher, S. (1969). The young male prostitute. *Pediatrics, 43*(6), 936-941.

Deisher, R. W., & Gandy, P. (1970). Young male prostitutes: The physician's role in social rehabilitation. *Journal of the American Medical Association, 212*(10), 1661-1666.

Deisher, R. W., Robinson, G., & Boyer, D. (1982). The adolescent female and male prostitute. *Pediatric Annals, 11*(10), 819-825.

Deisher, R. W., Wenet, G. A., & Boyer, D. (1982). Adolescent sexual offense behavior: The role of the physician. *Journal of Adolescent Health Care, 2*(4), 279-286.

deMause, L. (1982). *Foundations of psychohistory.* New York: Creative Roots.

Dimmock, P. (1990, August). *Myths about male victims* [handout]. Minneapolis, MN: The Treatment of Male Sexual Abuse Victims Workshop.

Doherty, W. J., & Baird, M. A. (1986). Developmental levels in family-centered medical care. *Family Medicine, 18*(3), 153-156.

Doherty, W. J., & Peskay, V. E. (1992). Family systems in the school in home-school collaboration: Building a fundamental educational resource. In S. L. Christenson & J. Connolley (Eds.), *New approaches in home-school collaboration* (pp. 37-46). Washington, DC: National Association of Schools of Psychology.

Dominelli, L. (1986). Father-daughter incest: Patriarchy's shameful secret. *Critical Social Policy, 6,* 8-22.

Doris, J. (Ed.). (1991). *The suggestibility of children's recollections: Implications for eye witness testimony.* Washington, DC: American Psychological Association.

Doshay, L. J. (1943). *The boy sex offender and his later career.* New York: Grune & Stratton.

Dumpson, J. D. (1949). An approach to antisocial street gangs. *Federal Probation, 13*(7), 22-29.

Ellis, A. (1962). *Reason and emotion in psychotherapy.* New York: Stuart.

Ellis, A., & Greiger, R. (Eds.). (1977). *Handbook of rational-emotive therapy.* New York: Springer.

Erikson, E. H. (1963). *Childhood and society.* New York: Norton.

Exner, J. (1986). *The Rorschach: A comprehensive system: Vol. 1* (2nd ed.). New York: John Wiley.

Faller, K. C. (1990). *Understanding child sexual maltreatment.* Newbury Park, CA: Sage.

False Memory Syndrome Foundation. (undated). *Mission and purpose.* Mimeograph.

Fehrenbach, P., & Monastersky, C. (1988). Characteristics of female adolescent sex offenders. *American Journal of Orthopsychiatry, 58,* 148-151.

Fehrenbach, P. A., Smith, W., Monastersky, C., & Deisher, R. W. (1986). Adolescent sexual offenders: Offender and offense characteristics. *American Journal of Orthopsychiatry, 56,* 225-233.

Ferris, T. (1988). *Coming of age in the milky way.* New York: William Morris.

Finkelhor, D. (1979). *Sexually victimized children.* New York: Free Press.

Finkelhor, D. (Ed.). (1984). *Child sexual abuse—New theory and research.* New York: Free Press.

Finkelhor, D., & Associates. (1986). *A sourcebook on child sexual abuse.* Newbury Park, CA: Sage.

Finkelhor, D. (1990a). Response to Bauserman. *Journal of Homosexuality, 20,* 313-315.

Finkelhor, D. (1990b). Early and long-term effects of child sexual abuse: An update. *Professional Psychology: Research and Practice, 21,* 325-330.

Finkelhor, D., & Browne, A. (1986). Initial and long-term effects: A conceptual framework. In D. Finkelhor & Associates (Eds.), *A sourcebook on child sexual abuse* (pp. 180-198). Newbury Park, CA: Sage.

Finkelhor, D., & Russell, D. (1984). Women as perpetrators: Review of the evidence. In D. Finkelhor (Ed.), *Child sexual abuse: New theory and research* (pp. 171-187). New York: Free Press.

Fisher, B., Weisberg, K., & Marotta, T. (1982). *Report on adolescent male prostitution*. San Francisco, CA: Urban and Rural Systems Associates.

Foucault, M. (1980). *The history of sexuality*. New York: Vintage.

Foucault, M. (1986). *The use of pleasure*. New York: Vintage.

Foucault, M. (1988). *The care of the self*. New York: Vintage.

Freeman, B. A. (1956). *Techniques of a worker with a corner group of boys*. Unpublished master's thesis, Boston University School of Social Work.

Freeman-Longo, R. E. (1986). The impact of sexual victimization on males. *Child Abuse & Neglect, 10,* 411-414.

Freeman-Longo, R., & Knopp, F. (1992). State of the art sex offender treatment: Outcomes and issues. In *Recidivism in sex offender treatment: A packet*. Orwell, VT: Safer Society Press.

Freud, S. (1896/1946). The etiology of hysteria. In E. Jones (Ed.) & J. Riviere (Trans.), *Collected papers: Vol. 1* (pp. 183-219). New York: The International Psychoanalytical Press.

Freyd, P. (1992, May 1). *FMS foundational newsletter*. Philadelphia: FMS Foundation.

Friedrich, W. N., Beilke, R. L., & Urquiza, A. J. (1988). Behavioral problems in young sexually abused boys. *Journal of Interpersonal Violence, 3,* 21-28.

Fritz, G. S., Stoll, I. L., & Wagner, N. A. (1981). A comparison of males and females who were sexually molested as children. *Journal of Sex and Marital Therapy, 7,* 54-59.

Gale, A. (Ed.). (1988). *The polygraph test: Lies, truth and science*. London: Sage.

Gandy, P., & Deisher, R. (1970). Young male prostitutes: The physician's role in social rehabilitation. *Journal of the American Medical Association, 212,* 1661-1666.

Garmezy, N. (1991). Resiliency and vulnerability to adverse developmental outcomes associated with poverty. *American Behavioral Scientist, 34*(4), 416-430.

Gebhard, P. H., Gagnon, J. H., Pomeroy, W. B., & Christenson, C. V. (1965). *Sex offenders: An analysis of types*. New York: Harper & Row.

Gelinas, D. J. (1988). Family therapy: Characteristic family constellations and basic therapeutic stance. In S. M. Sgroi (Ed.), *Vulnerable populations: Evaluation and treatment of sexually abused children and adult survivors: Vol. 1* (pp. 25-50). Lexington, MA: Lexington Books.

Gerassi, J. (1966). *The boys from Boise*. New York: Macmillan.

Gibbs, J., & Bennett, S. (1990). *Together we can: A framework for community prevention planning*. Seattle, WA: Comprehensive Health Education Foundation.

Gilbert, C. M. (1989). Sibling incest. *Journal of Child Psychiatric Nursing, 2*(2), 70-73.

Gilligan, C., Ward, J. V., & Taylor, J. M. (Eds.). (1988). *Mapping the moral domain*. Cambridge: Harvard University Press.

Gilmartin, Z. P. (1983). Attribution theory and rape victim responsibility. *Deviant Behavior, 4*(3-4), 357-374.

Ginsburg, K. N. (1967). "The meat rack": A study of the male homosexual prostitute. *American Journal of Psychotherapy, 21,* 170-185.

Goldman, R., & Goldman, J. (1982). *Children's sexual thinking: A comparative study of children aged 5 to 15 years in Australia, North America, Britain and Sweden*. Boston: Routledge & Kegan Paul.

Gomes-Schwartz, B., Horowitz, J., & Carderelli, A. (1990). *Child sexual abuse: The initial effects*. Newbury Park, CA: Sage.

Gonsiorek, J. (1982). Results of psychological testing on homosexual populations. In W. Paul, J. Weinrich, & J. Gonsiorek (Eds.), *Homosexuality: Social, psychological and biological issues* (pp. 71-80). Beverly Hills, CA: Sage.

Gonsiorek, J. (1988). Mental health issues of gay and lesbian adolescents. *Journal of Adolescent Health Care, 9*, 114-122.

Gonsiorek, J. (1989). Sexual exploitation by psychotherapists: Some observations on male victims and sexual orientation issues. In G. Schoener, J. Milgram, J. Gonsiorek, E. Luepker, & R. Conroe (Eds.), *Psychotherapists' sexual involvement with clients: Intervention and prevention* (pp. 113-119). Minneapolis: Walk-In Counseling Center.

Gonsiorek, J. (1991). The empirical basis for the demise of the illness model of homosexuality. In J. Gonsiorek & J. Weinrich (Eds.), *Homosexuality: Research implications for public policy* (pp. 115-136). Newbury Park, CA: Sage.

Gonsiorek, J., & Rudolph, J. (1991). Homosexual identity: Coming out and other developmental events. In J. Gonsiorek & J. Weinrich (Eds.), *Homosexuality: Research implications for public policy* (pp. 161-176). Newbury Park, CA: Sage.

Gonsiorek, J., & Weinrich, J. (1991). The definition and scope of sexual orientation. In J. Gonsiorek & J. Weinrich (Eds.), *Homosexuality: Research implications for public policy* (pp. 1-12). Newbury Park, CA: Sage.

Goodman, G., & Bottoms, B. (1993). *Child victim, child witness: Understanding and improving testimony*. New York: Guilford.

Goodman, M. E. (1970). *The culture of childhood*. New York: Teachers College Press.

Goodwin, J. (1982). *Sexual abuse: Incest victims and their families*. Boston: John Wright.

Gough, H. G. (1987). *California Personality Inventory (CPI)*. Palo Alto, CA: Consulting Psychologists Press.

Green, S. (1984). Victim-offender reconciliation program: A review of the concept. *Social Action and the Law, 10*(2), 43-52.

Greene, B. F. (1981). A primer on testing. *American Psychologist, 36*, 1001-1011.

Greer, J., & Stuart, I. (1983). *The sexual agressor: Current perspectives on treatment*. New York: Van Nostrand Reinhold.

Groth, A. N. (1979). Sexual trauma in the life histories of rapists and child molesters. *Victimology: An International Journal, 4*, 10-16.

Groth, A. N., & Birnbaum, H. (1978). Adult sexual orientation and attraction to underage persons. *Archives of Sexual Behavior, 7*(3), 175-183.

Groth, A. N., & Birnbaum, H. (1979). *Men who rape: The psychology of the offender*. New York: Plenum.

Groth, A. N., & Burgess, A. W. (1979). Sexual trauma in the life histories of rapists and child molesters. *Victimology: An International Journal, 4*, 10-16.

Groth, A. N., & Loredo, C. M. (1981). Juvenile sex offenders: Guidelines for assessment. *International Journal of Offender Comparative Criminology, 25*(1), 13-18

Gulotta, G., & deCataldo-Neuberger, L. (1983). A systematic and attributional approach to victimology. *Victimology: An International Journal, 8*, 5-16.

Gurman, A. S., & Kniskern, D. P. (Eds.). (1981). *Handbook of family therapy: Vol. 1*. New York: Brunner/Mazel.

Gurman, A. S., & Kniskern, D. P. (Eds.). (1991). *Handbook of family therapy: Vol. 2*. New York: Brunner/Mazel.

Haaven, J., Little, R., & Petre-Miller, D. (1990). *Treating intellectually disabled sex offenders: A model residential program*. Orwell, VT: Safer Society Press.

Hamilton, G. V. (1929). *A research in marriage*. New York: Albert & Charles Boni.

Hart, S. N. (1991). From property to person status: Historical perspective on children's rights. *American Psychologist, 46*, 53-59.

Hechler, D. (1988). *The battle and the backlash: The child sexual abuse war*. Lexington, MA: D. C. Heath.

Heider, F. (1958). *The psychology of interpersonal relations*. New York: Wiley.

Henggler, S.W. (1989). Sexual offending and violent behaviors. In S. W. Henngler (Ed.), *Delinquency in adolescence* (Vol. 18, pp. 72-83). Newbury Park, CA: Sage.

Herek, G. (1991). Stigma, prejudice and violence against lesbians and gay men. In J. Gonsiorek & J. Weinrich (Eds.), *Homosexuality: Research implications for public policy* (pp. 60-80). Newbury Park, CA: Sage Publications.

Herman, J. (1992). *Trauma and recovery*. New York: Basic Books.

Hoffman, M. (1972). The male prostitute. *Sexual Behavior, 2*, 16-21.

Homma-True, R., Greene, B., Lopez, S. R., & Trimble, J. E. (1993). Ethnocultural diversity in clinical psychology. *The Clinical Psychologist, 46*, 50-63.

Hubble, E. (1985). *The realm of the nebulae*. New Haven, CT: Yale University Press.

Hunter, M. (1990). *Abused boys: The neglected victims of sexual abuse*. Lexington, MA: Lexington Books.

James, T. E. (1951). *Prostitution and the law*. London: William Heineman.

Jersild, J. (1956). *Boy prostitution*. Copenhagen: G. E. C. Gad.

Johnson, R. L., & Shrier, D. (1985). Sexual victimization of boys: Experience at an adolescent medicine clinic. *Journal of Adolescent Health Care, 6*, 372-376.

Justice, B., & Justice, R. (1979). *The broken taboo*. New York: Human Sciences Press.

Juvenile Delinquency Evaluation Project. (1960). *Dealing with the conflict gang in New York City: Interim report no. XIV*. New York: Juvenile Delinquency Evaluation Project of New York City.

Kahn, T. J. (1990). *Pathways: A guided workbook for youth beginning treatment*. Orwell, VT: Safer Society Press.

Kaplan, M. S., Becker, J. B., & Martinez, D. M. (1990). A comparison of mothers with adolescent incest versus non-incest perpetrators. *Journal of Family Violence, 5*(3), 209-215.

Keller, E. (1980). *Sexual assault: A statewide problem* (LEAA Grant No. 4317013675). St. Paul: Minnesota Department of Corrections.

Kelley, H., & Thibaut, J. (1969). Group problem solving. In G. Lindzey & E. Aronson (Eds.), *Handbook of social psychology: Vol. 4* (2nd ed., pp. 1-101). Reading, MA: Addison-Wesley.

Kelley, S. J. (1988, April). *Responses of children to sexual abuse and satanic ritualistic abuse in daycare centers*. Paper presented at the National Symposium on Child Victimization, Anaheim, CA.

Kempe, R., & Kempe, C. H. (1984). *The common secret: Sexual abuse of children and adolescents*. New York: Freeman.

Kinsey, A. C., Pomeroy, W. B., & Martin, C. E. (1948). *Sexual behavior in the human male*. Philadelphia: W. B. Saunders.

Knight, R. A., & Prentky, R. A. (1990). Classifying sexual offenders: The developing and corroboration of taxonomic models. In W. L. Marshall, D. R. Laws, & H. E. Barbaree (Eds.), *The handbook of sexual assault: Issues, theories and treatment of the offender* (pp. 27-52). New York: Plenum.

Knight, R. A., & Prentky, R. A. (1993). Exploring characteristics for classifying juvenile sex offenders. In H. E. Barbaree, W. L. Marshall, & S. M. Hudson (Eds.), *The juvenile sex offender* (pp. 289-320). New York: Guilford.

Knopp, F. H. (1982). *Remedial intervention in adolescent sex offenses: Nine program descriptions*. Orwell, VT: Safer Society Press.

Knopp, F. H. (1984). *Retraining adult sex offenders: Methods and models*. Orwell, VT: Safer Society Press.

Knopp, F. H. (1985). *The youthful sex offender: The rationales and goals of early intervention*. Orwell, VT: Safer Society Press.

Knopp, F. H., Boward, B., Brach, M. J., Christianson, S., Largen, M. A., Lewin, J., Lugo, J., Morris, M., & Newton, W. (1976). *Instead of prisons*. Orwell, VT: Safer Society Press.

Knopp, F. H., Freeman-Longo, R., & Stevenson, W. F. (1992). *Nationwide survey of juvenile and adult sex offender treatment programs: 1990*. Orwell, VT: Safer Society Press.

Knopp, F. H., & Lackey, L. B. (1987). *Female sex abusers: A summary of data from 44 treatment providers*. Orwell, VT: Safer Society Press.

Kobrin, S. (1959). The Chicago Area Project: A 25 year assessment. *Annals of American Academy of Political and Social Science, 322*, 19-29.

Kohut, H. (1971). *The analysis of the self*. New York: International Universities Press.

Kohut, H. (1977). *The restoration of the self*. New York: International Universities Press.

Kohut, H. (1984). *How does analysis cure?* Chicago: University of Chicago Press.

Konker, C. (1992). Rethinking child sexual abuse: An anthropological perspective. *American Journal of Orthopsychiatry, 62*, 147-153.

Konopka, G. (1972). *Social group work: A helping process*. Englewood Cliffs, NJ: Prentice Hall.

Konopka, G. (1973). Requirements for a healthy development of adolescent youth. *Adolescence, 8*, 1-26.

Kurosawa, A. (Director). (1951). *Rashomon* [Film]. RKO Pictures.

Kurth-Schai, R. (1988). The roles of youth in society: A reconceptualization. *The Educational Forum, 52*(2), 113-131.

Kutchinsky, B. (1991). Pornography and rape: Theory and practice? *International Journal of Law and Psychiatry, 14*, 47-64.

Kvaraceus, W. C., and Miller, W. B. (1959). *Delinquent behavior, culture and the individual*. Washington, DC: National Education Association.

Landis, J. T. (1956). Experiences of 500 children with adult sexual deviation. *Psychiatric Quarterly Supplement, 30*, 91-109.

Lane, S. (1991). The sexual abuse cycle. In G. D. Ryan & S. L. Lane (Eds.), *Juvenile sexual offending: Causes, consequences, and correction* (pp. 103-142). Lexington, MA: Lexington Books.

Lane, S., & Zamora, P. (1984). A method for treating the adolescent sex offender. In R. A. Mathias, P. Demuro, & R. Allinson (Eds.), *Sourcebook for treatment of the violent juvenile offender* (pp. 347-354). Washington, DC: National Council on Crime and Delinquency.

Laws, D. (1989). *Relapse prevention with sex offenders*. New York: Guilford.

Leaman, K. M. (1980). Sexual abuse: The reactions of child and family. In *Sexual abuse of children: Selected readings* (pp. 21-24). Washington, DC: U.S. Department of Health and Human Services.

Lerman, P. (1958). Group work with youth in conflict. *Social Work, 3*(4), 71-77.

Lerner, M. (1957). *America as a civilization*. New York: Simon & Schuster.

Lerner, M. (1980). *The belief in a just world: A fundamental delusion*. New York: Plenum.

Lew, M. (1988). *Victims no longer: Men recovering from incest and other childhood sexual abuse*. New York: Nevraumont.

Lewis, A. N., Shankok, S. S., & Pincus, J. H. (1979). Juvenile male sexual assaulters. *American Journal of Psychiatry, 136*, 1194-1196.

Leiker, J. H. (1986). *A follow-up study on convicted juvenile sex offenders as adults*. Unpublished master's thesis, Utah State University, Logan.

Lightfoot, L. O., & Barbaree, H. E. (1993). The relationship between substance use and abuse and sexual offending in adolescents. In H. E. Barbaree, W. L. Marshall, & S. M. Hudson (Eds.), *The juvenile sex offender* (pp. 203-224). New York: Guilford.

Lloyd, R. (1976). *For money or love: Boy prostitution in America*. New York: Vanguard Press.

Loftus, E. (1993). The reality of repressed memories. *American Psychologist, 48*, 518-537.

Loftus, E., & Foley, M. (1984). Differentiating fact from fantasy: The reliability of children's memory. *Journal of Social Issues, 40*, 33-50.

Longo, R. E. (1982). Sexual learning and experience among adolescent sex offenders. *International Journal of Offender Therapy and Comparative Criminology, 26*(3), 235-241.

Lykken, D. (1981). *A tremor in the blood: Uses and abuses of the lie detector*. New York: McGraw-Hill.

Mackinnon, K. (1987). A feminist/political approach: Pleasure under patriarchy. In J. H. Geer & W. O'Donohue (Eds.), *Theories of human sexuality* (pp. 65-90). New York: Plenum.

Maclay, D. T. (1960). Boys who commit sexual misdemeanors. *British Medical Journal, 5167*, 186-190.

MacNamara, D. E. J. (1965). Male prostitution in an American city: A pathological or socio-economic phenomenon? *American Journal of Orthopsychiatry, 35*, 204.

Malyon, A. K. (1981). The homosexual adolescent: Developmental issues and social bias. *Child Welfare, 60*, 321-330.

Markey, O. B. (1950). A study of aggressive sex misbehavior in adolescents brought to court. *American Journal of Orthopsychology, 20*, 719-731.

Marshall, W. L., Hudson, S. M., & Hodkinson, S. (1993). The importance of attachment bonds in the development of juvenile sex offending. In H. E. Barbaree, W. L. Marshall, & S. M. Hudson (Eds.), *The juvenile sex offender* (pp. 164-181). New York: Guilford.

Martin, A. D. (1982). Learning to hide: The socialization of the gay adolescent. *Adolescent Psychiatry, 10*, 52-65.

Martin, E. P., & Martin, M. M. (1978). *The black extended family*. Chicago: University of Chicago Press.

Marvasti, J. (1986). Incestuous mothers. *American Journal of Forensic Psychiatry, 7*(4), 63-69.

Masson, J. (1984). *The assault on truth: Freud's suppression of the seduction theory*. New York: Farrar, Strauss & Giroux.

Matarazzo, J. D. (1986). Computerized clinical psychological testing interpretations: Unvalidated plus all mean and no sigma. *American Psychologist, 41*, 14-24.

Mathews, F. (1989). *Familiar strangers: A study of adolescent prostitution*. Toronto, Canada: Central Toronto Youth Services.

Mathews, R. (1987). *Preliminary typology of female sexual offenders*. Unpublished manuscript.

Mathews, R., Matthews, J. K., & Speltz, K. (1989). *Female sex offenders: An exploratory study*. Orwell, VT: Safer Society Press.

McCarthy, D. (1981). *Women who rape*. Unpublished manuscript.

McCarty, L. (1986). Mother-child incest: Characteristics of the offender. *Child Welfare, 65*(5), 447-458.

Mendel, G. (1971). *Pour decoloniser l'enfant: Sociopsychanalyse de l'autorité*. Paris: Payot.

Meyers, J. E. B., Bays, J., Becker, J., Berliner, L., Corwin, D. L., & Saywitz, K. J. (1989). Expert testimony in child sexual abuse litigation. *Nebraska Law Review, 68*, 1-145.

Millon, T. (1987). *Millon Clinical Multiaxial Inventory-II (MCMI-II)* (2nd ed.). Minneapolis: National Computer Systems.

Minnesota Department of Corrections. (1993). *State prison profile*. St. Paul: State of Minnesota Publications.

Minnesota Department of Human Services. (1986). *SHARP (sexual health and responsibility program): An adolescent perpetrator prevention program*. St. Paul: Minnesota Department of Human Services Publications.

Minuchin, S., & Fishman, H. C. (1981). *Family therapy techniques*. Cambridge: Harvard University Press.

More young men killed in U.S. than in 21 other nations. (1990, June 27). *Minneapolis Star Tribune*, p. 7.

Muuss, R. (1962). *Theories of adolescence* (2nd ed.). New York: Random House.

Nasjleti, M. (1980). Suffering in silence: The male incest victim. *Child Welfare, 59*, 269-275.

National Adolescent Perpetrator Network. (1993). Revised report from the National Task Force on Juvenile Sexual Offending [Special issue]. *Juvenile and Family Court Journal, 44*(4).

Nestingen, S. L., & Lewis, L. R. (1990). *Growing beyond abuse: A workbook for survivors of sexual exploitation or childhood sexual abuse*. Minneapolis: Omni Recovery.

New York City Youth Board. (1952). *Reaching the unreached: Fundamental aspects of the program of the New York City Youth Board*. New York: Author.

New York City Youth Board. (1962). *The summer of 1962: A report on the New York City's program of vigilance and services to youth*. New York: Author.

New York City Youth Board. (1965). *The changing role of the street worker in the council of social work athletic clubs*. New York: Author.

O'Brien, M. (1984, May). *Adolescent sexual offenders: An outpatient program's perspective on research directions*. Paper presented at the 13th Annual Child Abuse and Neglect Symposium, Keystone, CO.

O'Brien, M. (1986). *Model of adolescent sex offenders*. Workshop handout. St. Paul: PHASE.

O'Brien, M. (1989). *Characteristics of adolescent male sibling incest offenders: Preliminary findings*. Orwell, VT: Safer Society Press.

O'Brien, M., & Bera, W. (1986, Fall). Adolescent sex offenders: A descriptive typology. *Preventing Sexual Abuse*, *1*(3), 1-4. (Available from ETR Publications, Santa Cruz, CA)

O'Carroll, T. (1982). *Paedophilia: The radical case*. Boston: Alyson.

O'Donohue, W., & Geer, J. H. (Eds.). (1992a). *The sexual abuse of children: Theory and research*. Hillsdale, NJ: Lawrence Erlbaum.

O'Donohue, W., & Geer, J. H. (Eds.). (1992b). *The sexual abuse of children: Clinical issues*. Hillsdale, NJ: Lawrence Erlbaum.

Olson, D. H., Sprenkle, D. H., & Russell, C. S. (1979). Circumplex model of marital and family systems I: Cohension and adaptability dimensions. *Family Process*, *18*, 3-28.

Oregon Department of Family Services. (1986). Guidelines for treatment of juvenile sex offenders (Oregon matrix). In *The Oregon report on juvenile sexual offenders*. Salem: Oregon Department of Family Services.

Perry, N., & Wrightsman, L. (1991). *The child witness*. Newbury Park, CA: Sage.

Peters, J. J. (1976). Children who are victims of sexual assault and the psychology of offenders. *American Journal of Psychotherapy*, *30*, 398-421.

Peters, S. D., Wyatt, G. E., & Finkelhor, D. (1986). Prevalence. In D. Finkelhor & Associates (Ed.), *A sourcebook on child sexual abuse* (pp. 15-59). Newbury Park, CA: Sage.

Petrovich, M., & Templer, D. L. (1984). Heterosexual molestation of children who later become rapists. *Psychological Reports*, *54*, 810.

Phillips, E. L., & Wiener, D. W. (1966). *Short-term psychotherapy and structured behavior change*. New York: McGraw-Hill.

Pierce, R., & Pierce, L. H. (1985). The sexually abused child: A comparison of male and female victims. *Child Abuse & Neglect*, *9*, 191-199.

Pithers, W., Martin, G., & Cumming, G. (1989). Vermont treatment program for sexual aggressors. In D. Laws (Ed.), *Relapse prevention with sex offenders* (pp. 292-310). New York: Guilford.

Plummer, K. (1981). Pedophilia: Constructing a psychological baseline. In M. Cook & K. Howells (Eds.), *Adult sexual interest in children* (pp. 67-79). New York: Academic Press.

Pollock, N. L., & Hashmall, J. M. (1991). The excuses of child molesters. *Behavioral Sciences and the Law*, *9*, 53-59.

Pope, K. S., Butcher, J. W., & Seelen, J. (1993). *The MMPI, MMPI-2, and MMPI-A in court*. Washington, DC: American Psychological Association.

Prentky, R. A., & Cerce, D. D. (1990). Thoughts on the developmental roots of sexual aggression. *The Adviser*, *3*(1), 4.

Radbill, S. X. (1974). A history of child abuse and infanticide. In S. K. Steinmetz & M. Straus (Eds.), *Violence in the family* (pp. 173-179). New York: Dodd, Mead.

Rasmussen, L. A., Burton, J. E., & Christopherson, B. (1990, October). *Interrupting precursors to perpetration in males ages four to twelve*. Paper presented at the annual conference of the National Adolescent Perpetrator Network, Albany, NY.

Redl, F. (1945). The psychology of gang formation and the treatment of delinquents. In *The psychoanalytic study of the child: Vol. I* (pp. 367-377). New York: Internation Universities Press.

Reiss, A. J. (1961). The social integration of queers and peers. *Social Problems*, *9*, 102-120.

Resick, P. A. (1993). The psychological impact of rape. *Journal of Interpersonal Violence, 8*(2), 223-255.

Rogers, C. M., & Terry, T. (1984). Clinical intervention with boy victims of sexual abuse. In I. R. Stuart & J. G. Greer (Eds.), *Victims of sexual aggression: Men, women and children* (pp. 91-103). New York: Van Nostrand Reinhold.

Rosenberg, J. (1990). *Fuel on the fire: An inquiry in "pornography" and sexual aggression in a free society*. Orwell, VT: Safer Society Press.

Rush, B. (1974). The sexual abuse of children: A feminist point of view. In N. Connell & C. Wilson (Eds.), *Rape: The first sourcebook for women* (pp. 64-75). New York: New American Library.

Rush, B. (1980). *The best-kept secret: The sexual victimization of children*. New York: McGraw-Hill.

Ryan, G. (1986). Annotated bibliography: Adolescent perpetrators of sexual molestation of children. *Child Abuse & Neglect, 10*, 125-131.

Ryan, G., & Lane, S. L. (1991). *Juvenile sexual offending: Causes, consequences, and correction*. Lexington, MA: Lexington Books.

Ryan, G., Lane, S., Davis, J., & Isaac, C. (1987). Juvenile sex offenders: Development and correction. *Child Abuse & Neglect, 11*, 385-395.

Sandfort, T. (1982). *The sexual aspect of pedophile relations*. Amsterdam: Pan/Spartacus.

Sandfort, T. (1983). Pedophile relationships in the Netherlands: Alternative lifestyles for children? *Alternative Lifestyles, 5*, 164-183.

Sandfort T. (1984). Sex in pedophiliac relationships: An empirical investigation among a non-representative group of boys. *Journal of Sex Research*, 20, 123-142.

Sandfort, T., Brongersma, E., & van Naerssen, A. (Eds.) (1990). *Male intergenerational intimacy: Historical, socio-psychological and legal perspectives*. New York: Haworth.

Sanger, W. W. (1937). *The history of prostitution*. London: Eugenics.

Schoener, G., & Milgrom, J. (1989). Processing sessions. In G. Schoener, J. Milgrom, J. Gonsiorek, E. Luepker, & R. Conroe (Eds.), *Psychotherapists' sexual involvement with clients: Intervention and prevention* (pp. 345-358). Minneapolis, MN: Walk-In Counseling Center.

Schoener, G., Milgrom, J., Gonsiorek, J., Luepker, E., & Conroe, R. (Eds.). (1989). *Psychotherapists' sexual involvement with clients: Intervention and prevention*. Minneapolis, MN: Walk-In Counseling Center.

Schouten, P., & Simon, W. (1992). Validity of phallometric measures with sex offenders: Comments on the Quinsey, Laws and Hall debate. *Journal of Consulting and Clinical Psychology, 60*(5), 812-814.

Scott, G. R. (1968). *Ladies of vice* (rev. ed.). London: Tallis Press.

Scully, D., & Marolla, J. (1984). Convicted rapists' vocabulary of motive: Excuses and justifications. *Social Problems, 31*(5), 530-544.

Search Institute. (1992). *Training needs assessment for the strengthening our capacity to care project: Final report*. Minneapolis, MN: Author.

Search Institute. (1993). *The troubled journey: A portrait of 6th-12th grade youth*. Minneapolis: Author.

Sgroi, S. M. (1991). *Handbook of clinical intervention in child abuse*. Lexington, MA: Lexington Books.

Sgroi, S. M. (1975). Sexual molestation of children: The last frontier in child abuse. *Children Today, 4*(3), 19-44.

Shively, M. G., & DeCecco, J. P. (1977). Components of sexual identity. *Journal of Homosexuality*, *3*, 41-48.

Shoor, M., Speed, M. H., Bartelt, C. (1966). Syndrome of the adolescent child molester. *American Journal of Psychiatry*, *122*, 783-789.

Shotland, R. L., & Goodstein, L. (1983). Just because she doesn't want to doesn't mean it's rape: An experimentally based causal model of the perception of rape in a dating situation. *Social Psychology Quarterly*, *45*(3), 220-232.

Showers, J., Farber, E. D., Joseph, J. A., Oshins, L., & Johnson, C. F. (1983). The sexual victimization of boys: A three year survey. *Health Values: Achieving High Level Wellness*, *7*, 15-18.

Smith, T. A., & Wolf, S. (1988). A treatment model for sexual aggression. *Journal of Social Work and Human Sexuality*, *7*(1), 149-164.

Smith, W. R. (1984). *Patterns of re-offending among juvenile sex offenders*. Unpublished manuscript.

Smith, W. R. (1988). Delinquency and abuse among juvenile sexual offenders. *Journal of Interpersonal Violence*, *3*(4), 400-413.

Smith, W. R., & Monastersky, C. (1986). Assessing juvenile sex offenders' risk for reoffending. *Criminal Justice and Behavior*, *13*(2), 115-140.

Sohl, R., & Carr, A. (Eds.). (1970). *The gospel according to Zen*. New York: New American Library.

Spiegel, D. (1989). Hypnosis in the treatment of victims of sexual abuse. *The Psychiatric Clinics of North America*, *12*(2), 295-305.

Staats, G. R. (1978). Stereotype content and social distance: Changing views of homosexuality. *Journal of Homosexuality*, *4*(1), 15-27.

Starr, A. (1993). *What works with youth? A working draft of the research of the Community Fellows Program at Massachusetts Institute of Technology*. Unpublished manuscript.

Steele, B. (1986). Notes on the lasting effects of early child abuse throughout the lifecycle. *Child Abuse & Neglect*, *10*, 283-291.

Steen, C., & Monnette, B. (1989). *Treating adolescent sex offenders in the community*. Springfield, IL: Charles C Thomas.

Stermac, L., & Sheridan, P. (1993). The developmentally disabled adolescent sex offender. In H. E. Barbaree, W. L. Marshall, & S. M. Hudson (Eds.), *The juvenile sex offender* (pp. 235-242). New York: Guilford.

Streisand, B. (Director). (1991). *The prince of tides* [Film]. Columbia Pictures.

Strong, B., & DeVault, C. (1992). *The marriage and family experience*. St. Paul, MN: West.

Sutherland, E. H., & Cressey, D. R. (1978). *Criminology*. New York: J. B. Lippincott.

Swartz, B. (1989). *A practitioner's guide to the treatment of the incarcerated male sex offender*. Washington, DC: National Institute of Corrections.

Tharinger, D. (1990). Impact of child sexual abuse on developing sexuality. *Professional Psychology: Research and Practice*, *21*, 331-337.

The Forgotten Half. (1988). *Pathways to success for America's youth and young families*. Washington, DC: The William T. Grant Commission on Work Family and Citizenship.

Thompson, J. (1990). *The price you pay to wear tennis shoes to work: A phemomenological study of detached youthwork*. Unpublished doctoral dissertation, Union Institute, Cincinnati.

Thrasher, F. M. (1927). *The gang: A study of 1,313 gangs in Chicago*. Chicago: The University of Chicago Press.

Timnick, L. (1985, August 25). 22% in survey were child abuse victims. *Los Angeles Times*, p. 1.

Tobias, J. L., & Gordon, R. (1977). *Operation lure*. Mimeograph.

Toffler, A. (Ed.). (1974). The psychology of the future. In A. Toffler (Ed.), *Learning for tomorrow* (p. 15). New York: Vintage.

Trepper, T. S., & Barrett, M. J. (1986). *Treating incest: A multimodal systems perspectives*. New York: Haworth.

Trepper, T. S., & Sprenkle, D. H. (1988). The clinical use of the circumplex model in the assessment and treatment of families. *Journal of Psychotherapy and the Family*, 4(1/2), 92-111.

Tsang, D. (Ed.). (1981). *The age taboo: Gay male sexuality, power and consent*. Boston: Alyson.

Tufts New England Medical Center, Division of Child Psychiatry. (1984). *Sexually exploited children: Service and research project* (Final report for the Office of Juvenile Justice and Delinquency Prevention). Washington, DC: U.S. Department of Justice.

Umbreit, M. (1985). *Crime and reconciliation: Creative options for victims and offenders*. Nashville, TN: Abington.

Umbreit, M., & Coates, T. (1992). The impact of mediating victim offender conflict: An analysis of programs in three states. *Juvenile & Family Court Journal*, 43, 1-8.

Urban and Rural Systems Associates. (1982). *Adolescent male prostitutes: A study of sexual exploitation, etiological factors, and runaway behavior* (Final report to the Administration for Children, Youth and Families, Grant No. HEW 105-79-120). Washington, DC: Department of Health and Human Services.

Urquiza, A. J., & Crowley, C. (1986, April). *Sex differences in the survivors of childhood sexual abuse*. Paper presented at the Fourth Conference on Sexual Victimization of Children, New Orleans, LA.

U.S. Department of Justice. (1993). *Crime in the United States, 1992*. Washington, DC: Author.

van der Kolk, B. A., & Kadish, W. (1987). Amnesia, dissociation and the return of the repressed. In B. A. van der Kolk (Ed.), *Psychological trauma*. Washington, DC: American Psychiatric Press.

Vander Mey, B. (1988). The sexual victimization of male children: A review of previous research. *Child Abuse & Neglect*, 12, 61-72.

Vander Mey, B. (1992a). Theories of incest. In W. O'Donohue & J. H. Geer (Eds.), *The sexual abuse of children: Theory and research*. Hillsdale, NJ: Lawrence Erlbaum.

Vander Mey, B. (1992b). Incest. In E. F. Borgatta & M. L. Borgatta (Eds.), *The encyclopedia of sexuality: Vol. 2*. New York: Macmillan.

Veyne, P. (Ed.). (1987). The Roman empire. In P. Veyne (Ed.), *A history of private life: From pagan Rome to Byzantium* (pp. 5-233). Cambridge: Harvard University Press.

Wakefield, H., & Underwager, R. (Undated). *Magic, mischief and memories: Remembering repressed abuse*. Northfield, MN: Institute for Psychological Therapies.

Walker, L. (1989). *Terrifying love: Why battered women kill and how society responds*. New York: HarperCollins.

Waterman, C. K., & Foss-Goodman, D. (1984). Child-molesting: Variables relating to attribution of fault to victims, offenders, and non-participating parents. *Journal of Sex Research, 20*(4), 329-349.

Weeks, J. (1981). Inverts, perverts, and mary-annes: Male prostitution and the regulation of homosexuality in England in the nineteenth and early twentieth century. *Journal of Homosexuality, 6*(1/2), 113-133.

Weisberg, D. E. (1985). *Children of the night: Adolescent prostitution in America.* Lexington, MA: Lexington Books.

Welfare Association of Cleveland. (1959). *A community-wide approach; The United Youth Program, 1954-59.* Cleveland: Cleveland Group Work Council.

Werner, E., & Smith, R. (1982). *Vulnerable but invincible: A longitudinal study of resilient children and youth.* New York: Adams, Bannister, and Cox.

Whitaker, C. A. (1982). My philosophy of psychoterapy. In J. R. Neill & D. P. Kniskern (Eds.), *From psyche to system: The evolving therapy of Carl Whitaker* (pp. 31-36). New York: Guilford.

Whitchurch, G. G., & Constantine, L. L. (1993). Systems theory. In P. G. Boss, W. J. Doherty, R. LaRossa, W. R. Schuman, & S. K. Steinmetz (Eds.), *Sourcebook of family theories and methods: A contextual approach* (pp. 325-355). New York: Plenum.

Wickramasekera, I. (1980). Aversive behavioral rehearsal: A cognitive behavioral procedure. In D. J. Cox & R. J. Daitzman (Eds.), *Exhibitionism: Description, assessment, and treatment* (pp. 39-50). New York: Appleton-Croft.

Wienberg, M. (1972). Labels don't apply. *Sexual Behavior, 3*(2), 18.

Wilson, C., & Pence, D. (1993, October). *Uneasy alliance.* Paper presented at the Annual Midwest Conference on Child Sexual Abuse and Incest, Madison, WI.

Wolfe, F. A. (1985, March). *Twelve female sexual offenders.* Presentation at "Next steps in research on the assessment and treatment of sexually aggressive persons (paraphiliacs)" conference, St. Louis, MO.

Woods, S. C., & Dean, K. S. (1984). *Financial report: Sexual abuse of males research project* (NCCAN Report No. 90-CA-812). Washington, DC: National Center on Child Abuse and Neglect.

Wright, M., & Galaway, B. (Eds.). (1989). *Mediation and criminal justice: Victims, offenders and community.* Newbury Park, CA: Sage.

Wyatt, G. E. (1990). Sexual abuse of ethnic minority children: Identifying dimensions of victimization. *Professional Psychology: Research and Practice, 21*, 338-343.

Yochelson, S., & Samenow, S. E. (1977). *The criminal personality* (Vols. I, II, and III). New York: Jason Aronson.

Yokley, J. (Ed.). (1990). *The use of victim-offender communication in the treatment of sexual abuse: Three intervention models.* Orwell, VT: Safer Society Press.

Young, J. E., & Beck, A. T. (1982). Cognitive therapy: Clinical applications. In A. J. Giles (Ed.), *Short-term therapies for depression* (pp. 182-214). New York: Guilford.

Yourcenar, M. (1954). *Memoirs of Hadrian.* New York: Farrar, Strauss & Giroux.

Zehr, H. (1990). *Changing lenses: A new focus for crime and justice.* Scottsdale, AZ: Herald Press.

Index

abuse, client's description of, 66
  cycle, 128-131, 176-178
  definitions of, 37-39
  social environmental factors in, 102
abuse biography, 174-176
abuse-centric perspectives, 109
acting out, 70, 83
adolescence, as a fixed concept, 7
  history of, 5-10
adolescent health programs, 270
anxiety, 83
assessment, 57-71, 172-174
  need for, 154-155
  of serious psychopathology, 62
assessment/education program, 156-158
at risk, 266
attachment, 126
attribution theory, 191
"aversive behavioral rehearsal," 149
aversive conditioning, 148
Axis I, 69
Axis II, 69
  character disorders, 64
  disorder, 61
  problems, 61

barriers to identification of male victims, 45-49
behavioral, approaches, 148

assignments, 80
assignments, selection of, 86
assessments, errors during, 85
change, 94
  methods, 146
boundaries, 305

California Personality Inventory (CPI), 61
call service, 233
catamites, 228
cautions and guidelines, 198
child abuse advocates, 42
childhood, concept of, 6
child protection services, 28
children:
  as learners, 11
  as threats, 11
  as victims, 11
child sexual molesters, 134
civil law, 102
client-driven models of treatment, 34, 35
client-therapist exploitation, 44
client-therapist sexual abuse, 54
clinical judgment, 58
closure choices, 204-213
coercive approaches, 275
cognitive-behavioral, 89, 146, 148
  perspectives, 56

About the Authors

John C. Gonsiorek received a Ph.D. in clinical psychology from the University of Minnesota and holds a diplomate in clinical psychology from the American Board of Professional Psychology. He is a Clinical Assistant Professor in the Clinical Training Program, Department of Psychology, University of Minnesota. He is Past President of Division 44 (Society for the Psychological Study of Lesbian and Gay Issues) of the American Psychological Association and has published widely in the areas of sexual exploitation by health care professionals and clergy, sexual orientation and sexual identity, professional ethics, among others. He is in independent practice in Minneapolis, focusing on forensic evaluations, expert witness work, and individual psychotherapy.

Walter H. Bera received an M.A. in educational psychology from the University of Minnesota and has worked in the field of sexual abuse and harassment assessment, treatment, and prevention since 1978. He has worked in the Family Sexual Abuse Program of the Family Renewal Center, Illusion Theater's Sexual Abuse Prevention Education Program, and the Program for Healthy Adolescent Sexual Expression (PHASE) with adolescent sex offenders. He has produced original research, articles, plays, and videotapes, most recently coauthoring the video-based adolescent sexual harassment prevention curriculum *Crossing the Line*. He is a Licensed Psychologist and Marriage and Family Therapist in Minnesota and an Approved Supervisor in the American Association for Marriage and Family Therapy. He is completing his doctorate in family social science at the University of Minnesota; his dissertation focuses on male victims of clergy sexual abuse. He maintains a private practice in Minneapolis and provides training and consultation nationally.

Donald LeTourneau received a CSWE accredited social work degree from Bethel College in St. Paul and a master's of social work from the University of Minnesota Graduate School. He has taught youth studies courses at the University of Minnesota Center for Youth Development and Research and is past President and Board Member of the Minnesota Association of Child and Youth Care Workers. For more than 20 years he has helped develop community-based programming for a wide range of youth issues, including street outreach; shelter and transitional housing; employment and training; alternative education; outpatient mental health; health education and health care; gay, lesbian, bisexual, and transgender youth; adolescent prostitution; juvenile justice and delinquency; and youth development. With long-time colleague Jackie Thompson, he recently started the Institute for Youthwork, a private nonprofit organization that provides youth work consultation, program development, evaluation, education, training, and staff development.